MY TIME IS YOUR TIME

The Story of Rudy Vallée

THE STORY OF RUDY VALLÉE

MY TIME
IS
YOUR
TIME

by

RUDY VALLÉE
with GIL McKEAN

IVAN OBOLENSKY, INC., NEW YORK

© 1962 by Rudy Vallée and Gil McKean

All Rights Reserved

Library of Congress Catalog Card Number: 62-18783

Fourth Printing

Manufactured in the United States of America

Book design by Philip E. Schumacher

To my father, Charles Alphonse Vallée, and my mother, Kathryn Lynch, and all the stream of their ancestry who gave me my physical and mental traits plus, as importantly, the intelligence, energy, stamina, desire and ability to use them, I dedicate this biography.

RUDY VALLÉE

Contents

CHAPTER   PAGE

  I The Two Januarys   *"I'll Get By"*   1

  II Down-East in the Good Ol' Days   *"Wait Till the Sun Shines, Nellie"*   4

  III Saxophobia   *"Look For the Silver Lining"*   22

  IV Yale University "Part One"   *"I'll Build a Stairway to Paradise"*   30

  V The London Year and Yale "Part Two"   *"I'm Sitting on Top of the World"*   40

  VI To New York and the Heigh-Ho Club   *"There's a Rainbow Round My Shoulder"*   53

  VII Three Cheers for Radio—Two Cheers for Hollywood   *"I'm Just a Vagabond Lover"*   67

  VIII The Fleischmann Hour Is Born   *"Cheerful Little Earful"*   85

  IX Fay Webb and All That Jazz   *"Say It Isn't So"*   95

  X My Life and Times with *George White's Scandals*   *"Oh, You Nasty Man"*   103

  XI Songs Can Be Dangerous   *"We are poor little lambs . . ."*   115

  XII Hand Me Down My Crystal Ball   *"When the Pussywillow Whispers to the Catnip"*   134

CHAPTER

PAGE

XIII   Home Is Where You Hang Your Hat   *"A Wandering Minstrel I"*   147

XIV   London Revisited   *"A Foggy Day"*   160

XV   From One Sponsor to Another—More Movies *"We Could Make Such Beautiful Music"*   170

XVI   The Coast Guard Days in World War II   *"Oh, Say can you see . . ."*   180

XVII   The "Drene" Show for Procter and Gamble   *"Oh, What It Seemed to Be"*   195

XVIII   Eleanor   *"Some Enchanted Evening"*   203

XIX   Into the Heckler's Paradise—Night Clubs—Play-Acting—TV *"Dear Hearts and Gentle People . . ."*   212

XX   How to Succeed in Show Business by Really Trying *"I Believe in You"*   226

XXI   Life Begins at Sixty!   *"Life Is Still a Bowl of Cherries"*   239

MY TIME IS YOUR TIME

The Story of Rudy Vallée

The Two Januarys

"I'll Get By"

WELL NOW, GENTLE READER, WHERE TO start? Or, for that matter, why to start! Who am I to presume to pen my memoirs—but, then, who is *any*body to pen et cetera. Look, gentle reader, I've had a few kicks along the way, during a pretty wild segment of our recorded (sic!) time and maybe you'd like to savor them in retrospect with me. If so, I welcome you one and all. If not, stop reading *for nothing* right now!

If you are *straight* and still with me let's take a quick glance at the galloping events that made up the year of our Lord, nineteen hundred and twenty-eight. From the vantage (vantage!) point of this here and now post-nuclear day, things back then might look a bit strange but, take my word for it—that time, in its own sweet way, was kicks. For instance and to wit:

That January two men, one a Britisher and one who was German, were found guilty in London of being Russian spies. They received sentences of ten years.

There was trouble in one of Great Britain's African protectorates and as a result some 250,000 Negro slaves were freed by fiat.

High U.S. officials were heading south for an important, full-dress Pan-American conference.

A Senate committee was investigating the conduct of a high government official in accepting sizable gifts from vested interests.

The Communists were said to have massacred thousands of men, women and children in the Kwangtung province of China.

Does that sound like fairly recent history? The more things change the more they seem to stay the same!

It was a month like all months, full of both achievement and tragedy. While Colonel Charles Lindbergh was creating enormous good will on a flying trip through Central America, Ruth Snyder and Judd Gray were

1

put to death in the electric chair at Sing Sing Prison. A charming bit of medical naïveté may be noted in the fact that the State's surgeon declared that an autopsy had revealed that the brains of the electrocuted duo were normal.

Incidentally, people were then being exposed to an unusually fine group of popular songs, some of which are still in vogue to this day. Tunes such as "Let's Do It," "Diane," "Honey," "Lover Come Back to Me," "Sweet Sue," "When You're Smiling" were, as the saying goes, on everybody's lips. There were a few "pops" of a novel nature like "You're the Cream in My Coffee," "Diga Diga Doo," "Button Up Your Overcoat," and a weird one called simply "C-o-n-s-t-a-n-t-i-n-o-p-l-e"! The song-hungry public heard these in many ways: in vaudeville, in dance halls and cabarets, in nickelodeons, and a precious few hovered at home over a little contraption called a "crystal set" with their earphones on, riding the radio waves.

"Look, Ma! When the weather's right, I can get Cincinnati!"

I didn't know it at the time but '28 was going to be very good to me. Fantastic breaks were just around the corner and to make it as an entertainer you need them badly. This is another not-so-secret ingredient of success.

So there I was, a young-punk saxophonist from Maine, via Yale, knocking at the doors of New York booking offices such as Meyer Davis and Ben Bernie, trying to break into what appeared to me as the big time. You know the old chestnut about the hick who got the roof of his mouth blistered from looking up at the skyscrapers. I was just about that impressed and just about that hicky when confronted by the stone-and-steel mountain ranges of Manhattan.

I really must have made quite a strange picture in those days—a picture that John Held, Jr. might have drawn for *College Humor*. The costume consisted mainly of a derby worn with just the right tilt, a flowing scarf, a beautiful raccoon coat; at the same time, I was laden with a baritone sax, an alto sax, and a clarinet, all in separate cases, plus a canvas bag containing the parts which could be assembled into a "pipe-stand" to support the baritone so that I could play it standing up.

The previous month, December, 1927, I had begun to get three or four dates a week with various bands. We played coming-out parties, holiday dances, any sort of function which needed dance music. I was living in Morristown, New Jersey, mainly because I was in the midst of a romance with a gorgeous Swedish girl. It must have been true love because, to be near her, I was prepared to brave the horrors of commuting to New York or wherever the job might take me.

Most of the engagements I got as a reed-playing performer had come through the Ben Bernie office which was run by Ben's brother Herman. I had also played one dance date with a Vincent Lopez unit as well.

Bernie, Lopez, George Olson, and Paul Whiteman as well as Meyer Davis were what you might call orchestral cartels; that is, using their names as prestige, they would book a number of orchestras under their own name but would charge an additional sum actually to appear and direct the so-called "combination." Meyer Davis still runs such a business and does so most successfully. I suppose you might call it "ghost-conducting"!

Enter Bert Lown, a sort of small-time Meyer Davis, a man who was to have a profound effect on my career. I got an offer from him to front my own band at an exclusive new location which had just opened—The Heigh-Ho Club! From this came my perennial salutation, "Heigh-ho, everybody."

In order to take the Heigh-Ho Club job, it was necessary for me to get a release from the Bernie office for the three engagements I still had to play for them. The Bernies graciously consented.

The last date I played for them is one I shall never forget, not only for what it was at the time but what it came to mean in relation to a similar event that took place a year later.

Picture this—there I was, a down-east bumpkin (*I* considered myself pretty sophisticated by this time; after all, I'd been in the Big Town several months now!) engaged to play in the band providing music for the Jewish Theatrical Guild banquet. It so happened that ten of the bandsmen came from the Bernie office and ten from the Whiteman office. I was dazzled by the big names: much brass—generals, admirals, captains of industry and His Honor, Mayor Jimmy Walker. George Jessel, the nonpareil, was toastmaster. Lou Holtz was master of ceremonies; Vincent Lopez performed on piano; Van and Schenk came over from the Palace with their great routines—then followed star turns as the "names" of the entertainment world made their appearances. Had this not been a benefit, the talent cost might have been estimated conservatively at well over one hundred thousand dollars. And there I was, playing on a saxophone, earning a few bucks a night, not even close enough to bask in reflected glory.

One year later I was asked to appear with my band at the same affair and Mayor Walker asked *me* to permit *him* to introduce me to the gathering, since he had become a fan of mine! When I stepped out on the stage after his introduction, the entire audience—the brass as well as big-name entertainers—rose to its feet amid a storm of applause.

Of all the great thrills that have come to me in the course of my career, I think that evening probably stands out as the most dramatic and poignant. I was as close to tears that night as I will ever be.

In one short year I found myself taking a terrific stride on my way to the Big Time. It was due to two things: working like a neurotic beaver with too many engagements, and that strange new gadget called radio!

CHAPTER II

Down-East in the Good Ol' Days

"Wait Till the Sun Shines, Nellie"

IT WAS 1905 AND I WAS STUCK WITH THE number four. I was four years of age and I had been in a coma for four days. I guess I was trying to make four the hard way. They thought I was going to die. I will never forget until the day I *do* die the candles around my bedside, the hovering nuns, and the priest giving me the last sacraments. Possessed of an insatiable sweet tooth, I had indulged in too many of the one-cent prize packages that abounded in that day and age and the adulterated candy contained therein had laid me low. I was dying—I knew it and they knew it. And yet, somehow, I rallied and until the day I pass on for real I will remember with love what my Dad did for me. He persuaded the Catholic Convent Boys' Band, some thirty strong, to parade by my window which was well out of their normal line of march. It was on the first Sunday afternoon that I was strong enough to crawl to the window to watch them. Dad knew it was a maneuver that would cheer me up and hasten my recovery.

Even then, Dad must have known (although he never spoke of it) about my passion for music and anything pertaining to a band or orchestra. Heaven only knows how many sodas and ice creams he must have given to this little Catholic band to persuade them to deviate from their normal line of march. Suffice to say that the thrill and joy that I experienced as I peeked over the window sill in my bedroom and saw those green-coated boy musicians parade by, has never left me.

What a character my father was! I have met in my time more than my share of idiosyncratic human beings, but Dad was, as the saying has it, the most unforgettable character I've ever known.

I can see him now with his twinkling blue eyes set in a round, chubby, red face—the same oft-caricatured eyes that I have, with the heavy-folded lids slanting sharply down at the outer edges—looking for all the world like a fat little French priest. He would saunter down the streets of our little country town, his left leg slightly bowed out, his Homburg perched a bit aslant, his cane swinging with just the right jauntiness,

4

his spats setting off his gleaming shoes, a dark brown cigar with a long white ash in his hand, the whole outfit culminating in a large, flowing black tie fashioned into a large bow such as you might put on a prize cat! Even now as I watch a newsreel of Winston Churchill I somehow see my father.

Ah, those were the days! My flash-backs show me mental film-clips of Hubert Prior Vallee (that's what my parents had christened me) swinging with childish glee over the suspension bridge that spanned the river in Rumford Falls, Maine, or watching for hours the spectacular rush of water through the lumber flume that had been erected at the side of this same river, down which coursed the logs which lumbermen had slashed out of the forests far above. Occasionally to our horror down would tumble a hapless lumberman, his wildly decorated shirt gleaming in the sunlight.

Then there was a night, a night just foggy enough to make it a really mysterious adventure for a youngster, when we packed up and boarded a stagecoach for the small city of Westbrook in the great state of Maine. The moon backed in and out among the clouds and I felt like a hero right out of *Treasure Island*. The driver wore a wide-brimmed hat, needed a shave, and I was certain he would deliver the whole family into a pirates' camp before morning. However, I was not the least bit worried as I knew I could outwit any pirate living and see to our escape.

"I just hope we haven't left anything," my mother said worriedly. "Charles, did you put in the box full of the kitchen utensils?"

"Yes, dear. I put in the box with the utensils. And the box from our bedroom. And the children's toy box, et cetera. I put in everything you packed so don't worry. Up you go now, Kathleen. And now up *you* go, Hubert."

It so happened that I was not to have a chance to outwit the pirates. The stagecoach driver was just that and nothing more. In the beaming midday sun he somehow no longer looked like a pirate as he deposited my Mom and Dad, sister Kathleen and me in front of the two-story house that was to be the Vallee "estate" for the next twenty years or so.

That first night in our home, since our meager furniture had not arrived on the wagon-train, we slept on mattresses placed on the floor. When the last lamp was turned off, the world was as dark and eerie as the bowels of hell itself. Certainly the huge attic was infested with ghosts, bats, and other hideous monsters. I could handle pirates and other human beings but, as a simple matter of self-preservation, I spent the night sweltering with my head underneath the covers. Next morning I was surprised to see no trace of monsters and with a sigh of relief I looked out from my second-story window into the streets of my new homeland.

But school was to start all too soon and before I knew it my mother was sprucing me up and plastering down my unruly hair in preparation.

That first day at a new school where you don't know anybody, where even your *sister* is welcome as just somebody to say hello to! It's hell when you see the other children in groups, in their own little cliques, cronying up and looking at you quizzically. You feel as if you'd like to dig a hole and hide and never come up.

"Now, Hubert," my mother had said that morning. "First impressions are so important. Particularly with teachers. And remember, this isn't *Rumford!* It's Westbrook, a much larger town, and you've got to be on your toes. Oh, dear, I hope everything goes well at school!" She made one more desperate swipe with the brush at one of my curly cowlicks.

"Listen, Mother. Hubert will be all right, so stop fretting," my father said calmly. This always maddened my mother. Dad rarely got in an uproar about anything and, except for occasional brief temperamental fireworks, was always serenity itself. Mother was just the opposite, constantly in a stew, a real worrier. It always irritated her that Dad never seemed to have a really serious care in the world.

Naturally, sooner or later I had a fight with one of the kids at school —I even recall his name—Dibbie Dow! As our classmates urged us on we had a real knockdown brawl but I can't remember exactly why. I am glad to report I emerged victorious, as they say at Madison Square Garden. It was the only real fight I ever had in my life, false historians and newspaper reporters to the contrary. At least it's the only one I ever really *won*. When I got home my clothes were a mess. I told Mom what had happened and she gave me the devil and so did Dad. But underneath it all, I think he was kind of proud of me for sticking up for myself—me and my French-Irish temper!

In every kid's life there are teachers' pets and pet teachers. I think the feeling was mutual with Minnie Hodgdon and me. I will make no apologies for being Minnie Hodgdon's pet. She had wispy, graying hair tied in a neat bun at the back of her head. Even though I was her pet, she would brook no nonsense from me or any other student. She was firm and fair, the genteel type of teacher that the world needs so many of today.

She was the head of the Valentine Street School, a building to which I will pay obeisance for the superlative education I derived within its rough-wood interior. The rooms were heated by bulging iron stoves and how those glowing red sides would make the crowded schoolrooms at times almost unendurable. But Miss Hodgdon's teaching prowess and patience prevailed and she crammed a lot of learning into me in the third, fourth, and fifth grades.

It's strange how you remember a few teachers and forget all the rest. There was Miss Libby in the sixth grade. To her I owe, bless her, the pronunciation of Bulgaria as *Bool-gah'-ree-ah;* Serbia as *Sehr'-bee-ah;* Uruguay as *Ooo'-roo-gwai*—and of many other faraway lands, countries, and cities as they should be, and not as the average individual pronounces them today. To her I owe the ineffable feeling of superiority that I feel when I pronounce Buenos Aires, Afghanistan, Baluchistan, Montenegro, and other places that Miss Libby would never visit. Her correct pronunciation was due to her great linguistic ability and keen ear, as much of a pride and joy to her as it is to me today as I practice what she preached. To be able to impart, to those who have no ear for the nuance and accuracy of sound and speech, the critical pronunciation of these proper names that the average American murders so badly gives me great pleasure. It has, unhappily, lost me a few friends who resent my instruction.

Then there was Miss Pennell in the seventh grade, who though she rapped my knuckles until they were black and blue was never able to dissuade me from my determination to write with my left hand instead of my right. I wish she had had her way, as the Palmer Method that she sought to instill into our young hearts and minds would have enabled me to write with ease, whether with my left or right hand. Instead, there evolved the cramped and painful muscular efforts that I now employ. I am often forced to have recourse to the mechanical typewriter that forms the letters so easily for me.

When school let out I would run out like a convict suddenly released and lie in wait behind a huge snowbank for the Morrison Grocery Store sled. Oh, those Maine winters! Even though you'd get used to them more or less, sometimes the wind would blow the snow at you to almost cut the skin off your face. It would be very quiet and then I would hear the singing sound of the steel runners and dart out to catch an illicit ride on the sleigh. When the driver caught sight of me he would whip up the horses in challenge, looking back with sadistic delight as I scrambled for a free ride—yet rather hoping, I felt, that I would make it. On the days I was lucky I would cling grimly to the left-rear runner until I was near my father's drugstore and then swing off with as much aplomb as I could command. Sometimes when the footing was bad, I would reel into a snowbank and arrive like a bedraggled wharf rat at the Vallee Pharmacy.

I think the greatest thing in the life of a kid, better even than having a fireman as your father, is to have your dad own a drugstore. Think back to the days when *you* were a youngster. Wouldn't you have loved to run amuck among nine, count 'em, *nine* different flavors of ice cream in unlimited quantities? The variety became almost infinite when you considered the varied "toppings" of marshmallow, raspberry, strawberry, chocolate and so on, not to mention sundry chopped nutmeats and cherries. I must confess that, even now, my mouth waters as I write.

C. A. VALLEE, DRUGS. That's *Charles Alphonse* Vallee, mind you, my father and proprietor of The Rexall Store right there on the corner.

It was the store with the American flags draped in the windows and the Coca Cola and Moxie signs all over it. It dispensed pipes and tobacco, imported and domestic cigars, drugs and chemicals, medicines (some with the guarantee: "no cure, no pay"), and even money orders, along with countless other products.

Dad loved every minute of it. He had a way of describing the arrival of a new soda fountain, with its gleaming marble top, that made it sound like the creation of a new public building. And the staid state of Maine has never been quite the same since Charles Vallee introduced it to that insidious concoction known as the banana split. (He called it *spleet!*) All in all, I suppose he was the Howard Johnson of his day.

I suppose Dad figured that if I was old enough and big enough to get my hand in the huge gumdrop jar, I was quite mature enough to pitch in with the countless chores about the place. So I was apprenticed and I soon found out that all was not beer and skittles, or at any rate not licorice and peanut brittle.

Our day began at seven in the morning and operation number one was to sweep out the whole store from one end to the other. Then there was the ice. If an automobile runs on gasoline then a drugstore fountain in those days ran on ice. It would be 'way below zero outside but we'd still have to wrestle with the huge cakes of ice, dragging them down from the bulkhead and cutting them into four with the big ice pick. Each of these pieces was chopped fine in a large wooden tub then poured into some thirty buckets to be carried laboriously upstairs so the pieces might be packed around the ice cream. This was done the first thing in the morning and the last thing at night. I chopped thirty pails of ice in the morning and thirty each night and carried the buckets upstairs and packed them around each flavor of ice cream. With mountains of ice indoors twice a day and the sheets of ice outdoors during the bitter winters, it's a wonder I didn't go snow-blind.

Then there were the Sunday morning drunks—pitiable, bleary-eyed, hanging around outside like disconsolate cattle, waiting for us to open up so they might get a pick-me-up for the day. As they huddled there, I sometimes thought they must be having a prayer meeting for the Emerson Drug Company and their esteemed bromo-seltzer! Other early risers queued up for the newspapers we sold or for cigarettes, the most expensive of which brought five cents per pack.

Back in the bulkhead, in addition to the seemingly endless supply of ice, there were always boxes of backbreaking size to be opened and their contents stored on the proper display shelves. There were the heavy-bellied kegs of syrups that had to be manhandled and doled out into the soda-fountain receptacles. It seemed there were always jobs to be done— the tub-shaped dishes which held the banana splits and sundaes, for instance, as well as the beverage glasses, that became dirty at an alarming rate and had to be washed out in the sink. Up above this sink was a shelf of patent medicines, including a large bottle of Listerine which was dispensed for mosquito bites or some slight skin irritation. It was not until long after I left my Dad's employ that some bright soul invented the word *halitosis* and took this company to multimillion-dollar heights. In those days we were fortunate if we sold two bottles of Listerine a year!

Dad's idea of the stocking of films and cameras caused us on a Sunday morning to find ourselves loading box cameras for hours at a time for the little French mill girls who worked in the cotton, paper, and silk factories in our area. These darlings also sought to impress their boy friends with the latest in French perfumes that we sold. We would demonstrate this aromatic aphrodisiac in the graceful Charles Alphonse Vallee manner. He'd take the glass stopper and wipe it delicately across the back of his hand. Then, with a flourish, he would wave the scented hand in front of the bewildered customers to their giggling delight.

At the age of nine, I found myself initiated into this long grind which began at seven in the morning and wound up usually at ten at night. Sometimes, just as we were about to close the doors, a streetcar would pull up and dislodge a group of thirsty and sweet-toothed individuals who had just enjoyed the movies at Riverton Park, some five miles away. Overtime—without pay! My back was getting sore, my ardor for the drug business was cooling rapidly and I'd scream at the trolley-car jerks: "What the hell do *you* want?"

The fact that the other drugstores across from us had closed long before meant nothing to Dad. The Vallee drugstore was almost always open and we, the nine of us, were the expectant slaves, ready to serve the public morning, noon and night. Truthfully, Dad was the forerunner of the present-day drugstore which never seems to close and which seems to have within its confines every conceivable object that a human being might want—from a postage stamp to a fiberglass catamaran.

It must have been disconcerting and rather annoying to my father that, prior to my apprenticeship in the drugstore, all of my energies and enthusiasms were directed toward the field of music and entertainment. When I was four years old, I became the victim of severe earaches. Maybe psychologists or psychiatrists can theorize about it—for some strange reason the excruciating pain deep in my ears was relieved by the sounds I would make pounding upon some enameled metal drums I had. I certainly can't explain it, but it worked. This therapy which I had accidentally discovered led me to take a fiendish delight in pounding upon the toy drums: the clatter of percussion seemed to hold a terrible fascination for me. When I was about eleven or twelve years old, Dad gave me a real snare drum.

How or why I was enabled to teach myself the rudiments of a snare-drum roll, I will never know. Yet I found myself in the sixth grade drumming the students to and from recess. But my greatest thrill was the eventual possession of a complete drum outfit—bass drum, foot-beater, cymbal, snare drum, holder, sticks, and the orchestral bells—which enabled me to play with the high-school orchestra. I have always said that a father must possess a love that passeth all understanding in order to give his child so noisy and nerve-racking a present.

On Armistice Day in 1918, when the regular drummer of the Westbrook City Band was unable to get down to the public square in front of my father's drugstore in time to play for the celebration, someone had to be quickly found to take his place. There I was, in his stead, swelling with pride. I felt mighty grown up as I banged away with drumsticks in the marches I knew better than the bandmaster himself.

Was this band appearance my show-biz debut? Or was it my first appearance at the Star Theater? When I look back at the Star I realize that it was a brick architectural horror like any one of hundreds of such monstrous edifices which mushroomed in small towns almost overnight, spawned by the fabulous magic lantern. It had all the esthetic glamour of an immense shipping crate but in those days this was the town's TV set! The citizens had pretty damned good programming fare at ten cents per seat—Charlie Chaplin in *Easy Street* and *Shoulder Arms*, the latest Mack Sennett opus which might feature "Fatty" Arbuckle, Chester Conklin, Ben Turpin, and all that crowd, or the Star might go a bit arty (although they did not realize it at the time) with a blockbuster like D. W. Griffith's *Intolerance*.

Since the movies were silent, it was necessary to retain a small orchestra to implement the on-the-screen action with suitable mood music. In the beginning our small theater got away with a mere piano, played by a fabulous pianist, Lionel Doucette, who somehow segued from scene to scene and made a modicum of "sound-track" sense. A year later *we*, the Star, had an orchestra, mind you. Only five pieces, granted, but we made up for our lack of numbers with sheer volume. When an emergency occurred for one week, I was permitted to join this very select group. It was comparable to a kid of today suddenly appearing on a TV show. I was only a substitute for an indisposed musician but I fancied I saw even strangers glancing at me on the street as if they had seen me somewhere before. I was quite certain I had practically arrived.

At the same time, when not in school, I was helping my Dad. I would be, for instance, delivering special molds of ice cream and the salted nuts which my mother cooked (after we skinned the almonds) in salt and butter. It was, I guess, the forerunner of the present-day especially prepared nut industry which runs into millions of dollars. At the time, however, it was, as far as I knew, the special creation of my Dad. These high-calorie goodies I delivered to the wealthy mill-owning families of our neighborhood as well as those which Dad donated graciously to the nuns and priests of our French-Catholic church and ministers of the Protestant establishments on the important holidays of the year. In the winter I carried them in my sled through the heavy snows, through the mile-length of our city, and in the summertime deliveries were made on my little cart.

I liked to think of myself as the advertising manager when supervising the passing of countless handbills announcing special sales at our store. Old eagle-eye Hubert was always watching carefully to see that the less-interested of my staff did not merely chuck the bills overboard into the river. I required them to do as I did: put them, no matter how frozen their hands might be, into every mailbox where they were supposed to go.

By now Dad must have sensed that I wanted no part of the drugstore. At least one thing probably gave him a clue—I would put on shows in the little barn back of our house. In essence, they were pale replicas of the films and occasional theatrical productions that came to town. For Saturday afternoons, Dad had an idea for getting rid of old candies—and I would be carting bags of stale chocolates to be given away to those who attended the matinee at the local Scenic Theater before the Star was built. It was then that I felt I was in seventh heaven! I could be within the confines of the fascinating edifice known as a *theater*. It was the hub of Westbrook's modest entertainment wheel, with a proscenium that looked to me then as big as all outdoors!

Of course, if I had been an average, red-blooded American boy, I would have fixed my eyes on the filmic grandeur of the screen wherein Mabel Normand might have belted the wall-eyed Ben Turpin with an exceedingly mellow custard pie in a timeless Mack Sennett charade or have been entranced by Griffith's limning of Sherman's gory march to the sea in *The Birth of a Nation*.

Curiously, I was not watching the film on the screen or the production itself. I was much more interested in watching the way the curtain rolled up! And, too, I was always going up to the booth in which the film was projected and watching the way the operator shifted from one projection machine to the other, repaired the film and cranked the machines, bringing to life the motion pictures on the screen.

Almost before I knew it I was deeply engrossed in all things pertaining to the entertainment business—and music swelled up within me until I felt I would burst like an overfed song sparrow. As I walked home from the drugstore I would whistle the popular tunes of the time. I was flabbergasted and highly pleased to find out that some of the neighbors told my Dad they left their windows open to hear me each night!

Then came that night of nights—I was actually to perform in the pit of the Star. You can't imagine a more stupid or worse acoustical presentation. Of course, my mother and father were there in the front row beaming like klieg lights. I sang the melody of "When You Come to the

End of a Perfect Day" and my sister Kathleen sang harmony and played the piano.

All right, so it was only for a Firemen's Benefit. Nevertheless, it was immensely affecting to me. I don't remember any undue "stage" fright. I do remember applause at the end of our number and, well, it might have been, now that I think of it, just a trifle perfunctory. But I was too elated to even notice.

I sought music in every way I could, even to the point of begging my sister to teach me the piano. She had become quite proficient and kindly consented to undertake the job. But, unfortunately, I had no patience with the drudgery of scales and exercises. Our temperaments clashed—it was worse than a woman teaching her husband to drive! I think I was too stubborn. All the same, I would give my right arm today if I could really play this most important of all musical instruments.

In the year 1914 I technically lost my amateur standing as a performer. At the home of a local paper-mill executive, I received ten dollars for the rendition of a song entitled "The Sunshine of Your Smile"!

With this highly paid *coup*, could Broadway and Hollywood be far beyond?

It was about this time—oh, I suppose it was sometime early in 1917— that billboards began to appear around our streets suggesting that the youth of America join the Navy and, as they put it, see the world.

That year when the country went to war (a war to end all wars), the great songs, many of which are remembered and sung today, were items like "Back Home Again in Indiana," "The Bells of St. Mary's," "Dark-town Strutters' Ball," and that wild one with the Dixieland flavor, "Tiger Rag." However, as tin-pan alley grew more and more martial, we found ourselves singing, humming and whistling strange numbers such as "Goodbye Broadway, Hello France," "Over There," and "When Yankee Doodle Learns to Parlez Vous Francais."

In May of that eventful year, President Woodrow Wilson issued a Presidential Proclamation establishing conscription wherein all male persons between the ages of twenty-one and thirty, both inclusive, were to be subject to the draft. I didn't give it a second thought, since I was only fifteen.

It was the start of high school and it began to dawn on me that said schooling would be a waste of time, for I had chosen the "Gut" course —down-to-earth, bread-and-butter-basic, learn-a-trade.

The "Gut" course in Westbrook High School included curricula in mechanical drawing, forge shop, afternoons in machine shop, much chemistry, pattern-making and more mechanical drawing plus a great deal of study in the sciences. Also included was on-the-job training at the S. D. Warren Paper Mill, the largest paper mill in the world, in Cumberland Mills, one mile away. These long, dull years prepared one for the estimable and much-prized job of foreman at ten dollars a day. It was definitely the easy course!

Our manual-training instructor, Charles Johnson (who was later to become the caretaker of my lodge in Maine in 1930), impressed upon us the objective of seeking to better ourselves.

"Don't be satisfied in growing up and having to work for a dollar a day," he'd say. "Carrying your little lunch box back and forth from the mill every day. Pay attention to what I tell you—make good grades and you will be a mill foreman someday. Ten dollars a day!"

I took this course because all the rest of the boys whom I knew in the grammar school definitely agreed that this was *the* course if you wanted to have a "Gut-easy" career. I, to whom music and entertainment was the breath of life, plunged into a course which found me Monday afternoon in a duster, cranking away and trying to bring to life the fire in the forge in order to take out a shapeless piece of metal and beat it and weld it into the shape of a gate-hook; and on Tuesday, with the same duster on, putting a piece of metal into a lathe and turning it into a screw, bolt, or what have you.

I tired of this grind almost immediately. I had plunged into the course almost with my eyes closed, taking the path of least resistance in doing what most of my pals did. But I was just too stubborn to stick it.

It was probably the realization that I was a square peg in a round hole as I wasted away my time in this industrial course (combined with a thorough dislike for the montonous routine of my father's drugstore) that led me to seek a change. I was dazzled by the glamour of the billboards that showed a young fellow in a natty blue uniform, with his white cap at a jaunty angle, suggesting that I join the Navy and see the world. That, more than anything else, made me determined to do just this. It pays to advertise and Uncle Sam must have had a hell of an ad manager.

This climax precipitated itself at lunch at our home when Uncle Henry Randall, who was a Civil War veteran, and his wife, Aunt Mae, were our guests for a few short days. When I brought up the subject of joining the Navy, Uncle Henry heard the trumpet blow and seconded it warmly. My father, annoyed with my reluctance to work in the drugstore, felt that this was the time to call my bluff. Before I knew it, Dad and I were down in the office of the treasurer of the bank who was empowered to enlist men in our town for the United States Navy. That afternoon I was in Portland, Maine, six miles away, taking the physical. That same night on the *Calvin Austin*, an old side-wheeler, in charge of five other young men who had enlisted that afternoon, I was on my way to Newport, Rhode Island to begin a career as Apprentice Seaman in Uncle Sam's Navy.

The Services in 1917 were far more difficult and exacting than those of World War II. For a boy accustomed to the relative luxuries and enjoyments of life in a small town, with everything that a fairly successful small-town druggist could provide, it was tough to be thrown into competition with the rough-and-tumble element of men from the entire country. It was doubly disturbing now that we had declared war on Germany.

They decorated my desk at school with a flag. My entrance into the Armed Forces was followed by a flock of other boys from the home town. We were at war.

One day when I was swabbing the walls of the barracks, I looked outside and saw a group of young men in fine civilian clothes. I turned to my Chief Petty Officer.

"Say, Chief," I said, "what are those guys doing around here?"

"Oh, them."

The CPO, whose hash-marks on his sleeve bespoke twenty-four years of service and who was still an enlisted man, smiled a little wryly.

"In about three months time they'll be ensigns."

"How are they going to do that?" I was a little puzzled.

"Because they been to college," answered the chief. "Because they been to college, they are eligible to be commissioned officers."

I suddenly felt very lonely and left out. It unpleasantly brought home to me the fact that I had missed the boat in leaving high school, that the most important thing that I could ever hope to accomplish was to secure a college education. My God—I could stay in the Navy for thirty years and still might not be even a chief petty officer!

Ahead of me was the bleak and blank prospect of four years as a seaman in the Navy. I resolved then and there that when I finished this training (thinking, dramatically, if I came out alive), I would go back to school and never complain again about it or my father's drugstore work.

Then a strange thing happened. During the course of one of the periodic and methodical naval cursory examinations, it was discovered that I had acquired the measles! Then, for some reason, the Navy began looking through my records and came upon my birth certificate. How they had overlooked this document and its secret before, I'll never know. At any rate, they discovered at this rather late date that I had stretched my age from fifteen to seventeen in order to enlist. Before I knew it a special order, signed by the Assistant Secretary of the Navy, one Franklin D. Roosevelt, sent me packing back to high school.

The night I came home with my bag over my arm I embraced my mother as though nothing had happened and went to bed. For the next three days, relieved and happy to be home, I served the finest soda-fountain concoctions imaginable—in my Navy blues. This euphoria wore off a few weeks later as my same discontent with the monotonous routine of the drugstore reasserted itself.

But it was not until the end of my freshman year in high school (when I had made up the weeks I had lost due to my naval apprenticeship) that an agreement between my Dad and me for the summer work was to be destroyed by an act of the head drug clerk at the store.

You see, I had a yen for a motorcycle and it was to cost Dad some $200 for the finest machine of that day. In return, it was understood that I was to work in the drugstore all that summer. I must admit I was a capable clerk and could handle four or five people at the soda fountain to almost any other clerk's one or two. In addition to this, I could fill simple prescriptions, demonstrate perfumes, load cameras— and I knew where practically every patent medicine in the drugstore might be hidden.

Best of all Dad had taken on the most thrilling (to my mind) product the store had ever handled. I must say he was a most progressive proprietor—he was always on the lookout for new products to modernize his stock. In some way he put in a line of Victor records, complete with a demonstrator phonograph.

"Get your nose out of that gramophone horn," he'd yell at me. "Can't you see there are people waiting at the fountain!"

People would drop into the store and browse around while they waited for the streetcar. Most of the time they bought very little—but after we had the records and phonograph, I made it a point to "beam" the sound at these potential customers. By this devious device I sold a lot of records —but I really played them mostly for myself. I must have played Al Jolson's "Sahara" hundreds of times—I can still do it fairly well from memory. There were also records by the First Marimba Band, a talented group just up from Latin America. There was an artist whose Victor record label billing was "Sergeant Mike Markels and his orchestra." He had achieved quite a reputation as bandmaster in the Service in World War I and, after the end of the shooting, moved into the entertainment world still retaining his "rank" of Sergeant. He set up a band-booking organization whereby he spawned a number of Sergeant Markels combos, such as Meyer Davis (one of his biggest competitors) did at the time. Strangely enough, when I went to New York during a vacation from Yale, I was to ask this same "sergeant" for a job as saxophonist— unhappily to no avail.

At any rate, this phonographic product gave me pleasant respite from ladling out cherry topping and chopped nuts at the soda fountain. It was a pleasant, refreshing breeze blowing off Broadway, wafting its way into the hinterlands of Maine. Records were and are most wondrous things. I'll venture to say there are kids in Peoria and Albuquerque, etc., right now getting similar vicarious tastes of the sound from the Big Town.

Then suddenly in June of 1917 an event occurred that was to change the entire course of my life. Wasn't it Shakespeare who said, "There is a tide in the affairs of men, which, taken at the flood, leads on to fortune"? I'll wager as Aimee Boissaneau, my father's head clerk, walked briskly along to Dad's drugstore on that bright Monday morning, he had no idea that he was about to be the turning point in my life and root me out of the drugstore into the world of show business.

What Aimee could have been thinking about when he put lime juice into a chocolate-syrup jug without changing the label, I'll never know. Nevertheless, as I began that first summer morning of a contemplated long series of days in the drugstore (in exchange for the aforementioned motorcycle *plus* spending money) I carried the chocolate-syrup jug out to the soda fountain and started to pour chocolate syrup into the fountain receptacle.

Had it been milk or some other syrup, I might not have taken it so badly. But when a feeble stream of yellow lime juice poured out of the bottle, I blew my top.

"Who in hell is the idiot here who doesn't know the difference between chocolate and lime juice?" I demanded loudly.

I'll say one thing for Aimee. He may have been a dope about putting lime juice in a chocolate-syrup jug, but he never ducked the issue. He came out and instead of being apologetic about the whole thing (which would have soothed my ruffled feathers) he was even more belligerent than I.

"I did it and what are you going to do about it?" he shouted. "Who in hell are you to be telling off the head clerk, anyway!"

There is one thing about my make-up that most of my friends and enemies know. When someone pulls a boner and instead of being contrite, somewhat apologetic, seeks to defend the boner with an implausible and weak excuse—or no excuse at all—and gives me a fight, I find myself in danger of having a stroke. The French and the Irish are well-known for hotheadedness and I have both bloodlines with a concomitant low boiling point.

I was that way then and I am that way now. The quickest way to take the wind out of my sails, or the sails of anyone who is really annoyed about some stupidity, is simply to admit it and get it over with. Had Aimee done that, I probably would be in the drugstore today or might have retired as a small-town druggist in St. Petersburg, Florida, where my Dad used to go for his winter vacations.

My father, hearing the rumpus out at the soda fountain, came out to act as arbiter. To my complete consternation and rage, he sided with Aimee! That did it! In two seconds flat I had my coat on and was on my way astride the shiny new motorcycle toward Stroudwater River and "the old swimming hole." Even after a refreshing dip in the water, I was still burning about the incident. I made up my mind that I would not return to the drugstore and, instead, wandered down to the poolroom under the post office across from the drugstore. In the bowling alley there I offered to set up pins at three and a half cents a string. I got the job. I had been working two or three hours setting up pins at three cents a string when Dad found out what I was doing. He immediately called up the owner of the bowling alley and demanded that he let me go. The owner of the bowling alley, wanting no trouble with my father, told me that I just couldn't stay on, as much as he needed me. This happened again at another spot in town and determined my course of action.

I had never thought that I would run away from home, but I did. I stayed at the home of one of my chums and for the next two days spent my time swimming or hanging around another bowling alley which had closed for the summer. There I would listen to old Doc Stone, the blind pianist, do his wonderful songs at the piano. Perhaps it was fate, but I couldn't have chosen a more perfect retreat. To this bowling alley came Frank Girard, a boy of French-Canadian extraction, who for some reason had always looked up to me as a sort of leader.

"I've just quit my job," he told me. "I'm not at the Star Theater any more."

"I'm looking for a job," I told him. "Do you think they'd take me?"

"It doesn't cost anything to try," he said.

I immediately hot-footed it to the Star and talked to Fred Eugley who, coincidentally, had married Aimee Boissaneau's sister. Fred was a stocky, rugged individualist who would bow to no man, and in profane language he told me that if I suited him I could stay regardless of my Dad's wishes.

I was to be paid seven dollars a week. My duties included sweeping the theater in the morning, sweeping out the peanut hulls between shows, opening the cans of film as they came in three times weekly, rewinding the film, looking for bad places and breaks, cleaning out the projection booth, replacing the worn-out carbons in the projector lamps, taking tickets until show time and then standing in the hot booth cranking away (the machines weren't motor-driven at the Star). I would crank for the two-hour afternoon show and then come back again to perform the same duties for the four-hour evening shows. The day that Pat Bernier, the projectionist, nonchalantly gave the crank an extra whirl and asked me to grab it was a thrill I'll never forget. To stand there looking out through the square aperture watching the picture come to life on the screen by the magic of *my* right hand, was a joy that was probably only equaled by that of the man who made the film itself as he saw his creation come to life on the screen. Long before, I had purchased a little two-dollar motion-picture machine with one twelve-inch loop of film. Hour after hour during the long winter nights I would crank it endlessly, imagining my own productions and creating the musical background to fit the mood of the pictures. But here was the real thing, with the nimble fingers of my idol, Leo Doucette, the pianist down in the pit, bringing the barely audible tones of his mood music up to my happy ears. I was participating, an integral part of the program! And getting paid for it!

There were wonderful Mack Sennett comedies that had me laughing so hard that I fear the rhythm of my crank-turning must have suffered. One incredible Sennett jape had a lion running through a Pullman car and frightening the colored porters to the point where they literally turned white with fear.

A dream world, a dream factory in which I was ecstatically participating, it was all subliminal grist for the mill of a show-biz apprentice—whether that apprentice knew it or not.

There was no doubt about it. That day that Aimee Boissaneau got out on the wrong side of the bed was the turning point in my life. It was a little rough on my father who had bought the motorcycle and who really needed me badly at the store. But, if he had had his way earlier, maybe I would not have been a small-town druggist, either. I can remember the conversation I overheard between Dad and Mother when I was about five years old. It seemed that Father, who was one of a family of nine or ten boys with only one girl, thought that his greatest contribution to mankind would be to give a son to the altar of the Catholic Church. Can you imagine! Father Hubert Prior Vallee!

Mother, who had a brother, Father Lynch, already in the priesthood, saved the world from the astonishing sight of a crooning Cardinal. She stood fast in her desire to see me graduate from college, preferably Yale (I don't know where she got the idea of Yale!), and her argument to Dad seemed to me at that time a very cogent and flattering one. It was she more than anyone else who had detected early my great love for music and my desire to do something in the field of entertainment. She reminded Dad very punctiliously about the fact that as a baby I had sung myself to sleep instead of crying. She reminded him of all the shows I had put on in our barn and of how I would come home after seeing a motion picture only to recreate some segment of it, utilizing the kids in the neighborhood as my cast. And how, after the circus left town, I tried to create my own circus in our own back yard, with a menagerie of dogs and cats in improvised cages placed on the kids' wagons and paraded down through the streets to the amazement of our neighbors. To Mother that could mean only one thing: that her son was destined for a place in the world of show business—and she was to live to see her prognostication come true.

It is just possible that Mother herself had a touch of the entertainer in her. She was bright, attractive, dignified, animated. The rest of the family was often made to howl with laughter as in recounting the latest gossip she would mimic perfectly the neighbors involved. I often think that any gift I have for "doing impressions," as they call it, certainly stems from my mother's delightful personality.

At any rate, I had performed my duties satisfactorily at the Star Theater one. In fact, in true Tom Sawyer style, I was soon securing the assistance of some of my chums by reciprocal arrangement, permitting them to see the show for nothing. As we closed the theater on the fourth or fifth the pianola or piano-roll piano, used when Leo Doucette was occasionally absent from the regular piano, made my position as janitor a most pleasant for about four days. The fun of sweeping out the theater while I ran night, I stepped out into the dark to find Eddie Hebert, the Chief of Police, standing there waiting for me. I knew, of course, what he wanted but I was surprised when he told me that Dad had decided that if I wanted to stay at the Star I could. There was, however, the stipulation that I would have to return home. Mother was on the brink of a nervous breakdown! All Dad asked was that I assist him during the Sunday rush hours, which I was more than happy to do.

The summer segued into fall and I took on additional duties. I would take a streetcar six miles to Portland three nights a week carrying the two-reel comedy to the express office to have it reshipped to one of our sister theaters up in Rockland, Maine. I was to save the five cents carfare by bicycling the six miles each way. This physical effort seemed as nothing when counterbalanced by the jingling of the nickels in my pocket.

By this time we were well into the war with Germany and it was on a fall night in 1918 that I went into Portland, Maine, to the newly opened DeLuxe Strand Theater. This show place dwarfed our modest Star not only in capacity but in beauty. The picture playing there was a wartime shocker called *The Hun Within*.

Kathleen, my sister, knew the organist, a fabulous performer named Leo LeSieur, a boy who had come down from Montreal to set the natives of Maine on their ears with his gymnastics at the big console. After we saw the picture, Leo LeSieur introduced me to Bill Reeves, a chain-smoking manager, rough, but with a good heart. To my great surprise, he confessed that he knew about my working at the Star and asked me if I would like to be head usher at the Strand, supervising the activities and duties of four attractive young ladies and two young men. Oh, boy! Would I!

Looking around at the beautiful interior of the theater, I felt it was almost too good to be true. I was somewhat dashed, however, when he informed me that the salary would be the same as I had been receiving at the Star—seven dollars a week. With the subtraction of the carfare required to make the trip daily, this would mean that I would make much less than I had been earning out in Westbrook. However, the job was a pleasant one—merely standing in the entrance to the theater, taking the tickets, tearing them in half and instructing the possessor to go upstairs or down, according to his ticket.

There was only one drawback about this job at the time: I was going through the age of puberty and my complexion was suffering by the change. My face was so broken out that I was embarrassed when attractive young ladies handed me their tickets and I would turn the other way and mumble something as to their destination.

But this again was to be another turning point—another "tide in the affairs of men." Our chief electrician was a heavy-set individual named Richard Farr. Dick had very bad teeth. They were almost black, in fact. One day he approached me with a business proposition.

"You've been studying clarinet for a while, haven't you?" he began.

"Yes, I have," I said.

"Good. You see, I have been renting a C melody saxophone from the music store for five bucks a month. Would you like to take it off my hands?"

"But I don't know how to play a saxophone," I answered.

"Look, it's very similar to the clarinet. You practice on this thing a few short days and you will be surprised. Say you've got a date with a girl who plays the piano, see? You make a big hit with her accompanying her on the sax. Get it?"

"That sounds pretty good," I said. "But if the sax is so great, why are you giving it up?"

"I don't know why but every time I play this thing my teeth nearly kill me. Maybe it's the vibrations or something."

As I listened to Maestro Arthur Kendall and his twelve-piece orchestra play the overture on the big stage, I came more and more to love the orchestra and orchestral music. The thought of being able to play the saxophone, an instrument about which very little was then known and so rare that there probably weren't two performers on it in the entire city, made me feel fortunate indeed to be able to rent one.

The saxophone was brass and it had begun to get green and tarnished in spots but to me it was a thing of great beauty. The first time I put the reed and mouthpiece into my mouth and played a simple composition, with my sister at the piano, I was so overcome with the beauty of what I'd produced (at least *I* thought it beautiful) that I almost cried.

In a week I had mastered several compositions—popular ones of that day—and it was time for the Freshman Reception at the gymnasium down at Cumberland Mills. By now I had definitely decided to prepare to enter some college or university. By the addition of only one subject, French, which I was now taking, I would be eligible for some institution whose entrance requirements were not too stringent. I suggested to the committee for the Freshman Reception that, as a postgraduate, I would be very happy to secure the orchestra for the dancing afterward. I persuaded Dad to bring down some liquid refreshments (some of his *spiritus frumenti* which when mixed with certain attractive fruit punches became liquid dynamite). This we used to assuage the consciences of some of the union musicians I was able to secure for the engagement so that they would overlook the fact that they were playing with me and several other musicians who were not members of the union. I stood forth in front of this motley array, facing an admiring group of freshmen and upper classmen, and although my repertoire consisted of about eight or nine popular songs the instrument itself was such a novelty that I really was the hit of the evening. Soon the boys from the union were feeling no pain and we really put on a fine program.

My "career" was only beginning. Our plumber had a Saturday night engagement in Portland, where he and another banjoist surrounded themselves with a girl pianist, drum, bass, clarinet, and two violins. My budding talent on the saxophone had become fairly well-known in the area and Joe Hazelton, the plumber, had heard about it. He suggested that I become a part of the aggregation for the princely sum of five dollars for playing from eight to twelve at the Pythian Temple. Now I thought that I was really going places and my "fame" on this strange instrument began to mount.

So many people never quite seem to decide on their specific career until too late, if at all. I was fortunate to have enough musical experience under my belt at a relatively early age to give me an unshakable resolve to make the field of entertainment my business. Once I make up my mind I am a pretty stubborn guy. I now felt I had found my lucky star—and I was in the process of getting a good "fix" on it.

CHAPTER III

Saxophobia

"Look For the Silver Lining"

It was the first year of the Roaring Twenties. I was playing in all sorts of bands, bands with real jazzy names like "Welch's Famous Novelty Jazz Orchestra," "Harold T. Pease and His Society Orchestra," "The Crescent Orchestra," "The Vega Orchestra," and "The Famous Harmonic Orchestra." We played tunes like "Avalon," "I Used to Love You But It's All Over Now," "I'll Be With You in Apple Blossom Time," and "Margie."

I was getting the dread disease *saxophobia* but I loved it!

There was a recording that was to change the whole course of my musical career as well as my name. It was a Victor record entitled "Valse Erica" by a saxophonist named Rudy Wiedoeft. Up to that time I was in the position of a country fiddler, let us say, in a lonely spot in the Ozarks. This budding violinist imagines himself quite a boy with the bow, but upon hearing a record by Heifetz or Kreisler he really realizes just how bad he is.

The beauty of Wiedoeft's tone, the terrific speed of his tonguing, his clean-cut execution all hit me like a thunderclap. Instead of being annoyed, I was overjoyed to know that the instrument was capable of producing such a round and heavenly tone. I immediately set about the long and arduous task of perfecting my technique until I could become the equal or even the superior of the man I had heard on the record.

I proceeded to write Rudy Wiedoeft but as the days went by no reply was forthcoming. I wrote him seven letters, only to be greeted by complete silence from the master. By this time I had stuck a catalog picture of Wiedoeft up on the wall, and even as I gazed at him in admiration I vowed that some day he would acknowledge me as a worthy foeman. I suppose I was really annoyed that he would not answer.

At this time I was unquestionably inspired by a story which had appeared in serial form in *Collier's*. I was later to receive the actual book autographed by the author, who was evidently intrigued by my enthusiasm.

22

1. The infant Rudy with his maternal grandmother, mother, sister Kathleen and father.

2. A pensive portrait of Vallée at age eight.

3. Seaman Vallée, June, 1917 immediately following his discharge (underage) from the Navy.

4. Civilian Vallée proudly displays his first C melody sax, circa 1921.

5. A 1917 photo of Dad Vallée's drug store and staff.

6. The Yale Collegians pose in a formal portrait.

7. A rare shot of raccoon-coated Rudy, bandleader at the Yale Bowl, Fall, 1927.

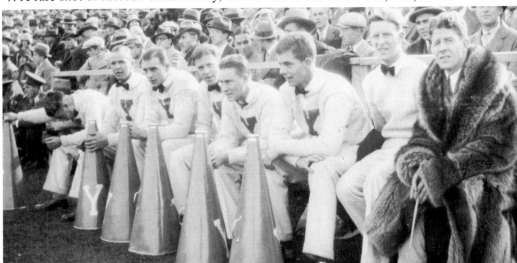

8. This cover epitomized Rudy's early preference for the dark sultry type female. Note remarkable resemblance to Fay Webb, his second wife. (see picture No. 18)

9. The Connecticut Yankees in bucolic splendor, Milton Point Casino, Rye, New York; the summer of 1928 finds them on the brink of fame.

The story was called *The Guarded Heights*. I suppose it might seem corny by today's standards but it moved me deeply then. Wadsworth Camp, its author, told of the son of impoverished, formerly wealthy parents, who were now permitted a small house on the vast Planter estate owned by a tycoon who practically ruled the world. The family was permitted to eke out an existence by doing menial work for the great Planter himself. The boy, a handsome six-footer, acted as a groom and was allowed occasionally to ride with Sylvia Planter, the luscious daughter of the great man. When Sylvia Planter is thrown from her horse, George Morton, the boy, blurts out his love for her as he sees her apparently in a faint. He finds to his great embarrassment that she has heard his protestation of love and takes the riding crop away from her as she tries to hit him across the face with it. He is thrown off the estate but not without first securing a photograph of Sylvia which he hides under his cap. The great man Planter, himself, has told him that he would destroy an army of such upstarts as George Morton if he ever so much as dared to look at his daughter.

The estate is near Princeton, and seeking out someone to help him, George Morton comes upon a tutor named Squibbs Bailey. Bailey sees in George the makings of a great football player. He lays out a routine of eight hours of study, eight hours of sleep, and eight hours of physical and mental football practice. On the nights that Morton is tempted to fall asleep or give up his colossal task of crowding three years' work into three months, he glances at the riding crop in the picture of Sylvia Planter and rouses himself to "climb the heights."

He becomes the greatest star in the history of the Princeton football team and goes into partnership with Sylvia Planter's brother. Even though he meets Sylvia at his first freshman dance in New York City, she still remains aloof and ignores him, pretending that she has never even met him. In the end of the novel he wins her, of course, in the true American tradition. It was this book more than anything else which inspired me in my long days of five and six hours of continuous practice to look at the picture of Rudy Wiedoeft on the wall and vow that some day he would be proud of me.

My eighth letter was written from the hospital in 1920, as I recuperated from an appendectomy, and to my great joy he replied. I was able to have a small phonograph by my bedside, constantly cranking the Wiedoeft records which I had accumulated. The day I came home from the hospital I defied the doctor's orders and opened a box which had just come from New York City containing a new French saxophone—the last word in manufacture. I blew the horn and the dire predictions of the doctor did not materialize. I felt no pain nor did I faint, as he had predicted I might. My mother was horrified on returning home from Portland to find me playing it, but since it didn't seem to cause any ill effects she too became reconciled. But I was to pay for that defiance of doctor's orders by having to undergo the operation all over again two years later, when it was discovered that I had, by playing the saxophone too soon, weakened the incision so that the protective muscles were forced away.

At this time there were probably not one hundred saxophonists in the entire United States, in contrast to the hundreds of thousands who now play either for fun, for profit, or to annoy people. There was actually no instruction to be had that could tell me the hows or whys of any of the things Wiedoeft did so easily on his records. One thing above all puzzled me—the fact that his tone on the records had the same wave-like emotional appeal that my own singing and whistling did. Yet, when I played the saxophone my tone was like the bleat of a nanny goat!

I tried everything I could possibly do to improve the tone. I experimented this way and that way and couldn't seem to hit upon the same effect that Wiedoeft gave in his sustained tone. Suddenly one night when the folks had gone to Portland and the snows were piled high around the windows, I stumbled upon the trick of producing the simple *vibrato* or wave-like quality which violinists produce by moving their fingers on the strings. This night when I discovered the trick of producing it by alternately relaxing and tightening my lower jaw on the reed, I was so delighted that I almost wept.

I discovered it on a Monday night and by Saturday had perfected it to the point where I could produce it almost mechanically without having to remind myself. I said nothing to anyone that Saturday night when I unpacked my horn at the Pythian Temple for our four hours of dance music. Everything seemed normal. However, when I began playing and sustained the first few tones the rest of the musicians turned and looked at me as though I had suddenly changed color. At the end of the first set, they crowded around me to ask what had happened. I explained it as best I could but I was careful not to give away too much of the secret. To me it was a revolutionary thing which should be guarded from the rest of the saxophone world.

Thus it was I became known as the "boy with the singing saxophone tone" and my crowning achievement was to have Arthur Kendall, the leader of the Strand Theater orchestra, ask me to play solos on the stage at a salary of ninety dollars for six days!

Up to this time Father had become more and more irascible as shortly after lunch each day I would begin practicing the long sustained tones which would drive almost anyone crazy. It irritated him to such a degree that he rushed up the stairs one day and insisted that I go "hire a hall." Strangely enough, I took Dad's suggestion literally. For a while I practiced in the old, unused Scenic Theater; later, in the lodge rooms of the Pythian Temple in Portland, six miles away.

When the offer to play at the Strand Theater at almost thirteen times the amount paid me for my long days and nights of playing head usher was tendered me, I really thought that I had arrived. My orchestrations were to be made by my idol, Arthur Kendall, for the full twelve-piece orchestra. When I opened the Sunday paper and saw the ad in bold type: "Saxophone Soloist, Hubert Vallee" (with my "co-star" on the screen, Gloria Swanson, in *The Lash*), I suppose my head may have swelled a trifle. I had a burning curiosity to see what my Dad's reaction would be when he saw the ad. Carefully I left the paper where he couldn't help but see it when he came home to eat lunch and then peruse the Sunday newspaper.

I watched his gaze fall upon the ad. While there was no reaction in his expression (I was back of him pretending to be doing something) I saw two tears steal down his cheeks. I felt myself choking up as I realized that Dad had finally come to admit that my long hours of practice had not been entirely in vain. He and Mother always went into Portland on Mondays to have lunch at the Elks Club and then attend the vaudeville show at Keith's Theater. But this Monday I could bet they would be at the Strand instead.

The theater auditorium was so dark I couldn't tell who was out there. It was a good house for a Monday afternoon. As the time came for the curtains to part, Dick Farr, who had started me on all this by suggesting that I take over his saxophone, stood at his switchboard flushed with triumph, trying to hide it with the nonchalant chewing of his tobacco. I had a feeling that he was about as thrilled as I was. I think even Arthur Kendall caught a bit of the excitement of the moment, as he knew that I had been out front in my many-buttoned bellboy jacket for almost a year and a half as head usher. This was the moment when the worm had truly turned.

There were no public-address systems in those days—there was no announcement; the orchestra merely began to play an introduction and I stepped out on the stage while a slide announced my name and what I was going to do.

How I ever got through those first solos I'll never know. I foolishly attempted some of the technical things that Wiedoeft had written, realizing that the audience expected some fireworks from me and that the playing of simple popular tunes alone would give them something of a letdown.

I think it was Winston Churchill or some other great orator who said the way to overcome any fear of your audience is to picture them all in long, red underwear. I didn't quite do that but I realized that they knew nothing at all about the saxophone and that probably only one or two in the entire audience had ever heard a Wiedoeft record. There were no radio stations in those days to broadcast records morning, noon and night, and the brilliant saxophone work so commonplace on the disk-jockey programs of this day and age were entirely lacking. So, in a way, I felt a little sense of superiority. When, in my extreme agitation and nervousness, I sometimes skipped whole passages, I knew that only Arthur Kendall and the musicians were aware that in the first place I wasn't really able to play these things and that I was so nervous I would have fumbled them anyway.

When I returned home that night, Father was waiting up to tell me how proud he was of me. His complete capitulation was in his simple statement that if I wanted the horn silver-plated or even gold-plated in the future, or if I needed another horn, I had only to ask him.

I had received advice from the University of Maine that if I was able to pass my French, I could enter as a freshman in the fall of 1921. I was going to have the thrill of attending a university where I felt my sax alone would carry me to some heights of popularity on the campus with the possibility of being pledged to one of the important fraternities. And since this was a coeducational institution, perhaps the plaintive notes of my saxophonic endeavors would win the heart of some fair damsel.

A violinist with whom I had played during my high-school days was already at the university. He suggested that I go up on the train with him and visit his fraternity house, Sigma Alpha Epsilon. I couldn't have made a wiser or happier choice. Naturally I brought with me all the phonograph records and pictures of Rudy Wiedoeft. The boys suggested that as a pledge I move into the room with my friend. During the hectic days that followed, every new pledge was brought into my room where I was displayed as the "genius" of the saxophone, and where I attempted in my bumbling way to play along with one of Wiedoeft's records.

You see, Maine is a state of small population where life comes hard— at least it did then—and the news traveled fast: the success of my appearance at the Strand Theater had made me indeed a state-wide celebrity.

The first day of matriculation I noticed a girl with a well-scrubbed complexion, obviously from one of the farm sections of Maine. Her looks—her long, golden tresses and the warmth of her complexion—hit me right between the eyes. I learned that her name was Avory Munro and the warm smile she flashed at me as we lined up to secure our assignments told me that this was going to be *the* girl.

Actually, I didn't have too much time or energy to see *any* girl. I was busy with my studies, and in addition to my practice on the saxophone I had my duties at the fraternity house—shoveling paths through the snow, freezing the ice cream when it came my turn, attending nightly meetings, and getting ready for the initiation which was to be a great event in my life. But as the fall wore on into the winter I occasionally did see Avory and we struck up a very happy romance.

In the fall, of course, we played with the band for football games. By winter I played the few dances that took place on or off the campus, with a band under my direction which included a group of musicians I had picked up. Again at Christmas time I was soloist at the Strand Theater for a week. There was also an appearance at the Star Theater in Westbrook as saxophone soloist with the City's Own Band. This was the same Westbrook City Band which I had watched so many times from afar and with which I had once played the snare drums in an emergency on Armistice Day.

After I received my first letter from Rudy Wiedoeft, I carried on a fairly continuous correspondence with a gentleman reputed to be Rudy's manager. Actually this "manager," Joe Davis, was a publisher who was later to release some of the songs which I recorded with my own Connecticut Yankees. Davis, sensing that I was really enraptured by the artistry of Wiedoeft, told me that he would arrange an appointment with the master.

When Easter vacation time came—it was in 1922—I took off like an excited bunny, bound for New York to bask at the feet of the god of the saxophone. After I had waited a little while in Joe Davis' office in the Roseland Building, he took me into the inner room where sat my idol. Wiedoeft was a man of about my height with clean-cut features, obviously of German extraction, and with a warm and winning smile. I was too embarrassed and nervous to remember many of the things I wanted to ask him. We chatted about the saxophone and made other pleasantries for a few minutes; then I asked him the all-important question. At that time I was undecided whether I would transfer to Yale or go to a band school in Ithaca, New York.

You see, I had become disillusioned with the University of Maine campus. My romance with Avory Munro had cooled considerably, chiefly because I had not been able to devote much time to seeing her. Also, because baseball was the all-absorbing spring sport at the moment, the star pitcher, Jack Jowett, a comparatively wealthy Sigma Nu frat man, had (on the evenings I had been working and studying) beaten my time.

I pleaded with Avory not to let our romance end so lightly but she made it quite clear in her firm way that "this is where you get off." With this emotional catastrophe in the back of my mind, I decided that I would get away from the campus and possibly study music as I had always wanted to do, get the training which I needed badly for success in my chosen field.

When I asked Wiedoeft whether he thought I should go to the band school or go on to Yale as my mother so fervently wished me to do, my idol thought for a moment and then replied, "You can always go to a band school but college comes once in a lifetime." He added that he had always wished he could have secured a college education and advised me by all means to transfer to Yale.

I summoned up enough courage to ask him if he might have another picture to add to the one in the Marine uniform he had sent me in response to my eighth letter. As he pulled open the drawer to look in vain for a photograph an empty liquor bottle rolled into view.

Embarrassed, Wiedoeft closed the drawer quickly. "Er, how would you like to come see me record at Brunswick Records tomorrow?"

This was almost too good to be true and of course I accepted. I told him that I was going to pay fifty dollars to make a personal recording at the Columbia studios so that I would have a lasting record of my tone and execution. He wished me well with it.

I left the building walking on air, though somewhat sobered by Wiedoeft's advice. I didn't give a second thought to the empty bottle but I realized later that it foretold the untimely end of this kind and wonderful personality. I was to come to know Wiedoeft very intimately, watch his star blaze and then wane as the saxophone itself receded in popularity. I was to have the privilege of acting as advance agent for him in London, England, for an appearance that he eventually made there.

Another time, while playing in Portland, Maine, he was to come out to our little house in Westbrook to play a gratis concert at a church in honor of my sister Kathleen. I was not able to be there since I was at college in New Haven. After the concert he cooked in our kitchen, as he was a master with pots and pans and recipes, and he kept the family up until early morning with his anecdotes and stories which he told so well in dialect. Rudy Wiedoeft was one of God's kindlier creatures, a man of great charm and personality, and I don't think he ever knew anything but friendship from those around him. But there was to be a tragedy in his life which was to destroy him long before his time, to take him away from the world of the saxophone and all who came to know him and love him so dearly.

As I watched him record, kidding with the rest of the band that he had gathered for the recording date, I realized he was not only a great artist but a lighthearted, warm individual who perhaps never realized how great was his genius, never knew the impression he had made upon the world of the saxophone and music in general. The loss of two of his three brothers in tragic accidents was probably the beginning of the end for this charming and capable man who covered his own personal feelings with a quip and a joke and a superb command of the instrument which he had mastered so thoroughly.

Toward the end of his life, Wiedoeft became interested in gold mining, of all things. He failed dismally at it. By that time the great sorrow and misery which was to engulf him had already begun. During the days when he stayed with my Dad and me at our apartment overlooking the East River, days that for me were filled with broadcasting, night-club and stage work, and the multitudinous things with which I was engaged, it was necessary for Dad and me to watch him very carefully lest he destroy himself completely. His death, which occurred while I was far away from him, affected me very deeply, and one of my proudest possessions is one of his saxophones, made according to his specifications. This was the man from whom I received my nickname. This was the man to whom I shall always be grateful for making me the "boy with the singing saxophone tone." This man was my inspiration on the saxophone, the inspiration which indirectly provided me with the means to secure my college education.

One of the obituaries of this fine man read as follows:

> "Rudy Wiedoeft, 46, known as the 'king of the Saxophone' during the 1920's, died Sunday night. He had long suffered from a stomach ailment. Wiedoeft, in addition to vaudeville and concert appearances as soloist on the instrument, also composed saxophone solos and taught the instrument. Among his pupils was Rudy Vallee, then known as Hubert Vallee, who dropped his first name in favor of his instructor."

CHAPTER IV

Yale University "Part One"

"I'll Build a Stairway to Paradise"

I DON'T SUPPOSE ANY OTHER COLLEGE freshman ever began his first day on the campus in quite the manner that I began mine. I came out of the darkened auditorium of Lampson Lyceum, where the dean of the Common Freshman Year had just welcomed us to the university. Ironically, this dean was the father of the boy who, nine years later, was to hurl a grapefruit at me in a Boston theater and almost kill me. Like an eager schoolboy, with my assignments and books under my arm I dashed out into the sunlight. There I saw a large luxurious (at least for that day) Cadillac with four men waiting for me. It sounds like a gangster movie and as if I was "going for a ride."

I actually *was* going for a ride but it was merely for a dance date at the Springfield (Massachusetts) Country Club. When I had arrived in New Haven to begin school, by a lucky chance I had made contact with Jack Cipriano who, along with partner Bill Bolton, had one of the best orchestras in the area. Cipriano was a lawyer and Bolton a city engineer and in their spare time they furnished "music *exclusively* for society functions and collegiate parties."

These two men, along with a George Bronfin, who was billed as "The Singing Drummer" (and, I might add, a wow with the girls, a real ladykiller), and John Nelson ("Sleepy") Hall, the toast of the Yale campus with his incredible gymnastics on his long-necked banjo although he couldn't read a note of music, were coolly waiting to be convinced of my musical ability at the dance that night.

During the ride of eighty miles, it was evident that the men had been talking about me in tones of great skepticism. This has been the curse and the bane of my entire existence. Somehow I have never inspired confidence. I don't think it is due to any weakness particularly evident in my face, but there is something about me, possibly a quiet reserve or shyness, that gives most people the impression that I can't do anything very well.

These men bombarded me with questions about my acquaintanceship with Wiedoeft and when I repeated what I had told Bolton—that I had turned down an offer to go to London with several Boston boys— I could see that they thought it a pretty farfetched story.

I decided I had better build up their confidence in me—honest to God, they sounded as if they were worried to be on the same bandstand with me! "Met Ted Lewis in Boston last spring," I said casually, when the right lull presented itself. "Great showman."

"Yeah," said George, "he must make a mint of money with all that clowning around."

"It's what I call relaxed showmanship," I said. "The way he uses his hands and the way he juggles that top hat around kills me."

"He's a good singer, too, in his own way," ventured Sleepy.

"You mean *stylist*, for crissakes," said George, our vocalist. "He's just a stylist."

"Anyhow," I continued, "I went backstage and he was very nice. We had a pleasant little talk."

"Really?" Jack was impressed. "How did you get to do that?"

"I just sent a note back asking was all. Of course, when I told him I was on my way to New York to see Wiedoeft, it didn't hurt any."

"You're a name dropper is what you are, Vallee," said Bill, a little annoyed.

"Maybe," I said. "Anyway, he let me handle his sax. It's really something. Got his name written on it in diamonds."

"Jesus, do you suppose they are *real* diamonds?" exclaimed Sleepy.

"They sure looked real to me. My God, I hear he's got the thing insured for thirty thousand!"

This intelligence seemed to impress them a trifle. We rode on for a few miles and there came another lull in the conversation. I felt it might be apposite to continue with some more show-business talk.

"Tell you a band I really admire," I said. "Paul Whiteman. He's really the cat's pajamas."

"You said it," said Sleepy. "I haven't heard him in person but his records are fine."

"I heard him at the Palais Royale in New York," I said, trying not to sound too excited. "Got a great sax man with him. Don Clarke."

When I mentioned I had seen Whiteman, whose records were being eagerly copied by just about every college orchestra in the land, Bill Webb, our colored chauffeur, turned his head around and started to ask me questions.

"For crying out loud, driver—keep your eyes on the road will you!" yelled Jack. "You're doing over forty!"

I was proud that I had gotten their interest. I started throwing out names of the men in the band I had met—Whiteman, himself, who later became my good friend, Henry Busse, Ferde Grofe the great composer-arranger, and Phil Ohman, the pianist who had just then joined the aggregation and was knocking out all his fellow musicians with his great ideas and ability.

By the time we reached Springfield I had done a lot of press-agenting for myself and the boys seemed a little bit reassured. But I was soon to rock them back on their heels—on the bandstand as I began assembling my saxophone, I casually asked for the tuning note of E flat on the piano. If I had suddenly asked them to turn the piano into an organ or had disappeared in a cloud of smoke I couldn't have caused more consternation.

Since time eternal it has been the custom of all musicians, regardless of what instrument they play, to tune to the note A. As the violin always tunes to that note (the A string is an open string on the violin and one best calculated to tune that instrument to its proper pitch) other musicians have tuned similarly. Being of a practical mind, a quality I have always had, to the displeasure of those who would set me down as a purely artistic and impractical fellow, I had long observed that in order to play A, it was necessary for me to use both my hands to finger the note. This made it impossible to blow the note and to adjust the mouthpiece to the proper pitch at the same time. Their dumbfoundedness on hearing me ask for E flat was intensely evident to me. They glanced at one another with apprehension and prepared for the worst. Tuning to E flat you can blow and tune at the same time. I deliberately did not attempt to blow the E flat in a way that would give any indication whether I had a good tone or a bad tone. By now the men frankly didn't know what to think. Bolton picked out a tune and tapped off the tempo. I played very softly during the first chorus, as Bolton was taking the melodic lead. Then they all turned to me for my turn at taking the melodic line, blowing out the melody of the chorus. It so happened that Bolton had picked a tune of a type to which I could do full justice. Halfway through my chorus, it was quite evident to any idiot that I had scored a touchdown with my compatriots. At the end of the first set of some four or five numbers they crowded around me to tell me how delighted they were. I had passed the severest test and was indeed one of their sacred group. The jobs that followed made it possible for me to make my way through college. The work and long hours were difficult but . . . well, it was the sort of on-the-job training which would fit me for a lifetime of music.

After the date we piled into our car, tired but happy, and proceeded back to New Haven, some two-and-a-half hours away. By the time we reached my dormitory it was close to four-thirty in the morning. After glancing over my assignments and studies, I discovered it was time to take a shower and go to chapel.

Thus began a long series of two and three engagements weekly. For example, we would leave at one o'clock Saturday afternoon to go to Amherst to play a tea dance following a football game. Then the band would go down to the Hotel Kimberly in Springfield for a dance from eight to twelve and back to New Haven at three or four in the morning. The remuneration for these engagements was usually around six or eight dollars but there were fortunately enough of them to take care of my tuition, room, and board.

Among my classmates were John Hay Whitney, the financier, John Ringling North, who later was to inherit the Ringling Brothers Circus empire, and the famed and unpredictable Lucius Beebe. The latter was the outstanding exhibitionist among the eight hundred of us and always made the rest of us keenly aware that he was the center of attraction. Suddenly, halfway through the year, he transferred. It is shocking to relate that he went to—Harvard! There, but for the grace of God— and all that!

I came to know a young fellow who was adept at playing the piano, the piano-accordion, and the banjo. His name was Curtis Peters and it was obvious that he was a poor but aristocratic young fellow who had prepped at Hotchkiss. He invited me over to his rooms to play saxophone to his piano and in the springtime he decorated with caricatures an up-stairs room over one of the fine tailoring shops in New Haven. This spot was to become our favorite hangout and was known as the Bulldog Inn. There, in conjunction with a couple of other musicians, we held forth each evening, happily grinding out the pop tunes of the day—"Anna-belle," "Swingin' Down the Lane," "Barney Google," "Yes, We Have No Bananas," and other like gems.

In the spring of '23, Peters approached me with the idea of playing at the Rendez-vous. It was the most successful supper club in New York City, where Gilda Gray was holding forth in resplendent glory, doubling from her part in the *Ziegfeld Follies*. This sounded great! I had seen the sexy ads for the place: "Egypt at the *Rendez-vous*—Gilda Gray Cordially Invites You to be Present at the Premier of Her 'Abor-iginal Voo-Doo' Dance." Like razzamatazz!

The Rendez-vous had been featuring the most popular collegiate band in the country, the Cornell Collegians. However, they were going down to the Lido Club at Long Beach in the summer and a band was needed to take their place. Peters assured us that Gilda Gray didn't know a note of music and that we would have no trouble filling the bill even though two of our musicians selected from the college ranks couldn't read a note. One of these boys, "Happy" Miller, became a famous motion-picture producer and writer under the name of Seaton I. Miller. He wrote *G Men, Two Years Before the Mast*, and many other films.

So we went up to New York on a Sunday and played for Gilda and the owner of the Rendez-vous. Well—Gilda may not have known much about music but she certainly did not dig our humble combo. We were told to come back some other time—and try again.

For the second audition, I wanted the job so badly I picked up a trumpet and tenor sax from New Britain and Hartford, Connecticut, both of whom could read.

P. S. We landed it!

During my freshman year I took biology instead of higher mathematics. Permission was granted by the aforementioned dean of the Common Freshman Year, Roswell P. Angier, who evidently sensed that I had no liking for, or understanding of, the dark field of mathematics. As any collegiate half-wit knows, biology is usually an easier course. In these classes where we proceeded to dissect the traditional frog (frogs must have an undying hatred for collegians) I made the acquaintance of Alfred deLiagre. He was obviously an artistic young fellow and was to prove it beyond a question of doubt by producing such hits as *Springtime for Henry*, *Petticoat Fever*, and *The Voice of the Turtle*. Another boy with whom I walked back from classes was a fat Irish lad named Lester Laden, who was later to play a very important part in my life as I was in his.

I had decided to major in Spanish. This subject had been my poorest in the University of Maine but I discovered it was taught at Yale by a group of ten or fifteen South American instructors who really knew their business. It was taught in such a way that one really learned how to speak it, write it, and read it. In fact, it is probably one of the most difficult courses in the entire university and one which demands an almost perfect final examination. In one portion of the exam itself, where a possible fifty mistakes may be made, one mistake and the student flunks the entire year! As a result, we really knew our subject; that is, those of us who weathered the first few months of it. It was one of the most pleasurable classes I could have attended and I decided to major in Spanish with the intention of going to South America to seek my fortune. An examination of the volume, *History of the Class of 1927— Yale College*, discloses the following statement along with my other biographical data:

> "*Vallee is planning to enter the*
> *music business in South America.*"

I honestly envisioned myself playing saxophone in a night club in Buenos Aires and perhaps owning a little music store on the side. At the night club, I would be flirting with and wooing the dark-eyed daughter of a wealthy cattle baron, marrying her and settling down to a lazy life out on the Argentine pampas.

I had a good deal going for me—by playing sax with the student orchestra in the Yale Dining Hall, I got my meals free. One evening, while the boys and I were quietly rendering some tasteful dinner music, an ominous quiet fell over the usually rather noisy room. When we finished the number you could have heard a wrist watch ticking. Then the diners began tapping in unison on the table with glasses, silverware, and other percussive paraphernalia. A few started throwing biscuits from table to table. Other objects followed, such as doughnuts soaked in coffee! The air was filled with bits of food and, before you could sing the first bars of "The Whiffenpoof Song," scores of tables were being overturned with the resultant din and clatter of broken crockery. The students marched out of the building into the street and, in the finest Yale tradition, engaged in combat with "town and gown." Their hurt was not assuaged until they had overturned a few streetcars. Although the ringleaders (and, inevitably, many of the innocents) were sorely disciplined, the riot was not in vain. The following year a new management was installed to cater and the cuisine improved a hundredfold. I still cherish the memory of their old-fashioned strawberry shortcake.

We went up to New York in June to take over the Rendez-vous engagement with Lester Laden playing an oompah piano. I do not mean to infer that he couldn't play piano but his technique on this instrument was about the same as mine. He was adequate for our dance music but heaven help us if we had been required to play anything really requiring a great technical command of the instrument.

Laden was rather annoyed with me. First, he felt I was not enchanted with his pianistics. True. Second, I was often late for a date due to subway commuting from the Brooklyn YMCA. True. Third, I was getting fifteen dollars more per week than even the leader. True. Come to think of it, he did have reason to dislike me!

Curtis Peters, who had led us for the first two weeks of the engagement, suddenly disappeared. He was discovered upstairs in the Rendezvous painting the interior decorations to be used for the new fall season. It became quite evident to us that Curtis Peters had no real love for music. He enjoyed doing some form of art work or painting more than creating music.

A few months later I discovered he was no longer in our Sophomore class and had gone to New York to join forces with a young fellow named Ross. They began publishing a little journal called the *New Yorker*. Thus our friend Curtis Peters was to delight millions all over the world with his sly and diabolically clever cartoons for the *New Yorker* under the name of Peter Arno.

My love life during all this time was not completely unappeased. While New York did not provide me with too many opportunities for dates

with attractive young ladies I had flirted with a few, and toward the
end of the summer when I lived at the SAE house at Columbia University
some of our Sundays were the swingingest. Others, I must confess, were
as empty as the romantic lives of the sailors who wandered along River-
side Drive looking for a date.

As I write these words one of the most remarkable occurrences I have
ever witnessed comes back to me. I must beg your indulgence as I retro-
gress for a moment.

To give you a bit of perspective, remember this was part of the twenties—the Roaring Twenties, as the phrase has it, although in this year of
our Lord, 1923, it was early enough in the decade so that the roar was
hardly a healthy murmur. But those dear, dead twenties were building
to the cataclysmic blow-off of '29 and were regularly getting wackier.

For example, New York City boasted (yes, boasted) thousands of
speakeasies, which had mushroomed from Prohibition, where you could
get a bottle of Scotch for about twenty bucks. Of course it was Scotch—
didn't the label say so? Oh, there might have been a little touch of
Tennessee moonshine in it just for bouquet, but who carped? Only squares
(though one didn't call them that then) used bathtubs for bathing—they
were designed as receptacles in which one made his own gin. Never
mind the outer, physical man—one's soul needed feeding.

Yes, indeed—the twenties were picking up momentum. Toward the
abyss, that is. In that year, 1923, Emile Coué was in full flower with his
own brand of the "power of positive thinking." Remember that slogan
of his which would cure everything from brain tumor to athlete's foot?
"Day by day in every way I'm getting better and better."

It was just conceivably symptomatic of these lightheaded times that
this period saw the emergence of the rather frenetic Charleston, a dance
which tortured many a sacroiliac.

Worthy of note, if not truly germane as part of these times out of
joint, was the founding of *Time* Magazine that year.

At any rate, staid historians are wont to charge off the Valentino
hysteria to its being a by-product of the mass lunacy of the twenties.
I do not buy this at all. In my opinion he happened to be one of the
most stunning *presences*, one of the truly consummate showmen, of
this century.

I had the privilege of witnessing this phenomenon on several occasions
that spring before college let out. Valentino, the Great Lover, had
become dissatisfied with the roles that were offered him in pictures.
He felt that they were not worthy of his talents, a feeling apparently
shared more recently by Marilyn Monroe and others who have protested
the parts given them, sometimes with as unfortunate results as those
which occurred in Valentino's case.

He had literally gone on strike from the studio and, sponsored by a company which made a mudpack known as Mineralava, had instructed his agents to book appearances for him at the largest auditoria and armories throughout the country. This tour had brought him to Bridgeport, Waterbury, New Haven, and Meriden, Connecticut. Although he carried his own orchestra with him for the tango he did in gaucho attire (the costume he wore in the famous picture, *The Four Horsemen of the Apocalypse)*, it was necessary for his manager to engage a band to play for the public dancing which followed his appearance. That was where we came in. Bolton and Cipriano had landed this plum and we not only played for the dancing, but accompanied a fashion show which took place before Valentino himself appeared.

As we drove up to the Armory in Bridgeport in our large black Cadillac the streets outside were packed with people—mostly women, of course. As we tried to alight from our car, they evidently thought that this was the vehicle bearing their romantic idol. We were almost cut in half by their pressure against the door as we tried to get out and it took the best efforts of several policemen to get us inside the auditorium even when they discovered that we were neither Valentino nor part of his entourage.

Inside the Armory was a scene of hysteria and devotion quite beyond description. The police had roped off a space in front of the band platform but every now and then as a door slammed, or somebody made a move, or someone thought he had caught a glimpse of Valentino, there would be a surge of several thousand bodies. Even a score of sturdy police were not able to cope with them. Time and again they pressed up to our band platform and almost pushed it over.

Finally the time came for the entrance of the god of the cinema. He came in quietly, quickly, from out of nowhere. Without the aid of a microphone he succeeded in speaking in a voice loud enough to be heard almost throughout the entire Armory. He explained why he had quit pictures (temporarily at least), and described what he was selling for his sponsor. He then proceeded to do a tango with a very beautiful young lady. I'll never forget the fact that he paid tribute to Richard Barthelmess, who strangely enough was Valentino's idol. He made it clear that he too should receive the same type of dramatic parts as those given Barthelmess and other personalities in motion pictures. Before we knew it, escorted by a phalanx of policemen he was gone. We were left with the drudgery of playing dance music to an obviously disinterested audience.

Before he left, however, Valentino very graciously agreed to dance with one of the town's debutantes, who had been chosen in the fashion show. Whether she could dance or not, she did some sort of a fandango with him and probably didn't wash her hands for years afterward.

As I sat each evening fairly near and watched his fascinating eyes and swarthy features, I could understand quite easily the great power he had come to have over women through the medium of the silver screen. What I didn't know was that seven years later, in 1930, in the same city of Bridgeport, I was to know almost this same adulation. I was to have my clothes literally torn off me as I alighted from a car to play a simple dance at the Ritz ballroom not very far from this same Armory. But that's another story.

We played again for Valentino in Waterbury, New Haven, and Meriden, with the same scene repeated each time. One of the musicians who played with us during the appearances in Waterbury and Meriden was a young Jewish boy of rather sullen demeanor, who had little or nothing to say about himself or the study of the saxophone. Nearly every musician who played the saxophone was as enthusiastic as I was and wanted to talk about it. This close-mouthed young man was obviously a very fine performer and a solid musician. At that time he was introduced to me by Bill Bolton as having the name Orshovsky. But the world was to come to know his brilliant clarinet work later on as well as his unpredictability both in speech and writing. His inability to settle down in the sacred state of matrimony led him to amass a record to surpass my own. When he became one of America's biggest band-leader attractions, he was known as Artie Shaw.

As the summer we played the Rendez-vous drew to a close, I made a trip to New Haven to talk to Dr. William F. Verdi, who had risen from bootblack and newsboy and worked his way through Yale University to become a highly esteemed surgeon. I wanted to ask him if he would operate on my ruptured appendix incision and make it strong again. He couldn't seem to understand why I didn't want to ask my father for help or why I wanted him to do the operation gratis. As I too was working my way through the university, I felt that there was a sympathetic bond between us. He finally agreed and did the operation for nothing. All I had to pay were the hospital charges. On Labor Day evening, I watched the fireworks going off over Savin Rock while I lay in the hospital with the bitter taste of an orange-juice-and-castor-oil infusion given me in preparation for the morning operation.

My second year at Yale was quite uneventful. I played any number of dances throughout the area and, coupled with my school work, it was a very tough grind.

My fraternity buddy, Carl Libby, had come down during Christmas vacation from Maine to play the dances with me and his presence by my side brought home to me the unpalatable fact that physically I was hardly God's gift to women. Proof? As we sat there playing our saxophones, Carl, a handsome devil, found girl after girl knocking over his music stand deliberately in an effort to make him raise his eyes to hers. More than one girl danced over to Bolton with her escort to ask him who Carl Libby might be. But for all his romantic looks he was more absorbed in playing the tenor saxophone than he was in flirting with these girls.

There I sat all romance, all affection, hoping that in the event they couldn't attract Carl's attention they might settle for me. They rarely ever did. I might produce from my instrument tones of incredible beauty, I might endow a simple popular melody with something its composer never knew it possessed, but these girls were acting as most human beings act. They were pursuing only the pleasant and attractive visual features.

Thus was borne home to me the fact (something that I now realize full well) that few people listen with their ears; one sketch is worth a thousand words. The handsome features of a Cary Grant or a Marilyn Monroe can win, at least at first sight, over a thousand other individuals with plainer features but with more charming and interesting personalities.

While the plain-looking individual may, through sheer charm, personality, and brilliance, triumph in the end, let no one ever doubt that the first attraction in most cases is physical and visual. Those Christmas and Easter vacations were to be lucid proof of the phenomenon for yours truly.

I just don't know what actually possessed me to do it. I had taken a fairly large-size megaphone and cut it down so that it would fit into the bell of the baritone saxophone on which I doubled. On dance engagements I would take the little megaphone out and sing into it. I featured songs I had heard on Brunswick records sung by Marian Harris who was to be a stylistic ideal and pattern for my own vocalizing. She had a warm, relaxed delivery, and was almost as popular in her time as Ruth Etting with both Americans and the elite of London. I also sang some of the "blues" songs as done by Al Bernard on Brunswick records.

There were no public-address systems available on these various dance dates so the megaphone gave my voice the needed amplification to sing out over the band. While my voice was not exactly a small one, I was never credited with the power of Enrico Caruso, who was said to possess high notes sufficient to shatter windows at fifty paces.

Unwittingly I had stumbled upon a device which was to become my lifelong trademark. Even now, when appearing in the Broadway musical, *How to Succeed in Business Without Really Trying*, in the number, "Grand Old Ivy," I cup my hands to my mouth, simulating a megaphone. Each time I do it, I sense a strange, nostalgic tremor among a large portion of the audience.

CHAPTER V

The London Year and
Yale "Part Two"

"I'm Sitting on Top of the World"

IN 1924, THE TIME THE LID BLEW OFF IN the Teapot Dome scandals, I decided to take a year's leave from Yale to go to London and play sax at the posh Savoy Hotel.

On the "bad-guy" side of the ledger at that time, there was enacted the lurid Loeb-Leopold case in Chicago; on the other side, J. Edgar Hoover was appointed chief of the Federal Bureau of Investigation.

People were reading Louis Bromfield's *The Green Bay Tree*, Ernest Hemingway's *In Our Time*, and Edna Ferber's *So Big*. It was the year Paul Whiteman gave his first concert of "serious" music at Aeolian Hall in New York with a world première of Gershwin's "Rhapsody in Blue" and the Broadway scene boasted such spectaculars as *Rose Marie, No, No, Nannette, The Student Prince, Lady Be Good*, a *Ziegfeld Follies*, and even a musical version of *Uncle Tom's Cabin* called *Topsy and Eva*. Theater marquees were hawking silent-movie products such as *Beau Brummel* with John Barrymore, *Girl Shy* with Harold Lloyd, Valentino's *Monsieur Beaucaire*, and the timeless epic, *The Thief of Bagdad*, starring the great Douglas Fairbanks.

It was mere happenstance that triggered my decision to make the London trip. (God, how our lives are the prey of coincidence!) For some time now I had been corresponding with Joe Brannelly, a Boston boy I had known, who had gone to London to play in a dance orchestra at the Savoy. He had offered me a job at the Savoy in 1922 at $140 a week, but I couldn't get a passport in time to sail, so I went to Yale instead. He told me that he was to return in the spring of '24 to recruit several more musicians, but I gave it little serious thought. After all, I was set for four years at Yale and that was that.

But then fate, as the saying goes, stepped in. In addition to dance dates with the Bolton-Cipriano "cartel" I was playing with Sleepy Hall, the Yale banjoist, who now had his own group. One Sunday afternoon as we were on our way to New York for an engagement at the Winter Garden on the bill with Al Jolson, I stepped out between the cars of the train for a breath of fresh air. And who in hell is standing there but Joe Brannelly! He had played a Yale fraternity dance the night before and was going to New York.

"Rudy," he said enthusiastically, "you're crazy not to come to London! If nothing else just for a year, for crying out loud!"

"But, Joe. I'm settled at college now. I've got to get my degree. I'm getting by with what I make playing my horn."

"That's just it! You're *getting by* and that's all. Take a year in London and you can put away some money so you won't have to kill yourself the last two years. You'll make good money at the Savoy, maybe pick up a few pounds at the recording studios—and there's a lot of English kids dying to learn the sax. There's money there in teaching."

He had me sold by the time we reached the clattering caverns of Grand Central Station.

I told my story to the Yale registrar. He was most understanding. "If you are sincere in your plans to return after a year," he told me, "then perhaps the experience will be good for you. Just save your money and then you won't have to do as much outside work to get through your last two years. You'll get more out of college that way."

There was the regret of graduating a class later but I felt it was not of crucial importance as I have found that classes are classes and men are men. The idea of seeing England greatly appealed to me and I have never rued the move.

Therefore, on September 7, I boarded the good ship *Olympic*, the second largest liner of its kind at that time, ready to regale the Britons with my sax. On the trip over, Brannelly, Carroll Gibbons, who wrote "A Garden in the Rain," and I played the tunes from the current musicals—we made quite a hit with the passengers, particularly with the new hits, "Tea For Two" and "I Want To Be Happy" from *No, No, Nannette*.

My year in London was a long succession of teaching four and five saxophone pupils a week, and playing tea dances one week at the Savoy with afternoons off the next week. But I played every evening: upstairs in the beautiful, pillared, red-carpeted main dining room, where dined such personalities as Tetrazzini, Marconi, Fokker, the German aircraft inventor, diplomats, artists, actors, etc.; or early in the morning downstairs in the large ballroom with its floor set on springs, playing opposite the large Savoy Orpheum, a band of some twenty-two pieces which rivaled Paul Whiteman's aggregation in its brilliance and beauty of tone.

I was given some great news by Clifford Essex & Sons, the music house that had arranged for my saxophone pupils and that featured large pictures of me using a certain American-made saxophone. They said that if I would stay in London several months longer, until the Prince of Wales returned from his African hunting trip, I would have the pleasure of teaching him the saxophone, "by royal appointment."

To anyone who has not been abroad, particularly in England, the words "royal appointment" may need a little clarification. Any merchant or manufacturer whose products or creations are used by the royal family may boast a specially stamped sheepskin that says that "by royal appointment, so-and-so is privileged to create this product for the royal family."

An Hawaiian American, Kel Keech, who played the ukulele exceptionally well, had been in London and had been secured by Clifford Essex & Sons to teach the Prince of Wales. I was assured that if I would only remain a few months longer this would also be my privilege.

I had seen the Prince of Wales the previous Thanksgiving Day at a luncheon sponsored by the American Society in London. Upon learning that William Lyon Phelps, one of the greatest Yale professors of all time, was to be the chief speaker, I had prepared a very elaborate practical joke.

To set this jape in proper perspective I must digress for a moment. The year after the dining-hall food riot, I was in the orchestra there one evening when one of the student headwaiters asked a strange favor of the saxophone section. It seemed that Professor Billy Phelps had asked for a volunteer from the class to arrange to play a composition which Phelps claimed was one of the first "popular" songs ever written, apparently by Robert Browning himself. Without thinking, one of the students volunteered to do it on his violin. Now he was on the spot since he hadn't touched the instrument in years and found he could not deliver.

"Could you fellows substitute for me?" the waiter asked. "It will get me out of a jam—and you can imagine the expression on Ol' Billy's face when three saxophonists walk in instead of a fiddler!"

This intrigued us and we set about arranging the piece for saxophone. But Phelps was to foil us. He had an equanimity that I have never seen equaled. I believe that if there had ever been a nuclear explosion near him and he were left alive, he would not have shown the slightest expression of amazement or consternation. On the appearance of us in his classroom, playing this tune, he merely marched around the room in time with the composition, smiling delightedly and tossing his watch chain as he always did in moments of enjoyment!

Thereafter, whenever I was playing a date and saw him in attendance, I would immediately begin playing the Browning composition with the orchestra vamping along with me. It was a sort of running gag between us.

This failure in the classroom to show surprise somehow nettled me. Now, in London, Phelps was to be the chief speaker, with the Prince of Wales, at the Thanksgiving Day luncheon of the American Society in the grand ballroom of the Savoy. So that day I made my way to the Savoy, pulled my sax out of my locker, wiped it carefully, and waited for the guests to file into the ballroom. As I peeked through the doors of our band shell, I could make out the Prince of Wales, later to become Edward VIII for a short time, then the Duke of Windsor. An equerry came in with an envelope for him, probably containing his speech, and I vowed that if he threw it away after the luncheon I would pick up a precious souvenir. (After lunch was over, I rushed over to the Prince's deserted table to find only the envelope, with its three ostrich plumes on the back, torn in four pieces. I placed them tenderly in my pocket.)

As the luncheon wore on there was still no sign of Phelps. I had resolved that, as he stood up to speak, I would pop out of the band-shell doors like a jack-in-the-box and play the Browning song *at least once* before the waiters and/or the police grabbed me. *If such performance would not cause the good professor to raise his eyebrows in some astonishment, then nothing would!*

But, gentle reader, I was doomed to disappointment, for all the elaborate rigging I had engineered. Phofessor Phelps had been taken ill in Paris and could not appear. However, won't you admit it was a good idea?

After graduation I came to know this storied teacher quite well. We spent many wonderful evenings together in New York and I enjoyed taking him to Leone's, one of my favorite restaurants, which specialized in a most delightful daiquiri.

"It is indeed ambrosial nectar," he intoned, doling out the words in his inimitable way as he savored every drop of it and every syllable of his pronouncement.

When I told him about my planned "Browning performance" which he had missed in London that time, his body shook with laughter and he assured me that for once he would most certainly have been taken completely aback.

Naturally it was not possible for me to teach my sax pupils, play tea dances every afternoon every other week, and full evenings night after night after night, without seeking relaxation and solace in the company of some fair creatures. Lovely girls were few and far between in London. You met them at some of the dives and night clubs that stayed open until the wee hours of the morning or you went to the tea dances that abounded in hotel rooms all over the city.

On Sunday afternoons the famous Jack Hylton band, which was rapidly attracting national attention, was playing at the Piccadilly Hotel.

Happily, it was quite possible to find many an attractive young lady there, alone and eager to dance. Most of them hoped that you would take them to dinner or even more but at least they were there and waiting. It was at one of these Sunday afternoon dances at the Piccadilly that I heard the strains of two songs that I was to bring back to America with me and make popular over here. One of them was called "Poem," which became "Moonlight Madonna" when an American lyric was written for it. The other was a song that today is associated with me and is generally played when I make an appearance: "My Time Is Your Time." I asked one of the saxophonists with the Hylton band the name of the publishers of the two compositions and began to do the tunes at the Savoy. When I returned to America I used them at the Yale dining hall and eventually on my own broadcasts.

London was, and is, a shopper's delight. Any time I could seize a moment off from the saxophonic chores, I would frequent the shops along Bond Street which catered to the sartorial needs of the man. As far as clothes are concerned (and in many other ways) England is a *man's* country. When I returned to Yale I had amassed a collection of around two hundred pairs of socks, about one hundred and fifty ties, eight suits, and a couple of coats tailored in the Chesterfield style then in vogue. At Christmas time I purchased some leather and silver gifts to send my good friend and benefactor, Dr. Verdi, he of the second appendectomy, as well as some baubles for my buddies Bolton and Cipriano. I also acquired a new gadget purveyed by Dunhill, the swank firm that ministers to those who worship the goddess Nicotine. It was in sterling silver, cost me a pound (five dollars at that time) and was called a cigarette lighter. It had been invented by a British army officer who had only one arm.

No matter how exciting living and performing in London was becoming, I clung to my resolve to return to Yale for my degree. As much as I wanted to, I decided that I could not wait for the Prince's return from Africa so that I might become the regal saxophone tutor (tooter?). I am sure I would have enjoyed his company immensely but my schooling had to come first.

The Savoy Hotel management, believing that my continual references to going back to college were only to secure more pay, had indeed raised my salary and secured another six months' extension for me. Nevertheless, when they were finally convinced that I was really going to return in the middle of said extension, the gentleman who had been most instrumental in securing the extension of my special musician's labor permit blew his top. He practically threw me out on my ear—the first time I had ever been fired from an engagement. I learned later that there was an opportunity to grab a good English saxophonist who was available at that moment and since my departure was to be only ten days away, they felt that they had to grab him. Nevertheless, I had planned a trip to Paris to take the boat from Cherbourg and I was not too unhappy.

I asked a very attractive English girl with whom I had been spending considerable time to make the trip to Paris with me. This, of course, was a supreme example of carrying coals to Newcastle or taking a sandwich to a banquet. Nevertheless, I doubted that I would find anyone in all of France as charming, as well-educated, and as loyal as this girl would be to me on my three-day spree in the city of good food, excellent wine, and much to see and do. Our visit, Eiffel Tower and all, was a very happy one. On the night before I departed, Sleepy Hall and his band came in for their second summer of playing in a gay Parisian spot before returning to Yale. Sleepy's boys and I had a rousing good reunion before I boarded the *Olympic* again to return home.

I got back from England in June of 1925 and got an engagement forthwith in the band at Old Orchard Pier, Old Orchard Beach, Maine. My London achievements must have given me something of a reputation and I was considerably flustered when Pete Martin, clarinetist-band leader of the orchestra, wryly informed me I was receiving fifteen dollars a week more than he was! Even though I didn't direct the band, my "international" experience must have been impressive because the combo would do practically anything I asked.

At the Pier I sang romantic songs for the first time—into a megaphone, of course. In England Joe Brannelly had run across a song from an American Doughboy Revue called "The Bing Boys," written by Nat Ayer, a Philadelphian in the AEF. The review had played London near the end of World War I and this song had persisted in popularity there. Brannelly taught me the lyrics and melody and I had brought it back and arranged it for the Pier orchestra. At least twice an evening I sang it and it has become a fixture among our country's standards: "If You Were the Only Girl in the World and I Were the Only Boy."

As at most summer resorts the dance crowds would congregate in front of the stage and listen to the vocalist on the ballads, and I would croon them out in my little nasal, plaintive voice while the spotlight played its varied colors upon me. It was a happy and wonderful summer, withal, that ended too soon—a glorious vacation with pay!

My college life in some respects was changed as I returned to Yale in the fall of '25 as part of the Class of '27. By scrimping a bit in London I had put away some money that would let me live a trifle better than before. If you will recall, one of the main reasons for the Savoy sojourn was to amass funds so I would not have to work so hard during the school term. All the same, I fell into the same old grind—playing dates off campus three and four nights a week when most students were going off with their cronies to theaters or night spots. I must have had

some sort of compulsiveness about work. All my life I have been able
to get along with very little sleep and in my waking hours I thrive on
hard work. Moreover, I enjoyed playing and singing so much I hardly
ever regarded it as a chore. On the nights when I was not working I
would be courting some girl in New Haven or running up to see a beautiful Jewish girl friend in Hartford.

Consequently, I had little time to know intimately the members of
my new class—it had been much the same with the Class of '26. And
more's the pity. There was Lanny Ross, who cut such a wide swath in
radio later on. H. C. Potter (whom I would have picked to become a
banker, minister, or architect) was a classmate in economics who became a fine director on Broadway and in Hollywood. Remember the
play, *Kind Lady*, and the motion picture, *Mr. Blandings Builds His
Dream House*, among many others? I have flattered myself that I generally am able to discover talent in embryo but, in this instance at least,
either I was temporarily blind or Mr. Potter was hiding his light under
a very large and opaque bushel.

Nevertheless, my life at Yale *was* changed—certainly changed as far
as my living quarters were concerned. My first two years found me
inhabiting mundane cubicles in very modest rooming houses, climbing
four flights in the old Berkeley Oval, or existing in the monkish cloisters
of Wright Hall. Now I was permitted domicile at the resplendent
Harkness Memorial Quadrangle.

It was quite a remarkable—well, dormitory. I hesitate to use such a
common word as *dormitory* for such a magnificent edifice. Reputedly
it cost eight million dollars and was erected in honor of the Harknesses'
son who had been killed in World War I. The Harkness family were
fabulously wealthy oil people and as a memorial to their boy they gave
this replica of a *Cambridge* building to Yale. Structured as it was of
warm-colored stone—red, yellow, and orange from various quarries
throughout the country—in the form of a large quadrangle with a moat
around the whole, it was quite as munificent a college lodging as one
might find at that time. For little more than a hundred dollars a semester
a lucky student could enjoy his own paneled, fireplaced room which
included porter service to clean the place and even make his bed. To
be able to write my letters on Harkness stationery was indeed proof of
the fact that I had truly "arrived" in the collegiate world.

Most important, however, my Junior year saw me arrayed in the
true hallmark of the successful collegian. I acquired, *mirabile dictu*, a
raccoon coat!

It may be cause for a yock today, when the raccoon coat appears in
a motion picture or a television show—but in those dim dark days it
was a very serious matter. Our football games were held on cold, raw
October and November afternoons. The Gulf Stream had not yet

brought its warmth to the New England coast and the sign of true grandiloquence was not only the pocket flask and the felt hat with the jaunty feather sticking out of it. Most important was the raccoon coat which denoted true opulence and success (at the same time keeping one's can warm) and I had finally decided to treat myself to one.

My first one represented my earliest excursion into that area of necromancy known as "getting something wholesale." Among my friends in the class of 1927 was a boy named Holliner, whose father was engaged in the mysterious art of the fur business. Holliner, who in a vague way worshiped me from afar for my saxophonic endeavors both in the dining hall and on the football field with the Yale band, was only too eager and happy to see to it that, at the firm's cost, I was to be arrayed in all my glory with that collegiate mark of distinction, the raccoon coat.

But in addition to my raccoon coat, sartorially speaking I was able to hold up my head with the best of them. For, as I have mentioned, on the afternoons that I was not playing tea dances at the Savoy Hotel or teaching some staid English character the warmth and heart of the saxophone, I wandered all over the streets of London looking for outstanding buys. I looked for a good price and I looked for good design in the fine English accessories such as socks and ties that I knew would cost me double or triple back at the Yale shops. I knew I couldn't operate like most of the other students in New Haven who had merely to send back padded bills to well-heeled fathers when they needed anything.

I had purchased quantities of tweed material and it had been made into collegiate suits in the Yale style by bewildered London tailors who thought I was out of my mind. As a Junior at Yale, I realized I now cut a really dashing figure. With these newly acquired accouterments I found it much easier to impress some of the fair damsels at the exclusive dances at which I was engaged to perform as a mere saxophonist.

More and more I came to realize that the Registrar and I had only been kidding ourselves about my taking it easy when I came back from London. I played as many, if not more, engagements in my Junior year than I had in the previous two years. I suppose the only difference was that I was now a gaudy fur-coated creature as I burst upon an astonished country-club dance gathering and set up my instruments.

Some of our engagements were in New York. More than one Sunday afternoon I found myself alone in that great city with nothing to do. And New York is no place to be lonely.

Roseland Ballroom at Fifty-first Street and Broadway was the mecca for such lonely hearts as I, and there I found attractive hostesses—fifty, count 'em, fifty! While it wasn't exactly ten cents a dance, you did at least have your choice of the most attractive ones provided you had the necessary ticket stub in your hand.

There was one phenomenon common to Roseland Ballroom that at
first intrigued me and then baffled me until I finally solved it. Almost
invariably in the course of the afternoon there would be some very attractive girl who seemed to take a sadistic delight in refusing every
man who asked her for a dance. You might well wonder why she was
there. She wasn't waiting for anyone. She just seemed to enjoy being
the unattainable!

When I saw such an attractive girl turning down the tall, handsome,
dark sheiks who were the best dancers in the city, I knew better than
to ask for a dance. But suddenly I stumbled upon a technique which
flashed into my mind one afternoon. Mine was a simple strategy upon
which you could bet your neck. In fact, on the occasions that I have
used this technique, I have made extensive wagers and have always won.

It consisted of the simple use of eight or nine words and it had always
been my contention that the girl *could not refuse* to dance with me; and
if she had any sense of humor whatsoever, no matter how soured she
might be on the world, she had to smile (if only wanly) when these
magic eight words were spoken. But if she failed to capitulate, she was
a heel indeed, and let me say, ladies and gentlemen, I have never known
this approach to fail. I'm not going to tip my mitt now; but later on, if
you're real good, I'll let you in on the Vallee Plan that always conquered.

This year was also outstanding for my presence at the Junior Prom
at which I both worked and danced. I brought from New York a girl
who could, in a later era, easily have passed for Elizabeth Taylor. She
was a model whom I had met through a wealthy freshman I had helped
keep in school and whom I had selected as Yale football band leader
three years hence.

This attractive brunette with the tiny waist and the wonderful sense
of humor was not only a girl who knew her way around; she was also
loyal and dependable. I had no worries as to what skulduggery might be
going on as I performed with the thirty-piece New Haven band on
our side of the large dining hall and I knew that when I went to find
her at the end of our set she would be there—either waiting at the side
lines, or if dancing, waiting for me to cut back in. This may sound like
boasting but this Prom was one affair that required an extremely careful
selection and I wanted a girl who would not give me, as the Jewish call
it, *tsoress* all evening by keeping me on the hot seat. Blanche McLeod
was that girl.

She was so attractive that the Pathé Newsreel people, who decided to
photograph that year's Yale Prom as the most elite collegiate event of the
year, kept the camera trained on us for quite a bit of footage. Blanche and
I really got a bang out of watching ourselves on the screen from the
balcony of a New York theater a few days later.

But now came spring and time to make a decision for the summer.

A very fine musician, who was to die of consumption before the year was out, organized us into the Yale Collegians and we set out on a vaudeville tour. Come to think of it, I never did have a vacation! The itinerary began very unhappily in hot, steamy Washington and then took us on buses to a few scattered dates in New England. Afterward, we made our way through Pennsylvania to Chicago where at last I had the thrill of seeing Bennie Krueger in person.

Krueger was a saxophonist whom I admired almost as much as Wiedoeft although he played in quite a different style. Where Rudy gave the instrument stature and dignity, Benny made it a device of comedy—he would make it laugh, cry, crow like a rooster or sound like a steel guitar!

Our doughty band of Yale Collegians had played two quick dates, one on the North Side and one on the South Side, when I learned that Krueger was acting as Master of Ceremonies at the Tivoli Theater. It was one of the Balaban and Katz chain of entertainment palaces decorated in an outlandish rococo that would have made a sultan blanch.

My idol gave a good account of himself on his horn and I relived the many hours I had spent listening to his Brunswick records years before. But still I did not meet him. On the same bill was a singer of lovely demeanor with a crystal-clear voice that had such warmth tinged with occasional cool aloofness, assuredness of pitch, tasteful vibrato and phrasing—such talent, in fact—that I knew after hearing only a few measures that she would be a great star. That was the first time I heard Ruth Etting.

All in all it was a pleasant summer in spite of the drudgery of backbreaking one-nighters. One thing that kept me going was looking forward to my Senior year at Yale when I would lead the band out of the tunnel of the Bowl into the bright sunlight and hear the cheers and applause of eighty thousand people—among whom I knew would be my mother and father.

Ever since my Freshman year when I walked into the gymnasium for the first rehearsal of the Yale football band, I had known that I was going to be its leader in my Senior year. It was quite a band, numbering around eighty pieces, and if it had any musical shortcomings it made up for them in enthusiasm. It was a typical college band in that a large portion of the members never practiced until a few days or weeks before the games in the fall—consequently, their embouchures (the proper placement of the lips to the mouthpiece) were in sad state, particularly at the beginning of the season.

No matter! After all, when a rabid football fan is huddled in his raccoon coat high in the stands and fortified by repeated infusions from his hip flask (*high* in the stands!), he is scarcely a music critic.

I had invited my parents down in 1926 for the most exciting game of the year, the Yale-Army fracas. It was a cold, crisp October afternoon when the band marched out of the tunnel onto the gridiron with yours truly at the head of the column. Of course, I had to be different—I was the first leader to wear a blue blazer instead of the usual plain white sweater affected by my predecessors. It was a lovely moment I shall always cherish.

After each game I would rush to what was probably the world's finest country club, the Westchester Biltmore in Rye, New York, where I was playing with a Bolton-Cipriano combo. We would perform for a long Saturday evening session in the main dining room or in the beautifully paneled grill. On Sundays we would play an afternoon tea dance and a short evening dance, again in the grill.

It was here at this club that I had the opportunity to observe the effects of a few of my vocalizings through the megaphone. One of the most sought-after debutantes stopped me as I walked through one of the spacious salons. The blood rushed to my temples as this most attractive creature, whom I had always regarded as unattainable, stopped me in my tracks to tell me with unmistakable sincerity that my songs *did* something to her.

The Westchester Biltmore engagement also afforded my first opportunity to try out some of my ideas upon an orchestra. True, our little band was only six pieces, but when Bolton and Cipriano played at a society dance in Bridgeport one weekend, I was elected to take charge. To my great delight, the *maitre d'* of the Westchester Biltmore instructed Bolton and Cipriano that he wanted me to lead the band the rest of the season! The two leaders obviously were slightly miffed at the fact that they were not indispensable, but rather than risk losing the job, they proceeded to let me direct its destiny. So well did our little group perform that we went down to New York again, as I had in 1922, and made several studio recordings at our own expense, to be sold at Yale bookstores.

The fall was to hold for me not only the thrill of leading the football band in the Bowl, but also the opportunity to duel with Bennie Krueger, saxophonically speaking.

It was the evening after the Yale-Princeton game and I was elected to lead a twenty-piece band which was to "oppose" Krueger's aggregation for the dance held in the large dining hall. Even while I dressed in my room in Harkness I was playing a Krueger record. I was so excited that in a few minutes I was actually to play opposite Bennie Krueger I could hardly tie my tie!

Well, our "duel" went through on schedule across the bedlam of dancing college men with their weekend dates but, save for a waving signal to each other as we finished our "sets," we never, to my deep chagrin, had the opportunity to speak to each other.

However, Bennie and I were to participate in what was history's shortest dialogue between idol and admirer. In the spring of '27 the Junior Prom committee decided to bring Krueger and a thirty-piece orchestra composed of New York's finest side-men up to Yale. Included in the group was Phil Ohman, the fabulous pianist I had so admired the first time I heard the Paul Whiteman band.

Krueger was in his usual fine form as he played the then popular "Somebody's Wrong." First, he played the melody straight as written, beautifully, cleanly, sweetly, followed by a series of stunning variations. He would then play it in a style representing a drunken man hiccoughing and stumbling home from a party. He would make the melody sound like a Hawaiian guitar and, in a comic way, would practically *talk* the lyrics on his horn. I watched with my mouth agape as I realized I was hearing an exhibition such as I had never heard before and probably would never hear again.

At about 1:30 A.M. the maestro and his boys were being fed in the Yale Rotunda, a section of the dining hall in which glass cases housed such memorabilia as the original drawings for Eli Whitney's cotton gin and the papers of President Taft. There were also numerous statues, plaques, and paintings memorializing famous Yale men.

I rushed there during an intermission to meet The Man. In those days I must have had a lot of nerve, even gall, because I was going to ask him if I could try out *his* saxophone.

As I approached him I became dazzled and grew suddenly timid. "Mr. Krueger," I blurted, "I play sax in the other band. In Eddie Wittstein's band. Er, I'm one of your greatest fans and I wonder—I wonder if I, er, might just, you know, sort of try out your mouthpiece and reed. Please."

He'd been touted to me as a tough New Jersey guy. I suppose I should have realized that he was preoccupied not only with eating but with his performance that evening. He just stared at me blankly as if he hadn't heard and calmly swallowed his mouthful of food.

"Nah," he said and continued eating.

I ran down the stairs with my tail between my legs and never approached him again that evening. Later on, in the forties, I was able to repay him for his influence on my saxophone playing: I got him a job as conductor for the bands I used on the Drene and Philip Morris network radio shows.

As I neared graduation, I became more and more melancholy. I had enjoyed Yale. I liked classrooms. I liked study. Some of my happiest moments had been in the awakening of my mind to new and adventuresome fields. I had perfected my knowledge of Spanish to the point that I felt South America was definitely my goal and had made a vow that Buenos Aires would be my next stop.

However, there were to be complications that would prove to me that my fortune was to be made here in America. First there was a beautiful girl of Swedish extraction whom I saw in the bookstore on the campus. She was a younger edition of Greta Garbo. I met her by the simple expedient of asking the young lady with her to introduce me to her. We had several happy evenings together and then when she returned to her native New Jersey and stood me up on a Sunday afternoon in the middle of my Senior finals, I realized that I was in deeper than I thought. I rushed to New Jersey in the middle of my most critical examination to find out exactly what was going on. And it was quite evident that she liked me but didn't love me.

In fact, the thrill of graduation and seeing my mother with tearful eyes and a proud smile on her sweet, dear face as she watched me receive my diploma was lessened by the fact that my mind was half at graduation and half in New Jersey. But I had at least made my mother's dream come true. After four long years of hard work both at my studies and the exhausting routine of earning my tuition and expenses each year, it had come to an end.

A few pages back I offered to let you in on the Vallee Plan for breaking the ice and getting a girl to dance with you. Simply smile warmly and say, *"May I have the sixty-fifth dance from now?"* Of course, you can use any preposterous number—seventy-third, ninety-first, etc. She will realize that she has been quite aloof and at the same time that she is much in demand and that you are willing to wait for the great privilege. It is simple and obvious—but it never failed to work for me!

CHAPTER VI

To New York and the Heigh-Ho Club

"There's A Rainbow Round My Shoulder"

In June '27 when I graduated, New York was giving Charles Lindbergh a welcome complete with thousands of tons of ticker tape, and the Federal government forthwith designed a commemorative air-mail stamp. Lindy started a trend. First thing you knew, Chamberlain and Levine had flown nonstop to Germany and Richard E. Byrd and crew had emulated Lindbergh with still another nonstop, as the saying was, flight to France.

That year there was a national controversy over Judge Ben Lindsay's so-called "companionate marriage," a marital tie easily dissolved if no children resulted, as an answer to the high divorce rate and mounting juvenile delinquency. President Coolidge in a fit of garrulity volunteered, "I do not choose to run for President in 1928." It was the year of the cloche hat, that bizarre headgear that could look like a football helmet or an inverted, close-fitting coal-scuttle. People were reading Sinclair Lewis's *Elmer Gantry*, Thornton Wilder's *The Bridge of San Luis Rey*, and Ernest Hemingway's *Men without Women*.

The Radio Corporation of America made a successful test TV transmission from Washington, D. C. to New York. And in that year the radio network known as CBS was founded.

Broadway musicals had another solid season with such gems as *Hit the Deck, Good News, The Connecticut Yankee, Funny Face*, and the timeless *Show Boat*.

In Hollywood the Academy of Motion Picture Arts and Sciences was founded and for the 1927-28 season it awarded the first Oscars to Emil Jannings for his performance in *The Way of All Flesh*, and to Janet Gaynor for *Seventh Heaven*, and the "best movie" was *Wings*. A special award was presented for *The Jazz Singer*, the famous Al Jolson picture which was partially, at least, a "talkie." The cinema was finding that the cat did not have its tongue after all.

It was the September of the famous "long count" at Soldiers Field, Chicago, when Dempsey again lost to Tunney, and the year Babe Ruth hit his sixty home runs.

There I was, the proverbial callow youth, sprung from the halls of learning into the big, wide, wonderful world. It was a little intimidating. I certainly hadn't forgotten my vow to invade South America but, until the opportunity was at hand, I must make a living.

My old friend Lester Laden had stayed on at Yale to take charge of student musical activity and he had planned a summer tour for the Yale Collegians. Unfortunately, though we were friendly, I had made a bad impression on him when we were working at the Rendez-vous in New York—he remembered all too well that I would often come in late for the engagement and made fifteen dollars a week more than he did. He wanted no part of me for the Collegians' tour.

Strangely enough he had used me the last semester of my Senior year. Just before graduation we had played a dance for my good friend Dean Angier at a party given for his children. It was quite possibly an event of portent. After we had been playing about three hours the Dean brought us plates of ice cream. Without realizing my boorishness and indiscretion, I inquired, "Is *this* all we're having?"

Apparently one of his sons noticed my rather uncivil question as well as his father's confusion and embarrassment and resolved that some day he would avenge this slight. What he actually did later at a Boston theater might have put him in the electric chair and me in my grave—but fortunately his aim was bad. But more of that later.

As matters turned out, Laden found himself short a saxophonist and, hat in hand (it must have galled him terribly), he *had* to come to me for the Collegians' tour. I was happy to accept with the usual condition that I wanted my price. It was considerably more than he wanted to pay but he had no choice and off we went.

One of our first locations was the Strand Theater in New Britain, Connecticut, sharing a vaudeville bill with the incomparable comedian, Fred Allen. His dry, brilliant wit delivered in his New England nasality was a sheer delight. I was so enchanted that I memorized his entire act. It has since become one of the best things I do professionally and I will launch into it at parties with little coaxing. With my own built-in New England-nasal voice it is relatively easy.

Suddenly we ran into the well-known plight of vaudevillians from time immemorial—no bookings. We were stranded in Pittsburgh, so while we marked time I got the boys rooms at the SAE house at the University of Pittsburgh for five dollars a week. Luckily, I had some money left over after college and was the only one in the group halfway solvent. I was the Collegians' FHA! On July 28 I threw a party celebrating my

10. Where it all started—the Yankees at the New York Heigh Ho Club in '28.

11. Vallée's visage as cigarette salesman was plastered all over New York in June, 1927.

12. Rudy in one of his favorite and most popular impressions—Chevalier, of course.

13. Home is the hero—Vallée's "homecoming" honored in a five-day celebration, Westbrook, Maine.

MOMENTS IN THE CAREER OF RADIO'S "ACE"

(1) The family group. With Mother and Dad (Mr. and Mrs. Charles A. Vallée) and brother Bill.

(2) The University of Maine awards the prized 'M' to Rudy for making 'The Stein Song' world famous.

(3) Rudy and some of his boys come to the platform to receive an ovation from thousands who welcomed them on their triumphant return from Hollywood.

(4) Rudy presents brother Bill with "S.A.E." emblem, as other fraternity brothers look on.

(5) Rudy meets and chats with The First Lady of the Land.

14. Rare photos from an NBC souvenir program booklet 1930.

15. A few of the thousand or more songs with which Vallée was associated.

twenty-sixth birthday at the frat house. That day Lindbergh was making an appearance at the stadium nearby but I was either too tired or too dispirited to go although I admired him greatly.

Fortunately, one of the boys in the group had initiative enough to keep us from starvation. He was a young fellow from Maine whom I had persuaded to transfer to Yale and I surely thanked God I had! As a result of a rush trip to New York he was able to dig up enough bookings to last us through the season.

On the way back to New York and the most welcome engagements, I dropped off in Jersey to visit my youthful "Greta Garbo." She was something less than ecstatic to see me yet did not spurn my attentions, leaving me wondering again just where I really stood with her! *Women!*

When I joined the band for dates in and around New York City, my punctuality left something to be desired. I have always been a very hard worker but on two occasions, when I was out shopping for saxophones, reeds and mouthpieces, the time slipped up on me and I missed our opening number. It got so none of the boys in the band would speak to me—not even my chum with whom I generally roomed and ate in cafeterias while the rest of the band "put on the dog" at expensive restaurants.

By the time we were to play the Fox Audubon Theater I was really in disgrace but there I found a chance to redeem myself. During the third show of our "four-a-day" I noticed, way up at the theater entrance, two young ladies who had been imbibing a bit too freely. When they took their places in a box up on our left I recognized one as Blanche McLeod, the Elizabeth Taylor type I had "made the news reels" with at the Junior Prom in '26; the other was going with our banjoist, a young wealthy boy named Neil Waterman. As they sat there with their feet on the box's red plush railing, taking swigs out of a bottle, violating the fire laws by smoking furiously, I knew trouble was brewing.

At the end of the show when we appeared for an encore, one of the girls leaned over and shouted, "Neil! Oh, Neil!"

The effect on the band and audience was catastrophic—all eyes turned toward the box and the Collegians were so rattled they couldn't play a note. *I alone knew something like this was going to happen* so I proceeded to play, with great gusto, the introduction to our encore number, "When Day is Done." After a few measures the boys recovered their wits and joined in. It was like the band playing "Nearer My God to Thee" on the *Titanic*, I guess. At any rate it prevented pandemonium and afterward the band congratulated me to a man. My sins were forgiven and I was back in the sacred circle.

While we were playing the Fox Theater in Philly, Laden began to brood about the audience's acceptance (or lack of it) of our vaudeville turn. He knew something was wrong but could not put his finger on it.

In desperation he called a nine o'clock rehearsal. The weather was unbearably hot which did not help matters at all and the rehearsal seemed of little avail.

As we began to leave the theater he heard me muttering, "I don't know why the hell we were brought here this early in the morning for nothing."

The taller and heavier Laden grabbed me by the collar and shook me like a water rat. "What are you complaining about!" he shouted. "You're getting fifteen dollars a week more than the rest of us—you and your nanny-goat voice!" He then proceeded to do a caustic impression of me singing "If You Were the Only Girl in the World and I Were the Only Boy."

Next morning, still in something of a huff, I arose early and went across the river to Camden, New Jersey, to visit the Export Department of the Victor Talking Machine Company.

"I'll do anything to get to Buenos Aires," I told the gentleman in charge of records for Argentina. "Anything—the shipping department or lugging wax masters around the place. I know music and I know Spanish fluently. And I've got to get to Argentina."

"My boy," he replied, "I hate to disillusion you but most of the records for Argentina are made right here in the United States. There's no job down there for Victor that would make it worth your while."

I was crushed at the time but now, of course, I'm glad it turned out that way. Neither of us knew then that within two years I would be Victor's top recording star.

After the Collegians' tour I led bands in and around Boston, playing the swank country clubs and socialite functions. But I was too far away from the Swedish lovely in New Jersey and, when I was offered one night a week with one of the Vincent Lopez orchestras in New York, I accepted. It paid only fourteen dollars but by staying at the SAE house at Columbia and patronizing the Automat I could get by until I found something more lucrative.

On my first date with a Lopez combo I showed I was still a starry-eyed country bumpkin. When Lopez dropped in to survey (in his nearsighted manner) the group booked under his name, I jumped down off the stand and asked him to autograph a program! I don't think he was aware that I was one of the musicians. If he had known, he'd have probably given me hell.

With only one engagement a week with Lopez, while I could *exist*, I was certainly not amassing any savings or indulging in luxuries. To augment my meager income I began a frontal assault on the various band offices. After cooling my heels in the reception room of the Ben Bernie organization for six straight afternoons, on the seventh (by buttering up the female receptionist) I was permitted to see Ben's brother,

Herman, who handled the business affairs in his cluttered inner sanctum.

"What do *you* want?" Herman scowled at me. This was completely rhetorical and funny since I was almost bent double with all my musical instruments plus a portable phonograph on which to play my records. But I wanted a job badly so I played serious. I took off my raccoon coat and put down my derby.

"Mr. Bernie, I'm a musician. Do you need a good reed-man? I also sing."

Luck was with me. They were putting together a group of musicians to replace Ben Bernie at the Roosevelt Grill while he went to Philly in a musical comedy. I'll always consider "Thinking of You" my lucky song for after I had auditioned about one-half of the chorus on sax for the Bernie brothers, I was in.

One of the Bernie dates was memorable. We went down to Baltimore to play a debutante party. Fortunately, the girl's brother was a Yale classmate—when he welcomed me with open arms, Herman and the rest of the band were very impressed.

At intermission, acts playing nearby theaters were brought in to entertain. One such was the Rhythm Boys who were playing Baltimore with Paul Whiteman. It was a crowded place and the trio working with only a piano was back against the wall of the gym and nobody paid much attention to their performance. Suddenly, however, one of them walked out to the center of the floor and delivered a popular song of the day, "Montmartre Rose." There were no amplifying systems in those days and I could scarcely hear his rendition. When he had finished, there was a deafening roar of applause which would have called for at least one or two encores. Instead, he walked off the floor past where we sat, his classic features expressionless, his patrician nose just a bit up in the air. You might have thought him deaf, so unaware he seemed of the sensation he had created. But then, this insouciance has always characterized Bing Crosby.

My days and nights might have continued in a similar vein—the mad dashes from Morristown, New Jersey, scorning redcaps who were rarely available anyway and who would have charged me a fortune to carry all my various musical gear; onto the Jersey trains to the Hudson tubes a bizarre, raccoon-coated figure barging in upon an astonished carload of passengers, then a long walk to the subway as I made my way to a date, a rehearsal hall, or a booking office; a squirrel on a treadmill, had it not been for an artist whose obsession was pirates, doubloons, and cutlasses and an enterprising young pianist who decided to book orchestras rather than run a checkroom for dances.

The former was Don Dickerman, a real Bohemian character. He was an artist who since boyhood had been obsessed by the colorful Henry Morgan and his pirate crew. As an outlet, he had set up the Pirate's Den in Greenwich Village complete with buccaneer décor including brigs and the roll call of a fake pirate crew. Subsequently, he created a club called the Blue Horse and another called the Country Fair, each with its own distinctive flavor, offering a particular type of appeal. The devotees of the "black bottom" and the Charleston in the F. Scott Fitzgerald era remember well these three hangouts.

Dickerman was at this time in his sixth or seventh marriage, evidently trying to outdo the renowned DeWolfe Hopper and set a record for Artie Shaw to shoot at. He was planning a smart supper club near Park Avenue catering to the elite—absolutely formal with no exceptions. It was to be completely exclusive as well. In other words, Herbert Hoover could not get in in a gray suit and Otto Kahn could not get in dressed in tails, if you get my meaning. Bigoted snobbishness might sum it up— but that's the way Dickerman felt it had to be in order to cater to the so-called Park Avenue upper crust.

It was really a most exotic concept for a supper club. Dickerman had been on the William Beebe expedition to the Galápagos and this influenced his decorations: there were large panels of silver or gold leaf over which were superimposed pictures of the intriguing underwater creatures Dickerman had observed through his bathyscope; there were also small statuettes and paintings apposite to the theme; to top it all off, behind the small bandstand against a background of cobalt blue, beautifully lighted, was a live white cockatoo which, whenever the drummer raised his sticks to any unusual degree, would raise his feathered crest in the air! It was perhaps a little too-too and a little too *frou-frou* but it had the makings of a snob hang-out.

In true night-club tradition this Heigh-Ho Club opened on New Year's Eve—the idea always being that the high holiday tariffs plus the healthy take in the checkroom and other concessions would accrue sufficient operating capital for even a couple of lean months following. However, it turned out that the opening was something of a bust—the dance floor was far from smooth and the band itself left much to be desired. In a few days the word was out—Dickerman was looking for a new band!

At this precise juncture Bert Lown entered my life. In retrospect, he kind of reminds me of the person Robert Morse plays in the musical, *How to Succeed In Business Without Really Trying*—a brash young guy on the make who makes it big, from window-washer to Chairman of the Board. Lown had been a typewriter salesman who also ran the checkroom at various Westchester County dances. His very analytical mind observed that the piano man in the band made more than he did, ransoming coats and hats. Therefore, he brushed up on his childhood piano lessons and was soon fronting an orchestra worthy of the best.

He had done quite well and had set up an office in the Roseland Building not far from where Wiedoeft and his manager were located. One day I was in the building visiting a booker called Jimmy Caruso. On the way out I saw the switchboard gal give me the big eye and she told me she had put in a good word for me with Lown. As this "operator" had been highly touted to me as a man-who-was-going-places, I naturally popped into his office in search of a few dates as saxophonist. It happened that it was the right day.

It seems he had recently been in the office of a song-plugger named, I believe, Tapps and had overheard the latter in a phone conversation with Dickerman. Lown got the picture—the Heigh-Ho Club was looking for a band and he planned to see that it was supplied by none other than Lown.

He looked at me for a moment without saying anything, as if he were assaying my embouchure. "So you play sax, eh?" he muttered. "I've heard of you. You're supposed to play pretty good. How'd you like a steady job?"

At that time I was quite content with my three or four dates a week and a chance to see the One Girl in Jersey when I wasn't working.

"I'd rather just do an occasional fill-in really. That's what I was looking for. A steady grind would tie me down."

"Okay, okay. It's too bad, though. I had something real nice for you—some of the best club dates in New York."

"Maybe some other time—and thanks." I started out of the office and then, for some reason, I figured I might as well ask for the moon. It never costs anything to ask. "Look, Mr. Lown. I might be interested in a steady job if I could lead the band myself."

At that moment Lown didn't even know if he could secure the engagement or, for that matter, whether I would suit the Heigh-Ho management. Nevertheless, great gambler and promoter that he was, he quietly remarked, "So you want to be the leader. Okay, you got it, Vallee. You got it."

Either luck was with me or Lown was the greatest living salesman—the very next day I was told to pick musicians for an eight-piece band, without brass. Don Dickerman was very positive about the instrumentation: two violins, two clarinets, and rhythm consisting of drums, piano, banjo, and bass. It was before the guitar had become an integral part of the rhythm section. I chose to pick only two men from New Haven. They were "townees," not Yale boys—a great pianist whose technique sounded like four hands playing and a tenor saxophonist who had made many engagements with me. The balance of the band were New York musicians chosen by Lown and the rehearsal date was set for January 8, 1928.

We met in a small rehearsal room in the Roseland Building with the high hope of creating (in a few hours!) a cohesive group that might win the job at the Heigh-Ho.

I could see the faces of the New York boys drop slightly as they looked me over. This reaction had become an accustomed one from people who generally did not conceive of me as being capable of handling them or a situation. Their consternation became greater when I did not take them through popular tune after popular tune, rehearse jazz choruses in the style of that day, or engage in obvious and usual methods of a band rehearsal. All we did was rehearse changes of key!

On those long days of college dances in and around New Haven, when the band was not led by Bolton and Cipriano (who generally played routine orchestrations from start to finish), the combo was conducted by a violinist. This worthy, so help me, God, for want of any ingenuity, would let us play twenty or thirty tunes *all in the same key for the course of an hour and a half*. It was like the Chinese water torture.

We had no music parts for these tunes but, in musicians' parlance, we "faked" them. Most of us knew the harmony and the melody to these compositions, anyway, but the difficulty of going from one key to another would have required some knowledge of where and how to *modulate*. Since we were together for an evening only, this leader took the easiest way out and never attempted to rehearse us in this simple expedient of key changes.

I made a resolution, after experiencing this soporific effect (not only upon us but upon the audience itself) of playing in one key for an hour and a half, that if I ever had a dance band I would make sure that we *never played two tunes in the same key*. We would mount steadily up! The increasing and dynamic effect of key changes going ever higher and higher is incalculable. The layman may never understand what is being done to him but he will feel the effect upon his spine and nervous system as well as upon what little or great amount of innate musical appreciation he may have.

After a thorough rehearsal of this method of bridging the gap from one chorus to another, I instructed the boys in how I would give them the key changes, by the use of the fingers of my right hand when it was not occupied creating notes on my saxophone.

It was agreed that a chap named Jules De Vorzon (who is now a real-estate salesman in Palm Springs, and on the side has a musical and mind-reading act with a guitar player) would do the singing in his "trained-voice style," singing songs such as those written by Victor Herbert and other musical-comedy composers.

It is important to understand that all the bands of that day had a vocal trio made up of "trained" voices. This was the result of a popular Victor record made by George Olson, "Who," from *Sunny*, in which he used such a group. The success of this record had been electrifying and as a result of its huge sale, Olson, Bernie, Lopez, and even Whiteman had followed sheeplike and had found themselves a trio of "trained" or "semi-trained" voices.

Quite obviously three voices, trained or otherwise, can never synchronize or express the feelings of the lyric, or even the melody, as well as one voice. Three voices are, indeed, three voices, each with individuality and personality. Though they strive to merge these into a single integral factor, there can never be the perfection of one voice singing simply and naturally and from one heart.

We probably would have had a trio in our little Heigh-Ho Club band (which I had decided to call the Yale Collegians) if we had had an adequate bass and tenor. Now the die had been cast that Jules De Vorzon was to do the singing, solo.

The evening of our debut was a Monday, January 8, 1928. It was shortly after New Year's when purses were still dented and heads just beginning to lose that throb of too much Prohibition-type booze. There weren't twenty people inside the Heigh-Ho Club. Dickerman sat there. He seemed to be a massive man, even though he was not the six feet in size that his frame appeared to be. The band was ordered to wear tuxedo pants and satin blouses in Russian style, buttoned up high around the neck with sashes around the waist. We had played for about an hour. De Vorzon had delivered himself of Victor Herbert's "Gypsy Love Song" and several other like compositions, when one of the waiters told me that Mr. Dickerman wished to see me. When I arrived at his table, he was scowling and evidently quite unhappy about the whole thing. He came to the point directly and simply said, "I don't like the singer."

I saw the job floating out the window. I reminded myself of my little megaphone in my baritone saxophone case and of a tune called "Rain." This tune, "Rain," had been featured by a leading publisher and had somehow come to the attention of the Yale Collegians in the summer of 1927. It had been sung by a trio of us in vaudeville in the best George Olson manner with the added effects of thunder and lightning overhead causing us to put on slickers while the band played proper "storm" music. Then after removing our slickers we went back to the final chorus of "Rain" vocally. Thus I had learned the lyrics and the melody and had even sung it at some of the spring dances at Yale with the pianist who was now playing with me at the Heigh-Ho Club.

In a few words I apprised the boys of the situation. Burwell, the pianist, remembered the song and we started a rendition of "Rain," first featuring the two violins, then my vocal, and then a chorus of two clarinets. Halfway through I switched to my baritone saxophone and then to the megaphone; after that a piano chorus and back to the megaphone for a final chorus.

The waiter again approached me and again I bowed low at the royal table of King Dickerman. This time Dickerman's face was wreathed in smiles. There, then and there, was made the decision that was to send me (through the medium of radio later on) to fame and fortune. The impresario very simply said, "*You* do the singing."

I think that to this day Jules De Vorzon believes that I double-crossed him. But these are the actual facts, so help me, God! The evening wore on. We tried many new things that I had many times wanted to do and at the end of the evening we were told to report the next night!

There it was—my big chance. After all the scuffling one-nighters and the uncertainty of the "road" I now had my own band and a steady job.

Ah, that band—it was the cat's pajamas. In those days some orchestras did a lot of comic bits in addition to purveying dance music. I had a good memory and in my eclecticism was not at all loath to take the best elements of the acts of Fred Waring, Mal Hallett (similar to Waring but in a more comic way), Paul Whiteman, and Vincent Lopez and adapt them for our own use. Oh, yes, we had all sorts of funny paper hats, gadgets, and props—I developed two war-song medleys complete with a flashbox containing flash powder which was ignited by an electrical spark agitated by an off-stage switch. The latter was also used in the Devil's number and the explosion was supposed to bring Satan up out of the ground.

In another tableau, a naval medley, one of the bandsmen, dressed as a sailor, spit out some "bad liquor" and, as it hit the floor, the flashbox went off. We all wore sailor hats and simulated a storm at sea complete with lightning, the sound of the raging wind, and foghorns. At the captain's order "To the lifeboats!" a terrified passenger appeared clad in a bathrobe with a hot-water bottle in his hand. Oh, I tell you, we were a caution!

So much for the dramaturgical part of our presentation. How about the music? First of all, due to the limited size of the bandstand and Dickerman's budget restrictions we were forced to get along without a brass section. At first blush this seemed annoying since it meant we would not readily be able to play the same arrangements as other bands. But it was a blessing in disguise. If we had had brass we would have sounded much like all the others—a lack of brass forced us into a style and sound all our own which was to take the East by storm. To get grist for our musical mill I haunted the song publishers for the latest and best tunes which we made into medleys of contrasting types and tempos. Before long we found ourselves developing into a smooth, facile combination worthy of taking on any of the bands in the city.

Even so the audiences were never very large at the Heigh-Ho. Dickerman's insistence on catering only to the upper crust was almost his undoing: there was little chance of word-of-mouth advertising reaching a "mass" market. But Bert Lown sensed that he was handling a band with an unusual quality and coaxed a small local radio station, WABC, into putting in a "wire" to broadcast our music from the club.

The station representative was a Mr. Sampson who happened to be a Yale man. It was shocking—here were two of us in show business when traditionally we should have been in Wall Street, in the advertising dodge, or at least lawyers like all the rest!

"There's only one thing, Mr. Vallee," Mr. Sampson added rather apologetically. "We're a small station and our staff of announcers is rather limited. Could you—uh—would you mind terribly announcing your own numbers?"

Would I *mind!* I was tickled to death. I had always spoken easily and naturally; this, in addition to the aid and training I had received by absorbing the incomparable style of the great Billy Phelps and from watching some of the great masters of ceremonies, made the prospect anything but a challenge. What might have been a contretemps turned out to be a boon. Moreover, it certainly could not be said I was influenced by any radio announcers of the day. Believe it or not, when I first went on the air *I had never heard even one radio program!*

And so with the naïveté of the pure amateur I decided to begin my radio salutation with the phrase used by the doorman outside the club: "Heigh-ho, everybody—this is Rudy Vallee announcing and directing the Yale Collegians from the Heigh-Ho Club at Thirty-five East Fifty-third Street, New York City." In those days there was no censorship either of tunes or of what was said over the air. Therefore, I programmed any music I wished, gave out prices on the menu, weather reports; in short, I talked about anything that came to mind. I was even able to mention other radio stations, something which is frowned upon today—now it's "*another* city station" or "*another* network."

Thus, on a chill February night in '28, we made our first broadcast. Since our club audience was small as usual and we had no announcer or "claque director" to direct and "milk" the reactions from the customers, we certainly had no idea how warmly our performance was being received in the homes with radios. As a matter of fact, I didn't give the broadcast a second thought—I presumed it was just a gimmick which possibly would amount to little. The boys and I played on until three o'clock, the usual quitting time, and went home.

The following afternoon I arrived at the club with an assortment of funny hats and props to go with some new routines we were preparing. The captain, who was taking telephone reservations, handed me a batch of a dozen or so letters. Fan mail! To my delight they were encomiums to warm the heart of any performer. I still have some of these very letters and their context was that we were "*different.*"

Even then I believe I had a sneaking hunch as to why we had so impressed the listeners. Let's take a look at what the "climate" was like at the time and try to derive some reasons:

Item: Listeners in New York, New Jersey, and Pennsylvania (the area WABC reached) were jaded as they listened each night to the same bands playing the same tunes the same way—the same "cute" announcers taking simple song titles and trying to coat them with a frosting of alleged wit and eloquence.

Item: Somehow the name "Rudy Vallee" suggested "Rudy Valentino" and, according to many letters, it conjured up for the female listeners a picture of a tall-dark-and-handsome performer to go with the radio voice.

Item: Although the voice spoke in the nasal manner of a Calvin Coolidge and philosophized like a college professor, it was nonetheless simple and direct. No fancy trimmings.

Item: There was no brass in the Collegians, only two strings, two saxes and the four-man rhythm sections—the sound we got was unusual, pleasant, and soothing.

Item: In a slightly down-east accent, I talked about simple songs and made them interesting by relating anecdotes about their composers or the songs themselves.

Item: I sang in French, Spanish, and Italian and instead of dealing only in the obvious popular tunes played by all the other bands, I found tunes the radio listener had never heard before.

Item: Our format never included the verse, that usually uninteresting introductory part of a song that leads up to the chorus, the big melodic part that everyone remembers, the meat of the song.

Item: We never played more than two choruses of a tune and they were never in the same key; rather, the keys always mounted higher, thus changing the musical colors much as the revolving spotlights in a ballroom change as they play upon the dancers.

I lack perception about many things but I would have had to be a four-ply *dumkopf* not to realize I had stumbled upon a pot of gold. As a double check I asked a friend who was close to Vincent Lopez if he had received similar letters as a result of his broadcasts. When I found he hadn't, I knew we were on the brink of something very big.

Before the week was out WABC dispatched Mr. Sampson to ask us to broadcast every night of the week. Of course, I gleefully accepted. Three weeks later, Station WOR, a large and important outlet, beseeched us to broadcast for *them* every night in the week. Great!

By this time we had garnered a sponsor! Each Sunday afternoon (on still another station) we were to broadcast for the Herbert Jewelry Store, in Harlem. I wanted to remain "different" and electrify our listeners on our first show, so I prepared an elaborate introduction. There was the sound of a clock striking midnight, then two shots rang out followed by the blast of a policeman's whistle. Two of us, impersonating a sergeant and a patrolman, began a dialogue praising Mr. Herbert's diamonds. Our boys in blue (a violinist and I) wailed that the product was so dazzling and tempting that they could scarcely blame a felon for breaking in to get them. The New York Police Department, however, took a very dim view of this realism. They informed our patron that once was quite enough. It was probably the first wacky commercial in history.

When spring had rolled around we were doing as many as twenty broadcasts a week! I was busily running up and down stairs, tearing up menus on the backs of which I would type out a thirty-minute routine of numbers and make copies of them on the gelatinous duplicators that restaurants use. I made up countless such routines so that our various programs (nine o'clock, eleven, and twelve-thirty A.M.) would not carry duplications of the same numbers.

Spring is supposed to be the time a young man's fancy turns, etc. but I was quite dejected. My sweet Swede from Jersey was dating several other guys, one of whom, horror of horrors, was a member of Hal Kemp's band!

If I had ever had any romantic illusions about myself (and what boy hasn't?) the Heigh-Ho Club engagement certainly dissipated them. (As a callow lad of sixteen I imagined I resembled Wally Reid, a popular movie star of the day!) One night at the club, shortly after a broadcast, a woman approached and asked me which one was Rudy Vallee. I was standing there in front of the band, holding my sax and, on impulse, I pointed to our tenor saxophonist, Joe Miller, a dark, good-looking fellow. He in turn pointed back at me and, with a faint snort of disgust, the woman walked away. She must have been a radio fan because it was quite clear that I in no way fulfilled her expectations in physical appearance.

This, with variations, of course, happened at least three times during that spring. Fortunately, I have a deep Irish sense of humor and was not too greatly disturbed. And happily, other gals did occasionally flirt with me as they danced by.

One enchanted evening late in May, while on the stand during a set, I heard a lovely sound of singing as if someone were playing a violin way out on the floor. I traced the sound to an attractive brunette who was humming along with the band as she danced.

Ah, *that face*—it bespoke good breeding, dignity, understanding, and a tolerant, compassionate nature. I judged her to be about twenty-eight or so and intuitively knew that she was interested in me.

I determined to meet her and, at intermission, strode toward the *maitre d'* to find out who she might be. *She* was there asking him to in-

troduce *her!* Thus I met Leonie Cauchois, a girl from a distinguished
and aristocratic family whose father had invented, of all things, the
tea ball! He owned considerable New York property and was involved
in a company purveying one of the finest coffees of the day. Leonie had
recently been divorced from a wealthy socialite (named McCoy) and
had a two-year-old child. All this data came later—what I was interested
in that night was meeting this immensely attractive, very dark brunette.

So ensued a week of whirlwind romance, as they say, enhanced by
the feeling of spring in the air. I must, for the record, further state that I
was somewhat on the rebound from Jersey's answer to Greta Garbo—I
figured I had had it in *that* area. There were a lot of pluses for the match:
all my friends and the boys in the band liked Leonie immensely; she was
a woman of charm and culture; she enjoyed cooking, and she played the
piano! And who is to say—perhaps this warm response from an attractive
woman was what I subconsciously needed as salve for my wounded ego.
For the first time I really found myself seriously contemplating taking
the final step.

Now, of course, I know full well that we would have been sensible
to continue our courtship for a longer period. We would have realized,
then, that it wouldn't work out—for the simple reason that I was still
carrying the torch for my Swedish girl. Nevertheless, on a Saturday
morning, less than a week after we met, Leonie and I were at City Hall
tying the knot.

Even though it was my nuptial day the Heigh-Ho Club had to have
its pound of flesh. Leonie had to wait for me during the tea dance and
the long dinner and supper sessions until three in the morning. This was
one hell of a way to spend a honeymoon! Finally the ordeal was over,
and we drove over the Fifty-ninth Street Bridge in the Sunday dawn
to a little place she had rented in Forest Hills.

A very strange thing happened as we reached the door of the apartment we had chosen in which to celebrate our spousehood. (I know now
that a ridiculously short engagement often leads to disaster.) With a
sinking heart I realized that this hastily conceived marriage was not to
be. Although I am tabbed a complete romantic, on occasion I can be
most realistic. Rather than go on with a marriage (as so many feel they
must do to save face) that was not to be a marriage in every sense of the
word, I told my bride the way I felt. Being a very understanding, sympathetic, and intelligent person, she agreed to an annulment which we subsequently secured. We have always been the best of friends—she later
married a naval officer and to the best of my knowledge has been most
happy. I still continued to see my Jersey gal but that too had changed
somehow and I realized we would never walk down the aisle together.

And so ends the first of four chapters in the marital adventures of Rudy
Vallee. Stay tuned to this station for further developments.

CHAPTER VII

Three Cheers for Radio—Two Cheers for Hollywood

"I'm Just A Vagabond Lover"

WE WERE WELL INTO 1928, THE YEAR that Herbert Hoover clobbered Al Smith by a score of 444 electoral votes to 87. The diplomatic boys were still writing up noble documents and actually signing them with a straight face: the Kellogg-Briand "Pact of Paris" was promulgated with major nations as signatories. It outlawed war as an instrument of national policy—*plus ça change!*

Everybody was getting in the act in aviation. The "coast-to-coast" speed record was broken, it seemed, once a week as was the "endurance" record as planes stayed aloft longer and longer by refueling in flight. "Endurance" achievements got almost as popular as flagpole-sitting and tree-sitting did years later. And, of course, Amelia Earhart became the first woman to fly across the Atlantic.

A politician named Franklin D. Roosevelt published a book entitled *The Happy Warrior: Alfred E. Smith,* and Stephen Vincent Benét wrote the Pulitzer Prize-winning *John Brown's Body.* The best-seller lists included Vina Delmar's *Bad Girl* and Roark Bradford's *Ol' Man Adam 'n' Chillun* which later became the timeless play, *Green Pastures.*

On the longhair musical scene the National Broadcasting Company formed the NBC Symphony with Walter Damrosch as conductor and New York saw the world première of Gershwin's sprightly *An American in Paris* scored for orchestra and taxi horns.

Broadway was thriving on such diverse dramatic fare as O'Neill's *Strange Interlude,* Hecht and MacArthur's *The Front Page,* and the sensational performance of Mae West in *Diamond Lil.* The musical boards were vibrating rhythmically to the tunes of *Rosalie, George White's Scandals, Earl Carroll's Vanities, Blackbirds of 1928, Animal Crackers,* and *Whoopee.*

The motion picture was undergoing epochal transformations as it found its voice in *Abie's Irish Rose* and Jolson's *The Singing Fool.* Silent films were still being released and included Chaplin's *The Circus,* and

67

Sadie Thompson which starred Gloria Swanson. Another ingredient was added as a young artist named Walt Disney created an animated silent cartoon, *Plane Crazy*, which featured the histrionics of a mouse named Mickey.

As Dickerman did not expect sufficient business during the hot summer months when the social set to which he catered would be away vacationing, he decided to close until fall. I was out of a job and had to cast about for ways to earn my bread, as today's musicians put it. Lown was frantic as he sought a summer engagement to keep the band together. By pulling a few strings, I was able to get us an audition at the Milton Point Casino, the very snooty club in Rye, New York, which I had turned down after my graduation in 1927. We won out over eight of ten bands but the job was *murder* all the way.

First of all, my pianist got sick on opening night but I was lucky enough to get Lester Laden (now a little more friendly) to sit in. It was foggy and rainy and I was a worn-out wreck from the long winter grind at the Heigh-Ho. Laryngitis had attacked my throat. The bandstand was shaped like the prow of a boat and was rather removed from the dancers, affording us no opportunity to get near enough for them to hear us. There was no public-address system and you could always hear the *swish-swish* of scuffling shoes as they moved on a floor covered with a thin layer of sand blown in from the ocean! And we in the band were treated like pariahs, forbidden to sit at the guests' tables or make telephone calls from the club.

This desolate summer was, however, relieved by one ray of sunshine— we were able to continue our Sunday broadcasts for the Harlem jewelry store. Radio was still pumping desperately needed adrenalin into us. In one broadcast alone, when the sponsor offered my photograph to listeners who would write for it, there were over fifty thousand requests. For a local station to "pull" that much mail in those early days of radio was truly fabulous.

Before our Milton Point engagement came to an end, the management began to realize we were much more popular, more of a "draw," than they had expected. They started to treat us almost like human beings and tried to sign us for the following season.

"You people don't have enough money to hire this band," I told them quietly. "There isn't enough money in the world to pay us to come back here."

The following year I was to return as guest of honor at this same club where I had been forbidden to mingle with the guests!

After the rather harrowing Milton Point episode, Bert Lown decided to turn our band ownership contract over to an individual who was to prove one of the most ingenious personalities I have ever known. He was not, however, inventive enough to get us a better deal at the Heigh-

Ho and we signed again for the same money and the same drudging hours.

To say that our boss, Don Dickerman, was a rather strange individual would be plumbing the depths of understatement. For some reason our broadcasts annoyed hell out of him.

"Look, Don," I would say to him. "We are reaching hundreds of thousands of people on every broadcast."

"What do you mean!" he would reply. It was in the days before rating bureaus like Hooper, Nielsen, and Arbitron were in such vogue that their thumbs-up or thumbs-down *pronunciamenti* determined the very existence of a show. "You're more likely playing to *hundreds* of people on radio."

"There's no use arguing," I said. "Even if it's only hundreds, it's free advertising. Besides, when we finish a broadcast, we give the customers a forty-or fifty-minute dance set."

"You fellows ought to enjoy just *playing* this club—never mind about the radio. You're entertaining the finest clientele in the country." I had shown him a wire offering me several hundred a week to emcee a show in a Detroit theater. "Would you really do this?" he asked aghast. "Would you *really* like to entertain that kind of people?"

More trouble! Several Yale alumni had come to the club and complained about our use of the name "The Yale Men" for the band. You know why? Because, to them, some of the boys in the orchestra didn't *look* like Yale men. We had also been using, as a theme song, "March, March on Down the Field," written by a close friend and alumnus, Stanleigh Friedman.

Dickerman, not unlike present-day TV sponsors who panic into changing their whole shows upon receiving a half-dozen critical phone-calls or letters, was always ready with a close ear for the idiotic snob-fringe. He "suggested" that we change our name.

At the Vanderbilt Theater I had recently caught a matinee performance of *The Connecticut Yankee*, the wondrous Rodgers and Hart musical with its viable melodies, "Thou Swell" and "My Heart Stood Still." As I came out of the theater after the matinee I suddenly realized its title wouldn't be the worst in the world for naming a band. I could picture exactly the way the billing would look on a marquee or on a record label. And so, to mollify Boss Dickerman and justify our Yale theme song, we became "The Connecticut Yankees."

All you had to do was think up some wild, new scheme for a night club and Don Dickerman would come a-running. Some Cuban money-men had decided to build a club on that troubled island and wanted him to come down as consultant. The "theme" of the place was to be, of all things, the court of King Arthur and his Round Table! It was to simulate an English castle complete with moats, drawbridge, and waiters dressed as knights in armor. All this, mind you, in Cuba! Naturally, Don took the first boat.

While he was away, the management fell to a loathsome *maitre-d'* who spoke six languages and was a scoundrel in all of them. He conspired to farm us out, so to speak, to other spots that would pay four and five times the Heigh-Ho stipend due to our radio broadcasts two and three times a night. Naturally, we got no part of this money—still only the modest contract salary at the club.

We had never been very ecstatic working under Dickerman but now with the new boss (who doubled as *maitre d'*) it became intolerable. Whenever there was any complaint during working hours it was magnified a hundredfold in a cabled report to Dickerman in Cuba. If a fair damsel so much as nodded or winked at me from the dance floor, the manager would notify Dickerman that I was constantly irritating escorts. Whenever I was told to make an outside appearance I was assured that they were made with Dickerman's blessing. But so maniacally dishonest was this managerial crook that he had the temerity to cable Cuba that I was leaving the club to perform periodically elsewhere!

It was a hectic regimen: I had accepted, for practically nothing, an engagement to play tea dances at the Lombardy Hotel from three to six, plus the full "day" at the Heigh-Ho with two and three broadcasts, seven days a week, as well as the Sunday broadcasts for the jewelry store. During the whole time I worked at the club I never took a night off for myself. It was a hard-working loyalty that was quite unappreciated as you will see.

The wear and tear began to tell on me. I began to have nightmares almost every night and once, in the middle of a particularly bad one, I jumped out of bed and struck my left eye on the corner of a marble table. Next day I showed up with a magnificent shiner and, naturally, no one believed my story!

The boys in my original band, the Yale Collegians, felt the Lombardy tea dances a little too much work to handle. Therefore, I picked up seven New York musicians as an alternate band to share the work. No one who listened to the broadcasts from the Lombardy or the Heigh-Ho could ever tell the difference in the bands. I realized it was not so much the individual muscians that counted, but rather the expression of our formula, a formula which was partly my invention through necessity and partly the result of chance.

About this time we were permitted to taste, but only barely taste, the sweetmeat of success; we were to get a network show with a sponsor!

Ironically, we would never have garnered this patron had it not been for the insidious character of the crooked *maitre-d!* Business was bad, so whenever he saw someone who looked like a big spender, the bars were let down whether the prospect was in formal attire or not. One night one such worthy entered the club. He had close-cropped red hair and went by the name of Burns. This gentleman really believed in sharing the wealth and always had a ten-spot for the checkroom girl and always sent up ten or twenty dollars to the band when he would request a couple of tunes.

"You guys oughta do commercial broadcasts," he informed me one evening when he had invited me to join him and his girl friend at his table. "You got a good band there and you oughta get yourself a sponsored show."

"We're sponsored right now," I said and described our jewelry show.

"Naw, I mean you should go network." He thought for a moment. "Say, I'm putting out a product pretty soon and I'm going to buy some time on the NBC Blue Network. Maybe you can fit in for the music."

"Up to now," I said, "NBC has certainly showed little interest in us."

"Don't mind that," he answered. "This is my show and what I say goes. I got an idea to revolutionize the drug industry—cod-liver oil *capsules!*"

I was summoned to his office to meet his advertising agency representative. Burns's place of business was in a brownstone in the East Fifties not far from the fabulous restaurant, 21. It was like something out of a B gangster movie—I was greeted at the door by two hoodlums who escorted me into a large room which contained a veritable tableful of telephones. Naive down-easterner that I was, I wondered idly why he needed so many phones since he didn't even have a secretary. Later on I realized that it was in all probability a bookie joint!

The ad executive proceeded to show me the magazine and newspaper campaign to announce the show which was to appear over a dozen or so stations—a sizable array of outlets for that period. The money wasn't much; about three hundred and fifty dollars for a half-hour show. Nevertheless, I was overjoyed at getting a network shot.

A meeting was set up with Keith McCleod, then head of the Blue Network's Program Department and subsequently involved for several years with the Red Skelton show. We all sat down together and kicked around a few ideas.

"You mean to tell me," said McCleod, giving me a fishy stare, "that you want to *announce* the show as well as perform with your band?" He had shown throughout the meeting that he had little enthusiasm for a union between the Connecticut Yankees and the Blue Network.

"Well, we've been pretty popular with that sort of format in our other broadcasts," I said mildly.

"I'm sorry, Mr. Vallee, but the Blue Network does not permit orchestra leaders to announce during commercial broadcasts and that's that. You'll be in the capable hands of Milton Cross or possibly Graham McNamee."

As we left the office I was chuckling to myself because I knew what might very well happen. Mr. Cross was assigned to our broadcast, so I dutifully supplied him with a list of the numbers we planned for the first show and gave him a little background on each tune, to use in the intros.

Halfway through the first show the network switchboards lit up like a Christmas tree as listeners demanded to know why I wasn't doing the announcing and why Mr. Cross was referring to the Connecticut Yankees as "The Clopin Eight"—yes, the network had even made us change our name for the broadcast.

Second Show: more of the same with Mr. Cross intoning in his best sepulchral manner something like ". . . and now the Clopin Eight, playing from a picturesque Spanish patio the lovely composition, 'Me Quieres.' " The switchboard almost blew a gasket with indignant calls and wires and letters of protest.

Before the third show, Mr. McCleod called and in a voice filled with disbelief and annoyance informed me that hereafter I was to announce the show. This may seem of little import to you unless you realize that it was such a radical departure for a great network—and it paved the way for a great number of radio personalities who up to that time had never been permitted this liberty.

Sad to say our "Clopin Hour" was not to last. There was some technical difficulty about taking cod-liver oil in capsule form and, after seven programs, the show was dropped. I could almost hear a deep sigh of relief from the network hierarchy.

When Dickerman returned from Cuba the fat really hit the fan, as it were. As the memoir writer says, I can see it now. He and his wife (I forget what "number" wife it was—a pretty little blonde) entered the club and took a table over against the wall. The place was pretty well packed and among the customers were George Olson and his wife who had come over to find out what all this "Rudy Vallee" talk was about. Dickerman just sat and stared at me and the band, his face clouded by a dark scowl.

I was singing "I'll Get By" and I stared right back at the boss, throwing the full meaning and intensity of the lyrics right in his teeth. If he wasn't appreciative of our hard work and effort to put over the Heigh-Ho Club then the hell with it—the band and I would get by.

Between sets I dropped over to his table. "Well, how was Cuba?" I asked politely. "Have a good time?"

"I had a good time in Cuba," he grunted. "That is, except for hearing a lot of bad news about the club here."

"Oh, really?" I said innocently. I hadn't learned about the chicanery of the *maitre d'* at that time. "What was the trouble?"

"I don't want to discuss it now. Just see that you and the band are downstairs at three in the morning after work. Got something I want to talk to you about."

It was about three-fifteen when we were all assembled on the carpet awaiting the storm. Dickerman was not a large man, but when he was angry he somehow assumed an appearance of monstrous proportion and

as he came down the stairs toward us in his majestic fury he fairly
loomed.

"I've know a lot of double-crossers in my day," he said, fixing me
with a baleful glare, "but you take the cake!"

"Now, wait a minute," protested my drummer. I was surprised at him,
of all the men, springing to my defense. We had battled constantly—he
felt our style was too corny, and constantly agitated for a change to a
more jazzy presentation like Ben Pollock's band. "Hold on now, Mr.
Dickerman," he continued. "While I don't agree with Rudy's taste in
music, I can sure as hell bear witness to his loyalty and hard work here."

"Okay, okay. All I know is something very smelly is going on. Maybe
it's that wacky new manager causing all the trouble. I don't care what
the reason is. I just want you all to pack up your instruments and get out
right now." He turned to the rat who had been running the place in his
absence and gave the most unkind cut of all. "George—see that they don't
take anything!"

The boys felt that the bottom had dropped out of their world but I
felt that our firing was for the best. While I did not actually find out until
later that our band owner and the *maitre d'* were working hand in glove
to secure our ousting from the Heigh-Ho in order to sell us elsewhere
at a much higher figure, I had a hunch that something like this might be
happening.

Over on the east side of Fifth Avenue, at 14 East 60 to be exact, there
was a very nice little spot called the Versailles, owned by Charles Morton
Bellak, a Hungarian who also had the hotel property surrounding the
club. It was called simply "14 East 60" and, although it had seen better
days, it was the choice of such English actor-gentry as Leslie Howard
and Nigel Bruce when they first came to America.

The Versailles, at considerable cost, Bellak had literally carved out of
solid rock. It had been decorated with beautiful murals of French garden
scenes. Today this space is occupied by one of the most successful night
clubs in the world—the Copacabana.

The Versailles had only been operating for a couple of months and its
music was being supplied by Eddie Davis and his pianist, Walter Gross.
This fine pianist, best known for his imperishable song, "Tenderly,"
informed me that the place was dying, with scarcely any business at all.
Here was my chance to prove once and for all the dramatic drawing
power of radio.

"What have you got to lose, Mr. Bellak," I told him. "Give me a
chance. You're not doing any business now. I'll pack this place for you
in a week. If not, we'll part friends."

Bellak pretended to be skeptical but it took only one Sunday afternoon
announcement on the "Herbert Blue-White Diamonds" show and a
couple of broadcasts from the Versailles itself to show the power of radio

popularity. By our fifth night we were doing turn-away business at the club.

On every broadcast we did I took great pains to announce that The Connecticut Yankees were to make a public appearance at Keith's 81st Street Theater. We had stumbled upon this engagement a few weeks before we were canned at the Heigh-Ho. Sammy Smith, a song-plugger who foresaw our great success, had prevailed upon Bill McCaffrey, the Keith booker, to give us a four-day weekend. McCaffrey had little enthusiasm for the deal; indeed, he didn't even own a radio. (He later became a teevee and radio agent!) He offered us a mere four hundred dollars but I didn't even haggle. I knew what was going to happen. Our radio listeners' mail was arriving in such an avalanche that I knew our appearance in a large and accessible place would cause a theatrical explosion such as Broadway had never seen.

On opening day they had to call out mounted patrolmen to handle the crowd. As the astonished McCaffrey watched the customers throng into the theater, he found himself being pushed clear out of the lobby onto the sidewalk by the crush of eager radio fans. Inside, our idolaters would half-rise from their seats each time we would play a tune we had featured repeatedly on the air. There were squeals, yells, and applause the like of which this staid old theater had never known. At the end of our second show that first night, the booker for all the Keith theaters in and around New York asked me into his temporary 81st Street Theater office and offered me ten weeks with their chain of houses. I thought I was asking for the moon when I demanded fifteen hundred a week for eight men but Mr. Godfrey, the booker, agreed. He laughed up his sleeve because he knew he was getting a bargain. I was happy also since our Yale Collegians on the road were lucky to get nine hundred for fourteen men!

A new ruling by New York radio stations was now promulgated whereby any night club which had a "wire" (that is, any club broadcasting "remote" from its dance floor) would be assessed a nominal fee to cover the expense of an engineer to set up microphones and arrange the technical details for radio transmission. When Bellak heard of this he blew his top.

"My God, but they've got a nerve!" he screamed. "They should pay *us* for supplying entertainment to the station. If that's the way they feel, they can take the damned wire out of here!"

I was very disturbed at the possibility that we might lose our life line, our umbilical cord to the public. We could have gotten a free wire which our current popularity and large following merited but I was too timid to demand it. Consequently I found myself making a deal whereby the Versailles would be able to broadcast without charge on NBC if I signed with the National Broadcasting Company's Artist Service Bureau.

With our smash success at Keith's 81st and the crowds packing the Versailles every evening, I began to be bombarded on all sides by various offers, stories for the newspapers and magazines and, best of all, an offer to record for Victor.

A word about the owner-manager system in those days—and, as far as I know, today. You would have thought that Abe Lincoln's legacy would have prevented this, for such agreements approximated peonage. For all the work I put out at the Heigh-Ho and the tea dances at the Lombardy (with broadcasts from each) my "owner" paid me the handsome sum of ninety dollars a week. Of course, he paid the band a union stipend—and pocketed what was left over. As I realized our "draw" and potential more and more, this arrangement began to gall. I felt that, since I had gotten the Keith engagements and the Victor recording deal on my own initiative, these contracts should be solely owned by me.

Prior to my signing with NBC, New Owner had put together a very fine band (it included the Dorsey brothers who had not yet become famous) for a sponsor audition. Since I was playing the Keith circuit, it was impossible for me to appear at the audition. Nevertheless, he "sold" me to front the band, as they say, "another" radio station for Van Heusen shirts. Oh, yes, he was a sharp one. If he had told me of his problem, I'm sure I could have secured a release from NBC for this one broadcast. But, no—such was his thinking that he introduced me to a gentleman who slapped a summons in my hand to "show cause" why I should not appear for Van Heusen. New Owner, who had studied a little law, interpreted the ownership contract to mean that he owned me for life; that no matter whether he secured the contracts or not, I was to pay him two-thirds of all I earned. The night he had me slapped with the summons, he told me that he "owned" me in perpetuity!

Through my Yale composer friend, Stanleigh Friedman, who was a top attorney for Warner Brothers, I got legal representation at court in the Van Heusen fracas. After five hours of sleep I arrived in court to face the lawyer for the shirtmaker, who entered as evidence the series of ads which had been placed throughout New York City inviting listeners to tune in on the show they were sponsoring starring Rudy Vallee and the Connecticut Yankees. Our dear band owner was in court licking his chops, secure in the knowledge that the court decision would prove his right to assign me anywhere without my consent.

I was due to play the Palace that day but I waited in court as long as I could—the decision of the court would, after all, have great bearing on my whole life as a performer. Finally, I got a call from the theater. "For God's sake, Rudy," a voice said, "you've got to get up here—court or no court. Van and Schenk have stalled as long as they can!" I grabbed a subway and made it. Just before I had to go onstage, I got a phone call telling me I had won. I was free from New Owner once and for all.

That evening he came to the Versailles to plead with me. "Jesus, Rudy, I've made three engagements for you. You can't let me down—it'll ruin me!"

I would have done them as a favor, but I realized that if I did it would imply that he still owned me body and soul.

Anybody else would have explained to the entrepreneurs that, due to "situations beyond his control," his artist could not appear. Not our fabulous ex-owner. Not and lose that money! You know what he did?

One of the bookings was in a New Jersey spot. At a dramatic juncture in the evening show, after the regular band had been playing several hours, this worthy burst in with his raccoon coat and flowing scarf. He asked for a drum roll and announced that I had been hurt in an automobile accident on the way to the club. He then proceeded to sing three or four songs and picked up the several hundred dollars for my "personal appearance"!

Another engagement he had sold me to was a druggist convention at the Hotel Astor. This time he stated that I had stolen away from my backbreaking chores at the Keith Theaters and the Versailles to take a plane to Maine to see my dear old gray-haired mother for the first time in years. By the time this sugar-cured ham had got through with his story, the audience was in tears (crocodile) and he again pocketed *my* personal appearance money. How he flimflammed the third date I never knew but it must have been a performance worthy of a Barrymore.

As I think of it, dear Mr. Bellak was not far behind in ingenuity. Up to this time he had been paying the band only union scale at the Versailles and paying me two hundred dollars a week. Now he approached me talking contract. He began to play on my vanity and I am only human.

"Rudy, you know what I'm going to do," he said excitedly. "I'm changing the name of the Versailles!"

"Really. What are you going to call it?"

"The Villa Vallee. That's what I'm going to call it. You're a big draw and don't I know it. What kind of contract you want?"

"Let me consider it," I said.

"Look, Rudy," he kept probing. "Just think—when your mother and father come down from Maine they'll see your name—*their name*—on a brass plate outside the club."

All he needed was some soft violins in the distance playing "Hearts and Flowers." I was hooked but I was calm and collected enough to ask for what I thought was a bundle.

"You've got a deal," I said, "but you've got to start paying the boys more than scale. And I want forty per cent of the cover charges."

Oh, I thought I was one smart cooky. After all, I had only to count heads in the clubs and multiply by five dollars (the "cover") and figure forty per cent of the take. I learned a very bitter lesson, though, on this deal—it taught me never to sign a contract without first having an experienced attorney examine it for loopholes and fine print! To show you how goddamned naive I was, I signed the contract after a most cursory examination of it backstage while my band was playing on the stand.

If I had really scrutinized the paper at all I would have realized that there were a dozen corporations involved, one to buy food, another to buy beverages, etc. By the time all parties were through maneuvering, there was little left of the "covers" for me. Furthermore, if the building were to be destroyed or burned down or if Bellak were to lose it (which he subsequently did!) he could then sell me to any other spot in New York City and pocket any amount above the cost of the band. I would in effect be his slave for years to come. Small wonder that, when I signed, Bellak and his little attorney exchanged warm smiles. When I showed this contract to the NBC attorneys they almost had apoplexy and I had no one to blame but myself. And so I was neatly trapped. The Versailles became the Villa Vallee.

As springtime approached and the weather got warm, business fell off mainly because the club was not air-conditioned. There were precious few "five-dollar covers" to be had even under my ruinous contract and I found myself working for practically the same union "minimum" that the boys in the band were receiving. I asked Bellak for a four-weeks vacation during the summer and he agreed. Business was so bad I could have just as well gotten six or seven weeks! It later developed that we were signed for a movie in California and it would require five weeks. Bellak, realizing he had me over a barrel, demanded a payment of five thousand dollars for the extra week—this, even though I was receiving less than two hundred at the club! I had no choice. I paid him.

In April, 1929, we had the privilege of playing the hallowed Palace Theater. Even though it is just another large theater, through the years it has acquired a glamour for the vaudevillian. To have "played the Palace" is to have achieved nirvana in show business. Those entertainers who fail to appear there die of a broken heart. It's that important!

We opened at a Sunday matinee, the day when all the performers not working always dropped in to catch the acts. In catering to this crowd the management scheduled lower prices. It was about as tough an audience of "pros" as you could find under one roof.

Two famous orchestra leaders caught one of our shows and the possibly apocryphal story got around as follows: they sat in silence while we went through a series of numbers. One turned to the other and remarked with a smirk, "This guy stinks—doesn't he?" We were then playing our eighth number to end the set and were killing the audience. "I dunno," answered the other. "He's been stinking up there for a long time!"

It was during our Palace date (I don't remember anybody exactly tearing up the seats with joy, but we were held over for three weeks) that a violinist, Phil Danenberg, suggested I listen to a small band then playing a tearoom in the city. I was looking for a replacement for our "relief band" which performed at the Villa Vallee during the hours we were in the theaters. The band sounded quite good. That is how I came to engage Will Osborne and how I wound up in another bizarre chapter of my career. It was so full of sound and fury and, of course, signified the usual zero.

It was a fine break for Osborne because he would have the club and the "radio wire" all to himself while the Connecticut Yankees were in Hollywood making the picture. I made his group over into reasonably accurate facsimiles of our group—they wore the same shawl-collared Russian blouses we had carried over as Heigh-Ho Club trademarks; they learned my finger signals for music cues, and they committed to memory all of our arrangements. When I engaged him he was merely a drummer—how could I know he had aspirations to become a singer? I even did what I could to get him the job on the Herbert Jewelry Hour while I was away.

Well, it seemed he learned a little too well. He happened to have a voice of a similar quality to mine and he rode it for all he was worth. When I returned from the coast the tempest was about to break, although I must say it had only teapot dimensions.

I can only assume that Will had a brilliant press agent. This genius conceived the idea of having Osborne accuse me of imitating him. He then garnered a tremendous amount of newspaper space by getting his client to challenge me to a ten-round boxing match! I believe there was some ill-contrived litigation such as a half-million-dollar libel suit and a request for an injunction against me, my publishers, and the *New York Sun* to restrain further publication of my book, *Vagabond Dreams Come True*.

To top it all Will always featured a heart-warming little ditty entitled "I'd Like to Break the Neck of the Man Who Wrote the Stein Song" just to keep the caldron bubbling. We both got a mountain of publicity out of this fracas but I believe it helped Will more than it did me. What annoyed me most of all was his claim that he was the first "crooner"— that I had stolen my style and technique from *him*!

The *New York Daily Mirror* had this wry comment on the battle of the century:

> ...How this radio feud is going to end nobody can guess.
> Maybe the boys will hurl plums at forty paces and handfuls
> of confetti at a city block. Anyhow the sugary-tenor feud is on
> and it's pistols and chocolate sundae for one...

Sic transit gloria mundi or, in other words, how the hell do I get into these things!

Osborne hassle or no, we continued to fulfill our Keith Circuit commitments. It was a devastating chore, with two shows a day plus the Villa Vallee stint including the three broadcasts—not to mention various rehearsals, Victor recording dates, and the Lombardy Hotel tea dances. It was a time of nightmared cat naps whenever a moment could be seized; it was a time when you would get frightened over the fact that you might do the wrong thing at the right time or vice versa; it was when you first experienced the horror of horrors—laryngitis. I found that the strain of constant singing began to take its toll—when I would steal a thirty- or forty-minute nap, I would awaken with a sorely constricted throat. Therefore, I had to stay awake and this too began to tell. To fill large theaters (there were still no public-address-speaker systems) with my simple, untrained voice became an ordeal, particularly after a night of forty or fifty "megaphone" choruses at the Villa.

The Keith engagements were without much event, though there were, of course, the usual weird, simple, wonderful happenings inevitable in that strange world called show business. We played Flushing for Keith and, on our opening day as I approached the stage door, the doorman, obviously taking me for a musician, asked, "When will Mr. Vallee be here?"

This encapsulated, is the story of my life! Look, I'm used to it. I would have to be a moron not to get used to it after all these years. But nobody will ever believe that "this-is-Rudy-Vallee" when they first meet me. I guess I've never had the good fortune to look impressive or command-ing. But I have compensated! In some sort of reverse reasoning I have accomplished a feeling of satisfaction—to have become a popular figure when my physical appearance, to many people at least, in no way indi-cated that I might be the personality that had won their approbation through a microphone.

Another amusing memory from Keith: the venerable Keith-Albee in Brooklyn. Without exception, in the rest of this theater chain we were, in a word, smashes. But there—well, they received us courteously but their fervor was judiciously restrained. There are few out-and-out smashes in that borough. Brooklyn (and I say this with great affection) is a coun-try unto itself!

We thought we were on a stern regimen before but then, in May, we were booked at the Paramount Theater, the so-called crossroads of the entertainment world. Ten weeks! Ten weeks of five and six shows a day— eleven in the morning to eleven in the evening—then to the Villa until four A.M. plus the usual broadcasts, recording dates, etc. We weren't getting rich but we were young and eager and somehow we managed to stay alive, indeed to thrive. After six weeks they shifted us (no re-criminations) to the Brooklyn(!) Paramount and, remembering the Keith-Albee hauteur, I was a little worried. It turned out to be a blessing in disguise, a chance for me to learn the fine art of really running the show. I was to emcee the whole program, which ran approximately an hour, and direct the augmented orchestra of twenty pieces.

Although I had directed the eighty-piece Yale Band, its repertoire consisted of nothing but marches and other relatively simple composi-tions. I had led dance bands too, but this function was primarily concerned with plain dance tempos. Fortunately, the theater had a real "pro" conductor on hand to coach me for a few days. He conducted the complicated routines of the various acts (adagio teams where two or three men toss a woman in the air and catch her—to music, tap dancers, singers, whatever the booker's net would bring him in) and I watched him, assiduously following the movements of his stick. It was a kind of finishing school for technical showmanship and I have found it the luckiest bit of training in my whole career. For two years I conducted for all the shows. Every week brought a new challenge at the Friday rehearsal— I never knew what sort of a line-up of acts I would have to introduce or what manner of pacing and cueing they would need.

But a good "finishing" school has to come to an end. Came our last night before departing for Hollywood, the land of starlets and citrus, and I got a call from, of all people, Don Dickerman, for whom I had worked and damned near killed myself at the now defunct Heigh-Ho Club.

"Rudy, I've got to talk to you," he said and his voice sounded strange, as if he were worrying about someone overhearing him, as if he had his hand cupped between his mouth and the phone. "In private."

"Well, sure, Don," I said. "Why don't you come over to the theater and pick me up after the last show. Around eleven. All right?"

It was a phone call out of the blue. Even though I am inclined to hold a grudge a bit longer than the average, I hadn't done much thinking about Dickerman. I must admit when he did cross my mind it rankled like hell as I remembered his parting words: "George, see that they don't take anything!"

Still, something in the tone of his voice told me he was in trouble and I was naive enough to want to do him a good turn to show that I had been and still was loyal.

As we left the theater and walked toward a cab there was a great mob of well-wishers packing the street outside. They knew we were headed for Hollywood and had come by to say their good-byes and good-lucks. Confronted by this scene, Dickerman must have realized we couldn't have been too damned bad when we worked for him.

The taxi pulled away en route to the Villa Vallee. Dickerman finally got to the point. "You see, I'm in a kind of spot. You know the Heigh-Ho folded, of course. I've got a great idea for another club though. But I need some money."

"Oh?" I muttered, not terribly enthusiastic.

"Now I've got these murals from the old club—you know those beautiful underwater paintings. Would you like to buy them?"

While the murals were unquestionably desirable, I had no place to use them. "What kind of club do you have in mind?" I asked.

"A nice small place in Greenwich Village. You know, warm, intimate. Want to call it the Daffydill Club. I've got a nice group of musicians

I can use. The California Collegians. Very talented. Can't you use the murals?"

"I've got no room for them. They're lovely but I can't use them. However," I added, "how much cash do you need?"

His face brightened. "About fifteen thousand."

"You've got it," I said. I hoped he would now understand me and the way I really am a little better. I felt that this act of investment would discharge the great obligation I still felt was due him—after all, he was the one who decided to let me do the singing at the Heigh-Ho which in turn led to our broadcasts and our big chance.

Well, just as he said, the Daffydill became a nice, warm, beautiful club. Of course, it wound up costing forty thousand before "we" opened it and who do you think we hired as the *maitre d'*? Yes, the same scoundrel who sent him the phony cables in Cuba about me.

When we had returned from Hollywood I tried to bolster the business at the Daffydill. We didn't work Sunday evenings at the Villa so I would bring some of the acts with whom we were appearing at the Brooklyn Paramount over to the dear old Daffydill and put on a show gratis. It wasn't enough.

In the spring of 1930 I happened to be in this club with one of my attorneys. Hal Kemp's band was appearing there at the time. It was a fine band but too large for the club and much too expensive for our budget. NBC agreed to broadcast Kemp's music from the club. I introduced Hal on the first program, and I really thought we were on our way. "You better start planning to close this place," said the lawyer quite calmly, the way lawyers always say things.

"What the hell do you mean!" I exclaimed. It was almost as if he had cast aspersions on one of my immediate family. This Daffydill was my baby!

"Look, Rudy. Face it—it's losing money. You keep it open and it'll cost you a fortune."

"So what. So we've lost forty, fifty thousand. Maybe we'll get it back if we keep plugging away."

"I looked at the books today. Took a good, hard look. If you close tonight, even take bankruptcy, it looks to cost you around ninety-eight thousand!"

And so it went, right down the drain in a time when taxes were very low and there was no chance to charge off the loss. I had paid my debt to Dickerman but it was a hell of a lot more expensive than any thrifty Maine Yankee could have imagined.

Hollywood has become famous or infamous for its smog problem. Many authorities and weather pundits attribute this to certain complex atmospheric conditions but only I know the real cause. It is not smog at all. It is what I choose to call the miasma of The Vagabond Lover! As the Connecticut Yankees and I made the picture for RKO in the summer of 1929 we were "acting" for all we were worth, but (and this is not false modesty) I apparently was very bad.

At the outset it looked as if the fee for the picture would be sumptuous. The representative from the NBC Artists Bureau came to me all aglow. "Rudy," he said, "I've got you a helluva deal! We're getting you and the band eleven thousand a week for five weeks. How about it?"

How about it! I never dreamed I could gross that amount. Looking back I see that I was hideously had. Monday morning quarterbacking tells me that we, as one of the hottest attractions of the day, should have received at least two hundred thousand plus transportation—and RKO should have given Bellak his five-thousand-dollar pound of flesh. Moreover, we should have had a percentage of the net profits of the picture. If this sounds vainglorious, consider the case of Jimmy Stewart in his portrayal of the band leader in *The Glenn Miller Story*—he made over one million dollars for it! Even though our picture was artistically a dud it made quite a bit of money due to our enormous radio following.

Well, no matter—it's all past now. What the hell!! It was kicks. To put it in modern parlance, we had a swinging ball making the picture. So that they might share in the fun, I took along my mother and father.

Our trip to the coast was a triumph. At whistle stops across the country we would make appearances on the back platform just like a presidential candidate. When we arrived in the old Union Station in downtown Los Angeles, we were met by the Mayor and a bevy of luscious chorines who were working in the RKO picture, *Rio Rita*. We disembarked and boarded a huge, white Rolls Royce as big as a hearse and, preceded by eight motorcycle patrolmen, wound through the streets to the Roosevelt Hotel. There we were serenaded by a popular dance band of the day, Aaronsen's Commanders, who played "I'm Just A Vagabond Lover." Touching?

I spent some time picking the songs and we embarked on the "epic" called *The Vagabond Lover*. The weeks went on, the cameras rolled, and somehow we got it done with the aid of a talented cast which included Sally Blane, Marie Dressler, and Eddie Nugent.

While making the picture I renewed my acquaintance with Mary Brian, a reigning Paramount star. I had met her at a dance at Yale when I was a Senior and was most happy to meet her again on more equal footing since I was now "in pictures" also. We had a number of dates and, of course, the columnists practically had us married. This was most flattering to a country boy but I suspect a studio press agent was behind it all. While dancing with Mary Brian one evening at the Roosevelt I noticed "across a crowded room" a beautiful, dark face, the very personification of the *College Humor* cover girl I had been smitten with years before. I kept staring at this seductive, oriental-featured girl until Mary noticed it.

"Like her?" she said.

"I can't take my eyes off her."

"Her name is Fay Webb."

"She has the strangest effect on me. I have a feeling I shouldn't meet her and know her. And yet—I know I must somehow." I was already completely infatuated.

Two weeks before the picture was finished Marie Dressler, who attained her stardom in our modest picture, introduced me to Miss Webb— but that is another harrowing story unto itself.

And so our great contribution to Western culture, *The Vagabond Lover*, was somehow completed, We headed back East routed, for some crazy reason, via Frisco and Salt Lake City secure in the belief that we had a great picture "in the can."

Every day the incredibly volatile stock market hit new highs and everybody was getting rich, "on paper." Everybody, that is, but me. I gave it little heed since I have never been interested in any kind of gambling or investment in securities. I have always been a conservative individual in such matters.

The character assigned to handle me for the National Broadcasting Company's Artist Service Bureau had previously worked for a Wall Street brokerage firm and still had the fever in his blood.

"Rudy, will you listen to me!" he would say. "All the smart people today invest in stocks and bonds. They're making a mint. You can do the same!"

"I'm not interested."

"Not interested! You've got over seventy thousand dollars in the bank downstairs. Just *sitting* there doing nothing. It could be earning a fortune for you if you'd just let it."

"I have no desire whatever to see it increased. I just want to know that it will always be there when I need it." I had heard from others that he regarded me as a temperamental artist and nothing more.

"Will you take my advice on this matter, Rudy?" His tone was condescending, as if he were speaking to a child. "For crissakes, if the stuff *we* buy goes bad, then the country will have gone to the dogs!"

My reply to him sounded naive at the time but it turned out to be pregnant with terrible truth: "And what is to prevent the country from going to the dogs?"

I suppose this man thought he was doing me a favor. I trusted him in business matters and somewhere along the line in the mounds of contracts, endorsements, releases, and what have you that I signed were intermixed investments and stock purchases.

One brisk October morning I took the hotel elevator to the lobby. Over a gentleman's shoulder I noted the headlines reporting the collapse of the big Bull Market of '29.

"Thank God I stayed out," I thought to myself.

Then I found out that I *had* been an unwitting investor! I was forced to cancel a trust fund I had started for my father and when I tried to pick up the pieces I found that a little over one hundred and fifty thousand dollars had gone down the drain—money I had earned by the sweat of my brow doing four and five shows a day. It hurt but, being young and healthy, I immersed myself in my work and refused to brood about it. The trusting soul, the wide-eyed country boy from Maine had been taken to the cleaners again!

The phone rang early one morning. "Mr. Vallee—there may be bad news," the voice said. I was wide awake now. "There's been a fire in the film labs. We don't know for sure yet but your film may have been destroyed."

It was a crushing blow! All that work for nothing! It seemed to me that it would be impossible for me to perform those epic scenes again with such mastery.

If only that fire *had* consumed our film it would have been the greatest blessing that could have befallen me. But unfortunately as fate would have it, our turkey was spared.

If I live to be a hundred I can never erase the première of *The Vagabond Lover* at the Globe Theater in New York. The place was naturally packed with friends, well-wishers and curiosity seekers who had heard us on radio. I made a short speech on stage before it began and then stood in the wings to watch the opus unfold.

About halfway through I became conscious of much movement among the audience and I discovered to my dismay that the theater was half-empty! I had been a party to a resounding flop.

Oh, it made a lot of money throughout the country because all our radio fans turned out to see what this guy with the adenoidal intonation was really like. Of course, since my contract did not provide for participation in the profits, I didn't get one cent over the salary.

The movie had a lot against it. It was static and unimaginative to a degree. The sound was bad. The performances of the band and myself were amateurish. I was almost laughable with the dead-pan sincerity that I thought was acting. Outside of these minor reservations it was a real gem!

The true, dyed-in-the-wool Vallee fans liked it; but even by the standards of that day it was the prize turkey of the year and it damn' near ruined us with the public. Fortunately, before the picture was shown, my band and I were given a new lease on life through a network show that was to endure for ten years.

My first cinematographic effort is now shown only in penitentiaries and comfort stations and they're still fumigating the theaters where it was exhibited.

CHAPTER VIII

The Fleischmann Hour Is Born

"Cheerful Little Earful"

IN OCTOBER 1929, AFTER A SERIES OF strokes the stock market finally collapsed of a cerebral hemorrhage—I say *cerebral* because the market, that is, the people had overtaxed the brain with the obsession of getting-rich-quick. "Coolidge prosperity" had foundered with a resounding crash, Hoover at the helm. Through my blind trust and, I suppose, stupidity I had lost a fortune in this monumental Wall Street bloodletting.

It was a year when Richard E. Byrd discovered the South Pole by the expedient of flying over it, the year Lindbergh married Anne Morrow, and the calendar of events also noted the sorry spectacle of the Chicago O'Bannion mob being gunned down in a rather pagan celebration of St. Valentine's Day.

The book business was very good. People had money to spend on them before the market disintegrated, and they had a fine selection from which to choose. *All Quiet on the Western Front, Look Homeward, Angel, A Farewell to Arms, Magnificent Obsession,* and *The Sound and the Fury* were notable.

Along Broadway the stand-out attractions were *Street Scene, Journey's End, Berkeley Square,* and *Strictly Dishonorable* in the realm of plays. The collection of musical comedies was rather weak although they included some imperishable songs: "Ain't Misbehavin' " from *Hot Chocolates,* "You Do Something to Me" from *Fifty Million Frenchmen,* "I'll See You Again" from *Bitter Sweet,* and "Can't We Be Friends" from *The Little Show.*

The movies were not only talking by now—they were singing! The nation saw the first wave of the big-big-big filmusicals and they supplied as many song hits as the Broadway boards. Remember "The Broadway Melody" from the like-named film, "If I Had a Talking Picture of You" and the title song from *Sunny Side Up,* "Tiptoe Through the Tulips with Me" from *Gold Diggers of Broadway,* and Chevalier's trade-mark "Louise" from *Innocents of Paris.* From the movie *Chasing Rainbows* the

85

nation garnered a pep song it was to whistle through the graveyard of the dark Depression years to come: "Happy Days Are Here Again."

Happy days were here again for me and the Connecticut Yankees and they came with blessed rapidity. At the very time investors were bailing out of office windows *sans* parachute, we were signed for a network show that was to run for ten years. Our first broadcast was on October 29, only two days after "Black Tuesday" when the panic selling on the New York Stock Exchange had amounted to more than sixteen million shares. The Thursday of our broadcast found the market so demoralized that the exchange did not open until noon and was not to engage in transactions again until the following Monday.

The show was for a product of Standard Brands—Fleischmann's Yeast —and it was to be presented on NBC, a part of the Radio Corporation of America whose stock was to drop that year from 101 to 28! I hasten to add that we had nothing to do with the depreciation—the Fleischmann Hour was a success.

Nowadays a person says "a job's a job—what the hell, it's a living." In those parlous times a job was a veritable precious jewel and every bit as scarce. We were tickled to get a network shot sponsored by *any*body! But to get a real dream of a client such as Standard Brands was certainly more luck than we truly deserved.

They were magnanimous and understanding beyond belief. I mean there were no sponsors' wives with helpful little suggestions on just how the show should be run. There were no creep executives who demanded that we program their favorite tunes. No member of the firm ever chose to dictate that we were to play all songs at the same tempo "so the family could roll back the rug and dance." They were as unhuckster as you might desire and I often wonder if they still make sponsors like that any more.

Thursday evening at that time was considered a dull night as far as radio audience was concerned. Our time slot was eight to nine Eastern Standard Time. When we began the show there were no ulcer-breeding rating systems such as Hooper, Nielsen, Arbitron, Trendex, etc. to mean life or death to a production—happily the only criterion we used was our own feeling. It was simple and I am sure completely unscientific but we judged the show on our own impressions of whether or not we were doing a good job, combined with the reactions of the sponsor and his advertising agency. We flew the Fleischmann Hour by the seat of our pants.

Our first show was broadcast from the organ loft of the Paramount Theater between our third and fourth stage appearances. Since we had made our radio reputation in programs from night clubs, we recreated this aspect by sound effects of glassware clinking, dishes rattling, and other such din. The magnetic, distinctive voice of Graham McNamee was chosen for the commercials and he was perfect. We had the good fortune to stay on the air in summer, winter, spring, and fall for some five hundred and twenty consecutive weeks. Must be some sort of a record.

For the first four years I received $2500 a program—after commissions, about $1200 to me. Compared to today's TV salaries I was getting peanuts.

For the first two years the hour was made up of long stretches of Connecticut Yankee music and my vocals, with one or two guest artists to do three or four spots per show. Then, in 1932, the sponsor and agency took a hard, objective look and decided on a new and radical format.

We became, in effect, the "Palace Theater of the Air." It was a program that was to discover and develop more personalities and stars than any radio show before or since. It couldn't miss! Remember, at that time NBC was the only coast-to-coast network in existence and at our beck and call was a gold mine of talent just waiting for the opportunity we could give them.

The pattern ran something like this: first an opening band number, then a comedian; a novelty spot—usually some newly arrived musical personality or possibly a theatrical or scientific figure; a dramatic spot either light or serious, with anywhere from two to ten actors; another novelty spot such as Fred and Adele Astaire tap-dancing over the air; finally came another comedy spot, to "leave 'em laughing." Of course, in between all these bits were band numbers and medleys by the boys and me, now augmented to thirteen pieces, mind you.

As we gained stature the show became important to all performers. For example, we were able to get the illustrious actor, Claude Rains, for about one-tenth what he could command in radio or TV today. It was possible to keep a talent like Fanny Brice as "Baby Snooks" for weeks as well as top comedians such as Howard and Shelton and Lou Holtz—or Lou Holtz and Carmen Miranda as a duo. We had Bob Hope, Red Skelton, and Milton Berle on the show. Strangely enough they never reached any great importance in these radio appearances. They seemed to need a show of their own to make it and, in the case of Hope and Skelton, they had to have motion picture appearances *first* to establish their physiognomies and "mugging" in the minds of the listeners.

Thanks to the progressive agency for Standard Brands, J. Walter Thompson, a wealth of talent was mined in their Monday and Tuesday auditions. Agents were scurrying everywhere beating the bushes to flush out possible performers. They brought in Bob Burns (the bazooka-playing comic) from the Coast and he was so successful that he landed his own show. There was the hysterically funny Joe Penner ("Do you wanna buy a duck?") who also got his own network series after only a few appearances. Ezra Stone as the "Aldrich Boy" ("Coming, Mother!") developed on the Fleischmann Hour and typically became the headliner later on as Henry in "The Aldrich Family."

Fading personalities of the legitimate stage got a new lease on life and newcomers such as the Mills Brothers, Alice Faye, Frances Langford, Dorothy Lamour (already gaining a foothold in pictures), and a host of others found their first foothold in radio on our broadcasts.

We presented key scenes from the latest Broadway hit featuring the original cast. Our dramatic spots were the work of a young genius named George Faulkner who dug up or created masterly sketches and monologues to fit the personalities. We had the first "we-the-people" series wherein we might let Frank Case of the Algonquin tell us his experiences as an innkeeper; Sherman Billingsley would recount the way he operated the Stork Club; a sandhog, in his working overalls and helmet, informed the audience of his faith in God which gave him the courage to work below ground and river in building the Holland Tunnel.

It was a dream assignment, one that so rarely happens to a performer. No discords, no wranglings, no conflicts. I was given every opportunity to present my own list of personalities—the aforementioned Faye, Langford, and Lamour as well as Al Bernie, Larry Adler, Benny Krueger, the beloved Rudy Wiedoeft, and many others whom I dug up or came across in my travels.

There was that rare delight in show business—complete freedom. We could try anything. As a vogue would change, we were permitted to plan a new attack. No personality was too unique or bizarre but that we dared program him. Orson Welles as an example, long before he achieved the heights, made his debut on our broadcast. Eddie Cantor, in one of our Florida broadcasts, first knew the taste of a coast-to-coast hookup. About the only star we somehow missed was Jack Benny. However, since he is only thirty-nine years old today, you must realize that he was much too young and immature to appear before our microphones.

When the program began we of course had to have a "signature" or theme song with which we would be identified. Someone wrote a very bad song about "Sunshine Vitamin Yeast" which we planned to discard as soon as I could find a substitute. I had plenty of help in the selection.

"Rudy, that 'Deep Night' is right for it," the agency said. "You've been doing it successfully for a long time now. It's *your* tune."

"I just don't see it," I said. "Not for a signature. Too slow—they'll fall asleep halfway through the first chorus!"

"What about 'Vagabond Lover'?" the client executive suggested. "You're really identified with that one."

"Neither is exactly right for this. 'Vagabond Lover' is too egotistical," I said. "I don't know—they're either too personal or too saccharine. I don't think they're *enduring* enough for a program every week."

Then a song occurred to me, a song I had brought back from London and had been successful with in the Yale Dining Hall. In essence, the song said: "We are here to entertain you for the course of an hour—" It was a song that had movement, being composed mostly of whole and half-notes—it was a song the public had come to associate not only with the Fleischmann Hour but with me: "My Time is Your Time." If there seems any excessive humility implicit in the title, make the most of it. I have always regarded myself simply as an entertainer. An entertainer should entertain. In "addressing" an audience I never wish to be obsequious nor do I wish to be patronizing. "My Time is Your Time" seemed to state my case, so to speak, and it still does.

In the summer of 1930 I decided to take a leave from the Villa Vallee and the Paramount Theaters. The wanderlust hit me I guess and I wanted a change. The tour of "one-nighters" in the East and Middle West, playing armories, auditoriums, and beach resorts, looked good to me even though this sort of trip often makes you feel it is an audition for a nervous breakdown. I suppose I took it to get away from the debilitating sameness of the nights in the smoke-filled night club which bore my name.

Just before I left, Paul Whiteman dropped by the Villa and I told him about the trip. He seemed dubious.

"Rudy, you're getting across fine here in the club," he said. "When you need to, you pick up a megaphone and everyone hears you. But what in hell are you going to do when you face three and four thousand people at once in a big place with lousy acoustics?"

"Paul, I've got the answer."

"If you've got it, let me in on it."

"It sounds like a real Goldberg contraption but it works. I borrowed an old carbon mike from NBC, hooked up a homemade amplifier with some radios, and I've got a sort of electronic megaphone. I had the legs sawed off the radios so they don't look so strange."

As crude as it was, it gave the voice some amplification. The crowds that heard us didn't know it but they were listening to the first public-address system ever used by a popular dance band on tour. It was a hot summer but we consistently broke existing records for box-office receipts and attendance.

It wasn't all gravy by any means. I had to furnish a relief band for the Villa at my expense and when Thursday rolled around I had to cough up the money for broadcast wire charges from wherever we did our show.

There were plenty headaches. We never missed any dates but sometimes we performed in a miserable condition with fever and sunburned skins from too much time at the beaches. Once, at Hampton Beach, New Hampshire, the weight of our two pianos almost caused the floor of the old hotel to collapse—right in the middle of a coast-to-coast broadcast!

I have a horrible memory of a date in Port Dover, Ontario—everything happened! First of all, to make the engagement on schedule, I had to engage a special train at a cost of five hundred dollars to get our group from Cleveland to Erie, Pennsylvania—then boat fares from Erie to Port

Dover and back. While in Canada a pair of tipsy reporters from the *Toronto Daily Star* interviewed me.

"Well, Rudy, whaddya think of Canadian women?" one of them asked.

"To tell you the truth," I said in complete honesty, "I've been so busy just *getting* here I haven't had time to really look. I haven't seen anything so far this evening in the audience to get excited about. But— the evening is young."

The next day the story appeared with a headline something like: CANADIAN WOMEN NOT SO HOT SAYS RUDY! All Canadian hell, quite naturally, broke loose. I mean, you can't go about sullying the fair name of Canadian womanhood, can you?

There was still another turn of the screw—the Port Dover promoter who had booked us into this disaster ran off with the gate receipts and we collected nothing! And we burned out our amplifying system on Canadian current!

But there were happy, thrilling evenings as well. We played Asbury Park and Atlantic City to crowds of five and nine thousand people respectively. It was in Asbury Park that I had the first opportunity to see Bennie Krueger since he had "chased me down the stairs" with his snarl at the Yale Prom when I asked to try his saxophone.

After our show at the auditorium I learned Bennie was playing a country club nearby. He was still one of my idols so I devised a plan which was partly a desire to pay homage to his greatness and partly, now that I think of it, to make him sit up and take notice of what that callow Yale undergrad had become.

Along with my pianist I dashed out to the club and asked the gentleman in charge of the dance if I might perform gratis. I was big "box office" at the time—it was a little like Harry Belafonte asking the local P.T.A. if he might be allowed to drop in for a few numbers at one of their fund-raising affairs. The entrepreneur was delighted and he asked Krueger and his band to stop playing while he introduced me.

I did six or seven songs and then addressed the crowd. I told them I had just dropped by to pay tribute to Bennie, one of the great artists of the day. To say that Krueger was nonplussed would be rash understatement. You could have knocked him over with a damp saxophone reed. He was enormously pleased and we became very close friends from that day onward.

When the tour wound up in the fall we found to our chagrin that several of our promoters had either defaulted on guarantees or disappeared with the gate receipts for the evening. But, all in all, it was a successful tour full of a great deal of romance, adventure, and excitement for the boys and me.

But it was the theatrical tour of '31 that was to prove one of the most exciting and *fruit*ful of all. It was to take us from Boston to Florida, New Orleans, Chicago, Detroit, Rochester, and points in between.

On opening day in Boston at the Metropolitan Theater one of the god*dam*dest things happened to me! The son of my good friend at Yale, Dean Roswell P. Angier, was in the audience. I was playing saxophone and we were doing a chorus of the tune "Oh, Give Me Something to Remember You By." Perhaps the title of the song triggered him or perhaps he was imbued with a courage born of alcoholic stimulus. No matter. All of a sudden a large, yellow grapefruit came hurtling from the balcony. With a tremendous crash it struck the drummer's cymbal and was cut practically in half. Young Angier had become a critic. He either found my rendition unsatisfying or he was repaying me for my rudeness to his father at the Yale party years ago.

Now a grapefruit may not sound like a particularly lethal weapon but if it had struck the gooseneck of my sax squarely where it curves into the mouth, it might have driven it back through the vertebrae in the back of my neck. A glancing blow might have broken every tooth in my head as well as my jaw.

I was pretty damn shaken I can tell you. As the incident occurred just as we were finishing the show, two stagehands pulled the massive curtains together and stood looking at me while my drummer quizzically eyed the grapefruit in his hand.

"Open the curtain," I said. The theater was in an uproar as the audience wondered just what in the hell was taking place.

"Ladies and gentlemen," I said as calmly as I could, "this is our fifth show today. We have been rehearsing since early this morning after a train ride from New York." The audience began to quiet down a trifle. "Our efforts here today whether successful or otherwise are honest and from our hearts. All we ask is the courtesy of your applause if you enjoy the things we do. We also ask the courtesy of your silence if you are displeased."

My words were greeted by a roar of approval and I launched into an all-out impression of Al Jolson, theorizing that my previous vocalizing perhaps had been lacking in virility and masculinity. More important, in the Jolson impersonation I naturally moved rapidly about the stage. I believe it was W. C. Fields who used to say out of the corner of his mouth, "You can't hit a moving target." I was no fool!

Some newspaper writer summed up the whole preposterous incident with:

> ... we have just found out why that Rudy Vallee was grape-
> fruited that night in Boston. One of the English teachers suggests
> that a Harvard professor didn't like that sentence of the song
> Rudy was singing, ending in a preposition ...

The ridiculous story was front-paged everywhere but I got the last laughs as it were. For weeks afterward I never failed to fracture the audience as I did the "Oh, Give Me Something to Remember You By"— with a wastebasket over my head!

The rest of the tour was much more pleasant and free of combat. From Boston we jumped to Miami where Eddie Cantor graced our Fleischmann Hour in his first coast-to-coast broadcast. A Florida tobacco tycoon brought me a young lady to audition from Tampa. I would have had to be stone-tone-deaf not to realize her great singing potentialities. Even though we had already selected a New Orleans girl for the broadcast from that city, we took this new find along also—and Frances Langford began her career. It has always been sheer delight to me to recall the chic, smartly coiffured interpreter of songs that later emerged from what she appeared to be when I first saw her—a rather plain girl in flat heels, a beret atop the hair with a bun in back, ill-fitting clothes—a latter-day Cinderella.

We hit New Orleans and descended into the maelstrom called Mardi Gras. The grind was beginning to tell on me and old Laryngitis began to rear its ugly head. With each performance at the Saenger Theater it grew worse.

Word must have gotten around about my condition because one morning, while I was shaving and dressing in my room at the Roosevelt Hotel, the doorbell rang and I was greeted by a State Trooper.

"The Governor wants to see you right away," he said.

"What's it all about?" I asked, wondering what on earth I had done wrong.

"He just said for me to come get you. I'm not in the habit of asking the Governor *why* he tells me to do something."

We made our way to the Governor's suite at the Roosevelt and there was Huey Long, sitting up in bed to receive me in a gaudy silk dressing gown.

"Hear you been having a little throat trouble, my boy," he said in what might be described as a soft bellow. A smile broke over his pudgy face with its turned-up nose. "Got just the thing for you. You know we want to be real hospitable to out-of-state visitors even though they *are* Yankees." He started to chuckle. "Now you just set down over there. The ol' Kingfish's remedy is on its way up here from the drugstore right now."

Since it was on more or less regal command, I took the medicine. Governor Long neglected to tell me that the chief ingredient was Epsom salts. My condition only grew worse. The laryngitis *did* help my impression of Maurice Chevalier—the more my voice cracked, the more lifelike the bit.

At the Saenger I ran into a minor bit of history in the making. After each show a young collegian would come backstage and inform me of reactions and comments he had been jotting down as he elicited them from members of the audience. He had been hired by our sponsor to ascertain what the public actually thought about a radio personality. It was the beginning of the "rating" system!

In Chicago the throat was so debilitated we had to get hold of the specialist that used to treat John McCormack. He sprayed a concoction called Aero Oil directly on the vocal chords and I was able somehow to get by.

The tour progressed then via Detroit to Rochester where just about everything is named "Eastman" something or other and it was the name of the theater where we played. The Victor Company placed a phonograph and a stack of records in my dressing room. One of the disks was by Gus Arnheim and his orchestra and at the bottom of the record label was the name of the vocalist in exceedingly small type—Bing Crosby. The performance was fabulous and I called in the members of my band to hear it. The "Yes" boys promptly denounced the singing as "lousy." However, I didn't need the comments of the men who were always honest with me to realize that this young man was going to push Pappy Vallee right off his throne.

On our next Thursday broadcast I did the same song Bing had done on the record and congratulated Gus Arnheim over the air waves on his new "find." Crosby had come a long way since I had been so impressed with him at the Baltimore debutante party four years before.

Back to dear old New York and the stern regimen of the Villa Vallee, the Brooklyn Paramount and the broadcasts—back to five and six hours sleep a day (counting cat naps) and three and four benefits on Sunday. I averaged at least one hundred and twenty-five benefits a year in those days!

I had hardly settled down in Gotham before I was slapped with a hundred-thousand-dollar lawsuit by a Ziegfeld chorus girl who claimed I had jilted her. Way back when I was still at the Heigh-Ho I had observed this attractive young thing and been a trifle smitten. She too was quite aware I was ogling her rather hungrily. Nothing happened then and I put her out of my mind. Later on she appeared at the Villa accompanied by Larry Fay, a notorious gangster who traveled about in a bullet-proof automobile. I was still casting admiring glances at her but I was more circumspect about it since Fay could have had my head blasted off with no trouble at all. I wasn't nearly careful enough and Fay caught on. Fortunately he was amused and invited me over to his table where he made it clear I was free to see the young damsel again as far as he was concerned.

This I did on a number of occasions and we became very good friends to put it mildly. I don't know—I may even have ventured a few serious remarks about our future. However, after I had met Fay Webb on the

Coast, I thought I had made it clear that our romance was a fading ember. The action never reached court. We were able to get sufficient evidence to link her with Kiki Roberts, the gal friend of "Legs" Diamond, and the suit was dropped.

One thing resulted from this suit. I realized I could become a prey to any conniving woman whom I happened to go out with more or less steadily. I deduced that I should get married and settle down if I could find the right girl. I could quit the sex rat race and no longer be a target for any money-grubbing wench that happened along.

By this time the Villa Vallee was on shaky foundations, as Bellak (who more or less *owned* us) found himself at the point of losing the hotel at 14 East 60 in which the Villa was located, as well as his two other small hotels on the East Side.

Suddenly Bellak threw us out of the club! He added insult to infuriation by presenting me with a bill for the room I had lived in, the occasional food I had consumed, and the room my father and mother had occupied once in a while when they came down from Maine. What made it so maddening was the fact that Bellak had always made it clear that all this largess was completely gratis.

Our main concern was to prevent Bellak from selling us like chattel to some other location for a large fee, paying only union scale to the boys and peanuts to me and pocketing the difference. This could have meant a very pretty penny to slave-owner Bellak; I had turned down five thousand a week at the Roosevelt Grill two years before because I had signed for the Villa with the promise of "all those cover charges" that never seemed to materialize.

And so back to court. I wonder how many hours I have spent in litigation. I could have been *sleeping* all that time instead of listening to long-winded lawyers! At any rate old Bellak was defeated before the judge and we were free to make our own bookings. For the next two years the Pennsylvania Hotel became our stamping grounds, both on its delightful roof and down in its grill.

CHAPTER IX

Fay Webb and All That Jazz

"Say It Isn't So"

THEN ENSUED A VERY DISASTROUS PART
of my life. Even now, some twenty-five years later, it is not easy to write about it.

It all began in a way while I was still at Yale. A romantically inclined, soft-headed collegian, I fell in love with the drawing of a dark, sultry girl that graced the cover of a copy of *College Humor*. It took me years, painful, wrong-headed years, to get over this obsessive infatuation with a *type*.

Fay Webb epitomized this type to the *nth* degree. When I had first seen her that night in Hollywood two years before I had fallen quite as hard as any man has ever fallen. I was hooked completely. I was like a dope addict who had found a fix after waiting too long. Even if I had known the unspeakable anguish I was in for, I still believe I would have gone right after her.

She was an extraordinarily sexy-looking young woman with dark hair, dark, heavy-lashed eyes and luscious lips which could contrive one of the most enthralling come-hither smiles I had ever witnessed. Fay was under contract to MGM at the time. A number of publicity stills had been made of her in which her exquisite body was exploited but she had made no appearances on the screen. Her father was Chief of Police in Santa Monica and it was said that she had been signed by MGM as a form of baksheesh to the men in blue.

As I have said, I met her through Marie Dressler when I was in Hollywood, and we were off to the races. She had paid a few visits to New York when suddenly her father (she *said*) made the arbitrary decision that if I was to see her again marriage would be necessary.

I was not too dismayed at this stipulation. However, there was only one cause for reluctance. In a sense I was a romantic image to many of the fair sex who listened to our programs and marriage might affect the acceptance of the show. I felt I had a certain debt to my sponsor not to meddle with this status quo under which the contracts had been signed.

95

I decided on a secret marriage so I could have my cake and eat it too. One night in July, 1931, we made a midnight trip to a Justice of the Peace in a little New Jersey town and the deed was quietly done. I was so excited that I tipped the J. P. several hundred dollars, later to find that my NBC manager had done likewise. *Unknown to me, both the manager and Fay had informed the newspapers!* By the time we returned to New York I landed smack in the middle of a press conference and the world eagerly devoured the story in the morning papers. A nice wedding present! I think I was more annoyed about the double tipping than the publicity double-cross.

For a few short weeks we honeymooned at my New York apartment after several days in Atlantic City. We couldn't get away for any sort of real wedding trip because I was tied up with the Hotel Pennsylvania booking and the weekly radio show as well as rehearsals for *George White's Scandals*. I was very happy and I thought Fay was as well but, in retrospect, I believe she was happy for a different reason. Now that I consider it, I don't think she ever had any deep, loving feeling for me at all. She was instead pleased with her "catch"—a celebrity, a cynosure of American womanhood, a breadwinner who brought home the bacon every week.

Then, after what I felt was an unseemly short time after our marriage, my wife unaccountably decided to visit her family in California. I was a newly-wed—and alone.

If yours is a humdrum job at a small salary and you've envied a celebrity—don't! I've got news for you straight from the horse's mouth. I was supposed to be the toast of New York. I was appearing in a Broadway musical, leading one of the most popular dance bands in the country at the Pennsylvania Grill and one of the nation's top radio stars—yet I was the most lonesome, unhappy person in gay Manhattan.

In the *Scandals* there was bitter-sweet irony every time I sang the song "This is the Missus" because I was coming home every night to an empty apartment in which hung *her* clothes with the suggestion and aroma of everything that was the missus—but she wasn't there. At the Grill I was asked to visit the tables of attractive women who seemed to be utterly oblivious to the fact that I was married; they were only too eager to pinch-hit for the missing Mrs. Vallee. On the Thursday broadcasts I often had to deliver torch songs of the day which embodied wordage that was terribly apt and pertinent to my sorry situation. The popular tune of the day, "Stop the Moon, Stop the Train, My Gal's Gone," that I had to sing was autobiographical to say the least and another, "The Thrill is Gone," was dreadfully close to home.

No, don't ever blindly envy a celebrity until you know all the facts. Once when Fay was in town we invited a group of friends over for dinner. I was to appear later after the broadcast.

"Well, how do you think the show went tonight?" I asked when I arrived.

There was a very painful silence as the guests exchanged embarrassed glances. My own dear wife had turned off the radio almost before the program began!

I suppose I have only myself to blame. Perhaps I should have listened to the gossip and rumors that were rife about Fay in Hollywood. My well-meaning friends had implored me not to go through with the match but no—I was just too bloody bullheaded and, I might add, too bloody much in love. And so even after she left for California I went around laughing on the outside but bleeding on the inside!

Then came the coup de grâce. A charming columnist on one of the cheap, yellow New York tabloids (the late top Hollywood producer Jerry Wald) saw fit to bare the innermost secrets of our marital life in print to the drooling delight of the sensation-seeking morons who made up his readership. I later found out he had secured the low-down for the low blow from my own manager! My bruised and battered ego hit bottom.

It has always been my theory that when a woman loves a man, she will cheat, steal, kill, and scrub floors for him; and when my bride evidenced not the slightest interest in my work or anything that pertained to me I naturally found it a bit chilling. But I still would not admit defeat—I would invent a thousand excuses for her behavior because I was still a starry-eyed idealist in believing this marriage could be a success.

The whole affair was maddening. We were separated although we had had no argument or quarrel. Finally, by persuasion, gifts which were really bribes, and every other form of entreaty I could master, I coaxed her back to New York. I still hoped, in my stubbornness, to prove all the wiseacres and prophets wrong.

Someone finally suggested to me that there was only one way I would ever really know how she felt about me. He suggested tapping her telephone wire and recording the conversations. I was just about at the end of my tether and I *had* to know the truth.

On the night of one of the last "listening sessions" I returned from a dance date in Delaware, New Jersey. The location of the engagement was full of irony; it was the Black Cat Ballroom at the intersection of Routes 13 and 113 and the calendar said Friday the thirteenth of March! When I heard the shocking recordings *in her own sweet voice* as she talked to her boy friend and made snide remarks about me, I knew there was not the slightest hope in the world that I could make my dreams come true. I was ready to throw in the sponge.

As soon as I informed her that I knew everything she had said on the telephone for a period of many weeks, she was the picture of abject supplication. She cried, "Rip the phones out of the house!" As though that would do any good. I then called her father and told him to come and take his daughter home at my expense. Then Fay spoke to her mother. The first question her mother asked my wife as I listened to this conversation was "What have *you* done?"

When her father came to take her home she was more than content with the weekly settlement that our crazy laws demanded I should make upon her.

We had come to the parting of the ways once before and had agreed that she was to go to Reno for the usual termination of a marriage. A few days before her departure for Reno, Irving Berlin's manager had called me to ask me if I would listen to a song that Irving Berlin had written.

Berlin was in the doldrums of his song-writing career, and according to his manager Max Winslow, felt that he had "written himself out." Whether this was a subterfuge or whether Irving Berlin who, in my opinion, is a true genius (and I use that word very sparingly) in the art of fashioning melody and lyric, had actually come to the conclusion that his very great gift of creativity had indeed come to an end, I do not honestly know. But I did listen to Irving Berlin do the song for me, a number which I intuitively and instinctively knew was a truly inspired melody and lyric. I agreed to do it on my next Thursday broadcast.

On that Thursday as my wife, my lawyer, and her father sat in an office in the late evening, my attorney turned on his radio. The poignancy of Irving Berlin's lyric and melody of "Say It Isn't So" hit all three of them with the impact of an A-bomb!

My attorney had not engineered it so, but every word of this song hit home. Fay's eyes filled with tears as she listened and yet she signed the separation agreement. Still it was I who weakened, and begged her to return from Reno. She did, and we made another vain but inglorious attempt at a marriage that was doomed to failure. This time really finished it. Although I nearly weakened on several occasions when we met after her father arrived to take her home, she did indeed return to California and, except for the times that we faced each other in court, our pretense of marriage was at an end.

I think that Fay Webb would have gone on accepting the terms of our separation agreement until she found and married someone else. Nevertheless, an innocuous item in the great Winchell's column was to foretell a legal battle without a parallel in matrimonial and judicial history.

The Winchell item very simply said that "Fay Webb is hitting the nightspots with her lawyer." Frankly I thought nothing much of the item. Then I was suddenly served with papers in New York City—papers that claimed, in spite of the phone conversations I had heard and her willingness to accept the more-than-fair settlement we had made (which she had made in the presence of her father), that this settlement had been obtained under *duress and fraud!*

My New York attorney warned me that if I entered California I would be completely hamstrung by the jurisprudence of that state. I have become a confirmed Californian as I write this today, so I speak as a citizen. All the same it is true (and I think any fair-minded California judge or lawyer will admit it) that of all the states in the Union, California is the one that still lives most in the shadow of olden days and attitudes. In an old California gold-mining town a good woman was enshrined on high and any man who looked askance at or even dared accost the virtuous goddess was liable to be strung up without due process of law. This attitude still prevails!

I do not pretend to be an authority on marital law but I do know that many attorneys, among them Californians, have bitterly said that in marital problems in that state the man does not stand a chance. Therefore, when I contemplated going to the Coast to make a picture, I was warned that to go into that state was to deliver myself into the arms of my adversary. But I felt I had to wipe out the taste of the ill-fated *Vagabond Lover* and although the picture which George White had sold to Fox Studios offered me a very small recompense, I accepted the role and prepared for the worst.

They timed it beautifully. It was not until the last three days of the picture that I was served with sealed papers which threatened to destroy the career of Alice Faye (a career which bade fair to be great and promising in this, her first picture) if the contents were revealed.

Alice Faye and I both knew that we had nothing to hide, nothing of which to be ashamed. It was a credit to her honesty and courage when I asked her, "Should we authorize the newspapers to open these papers?" that she, without any hesitation said "Yes." The papers contained nothing of any consequence and, through the brilliant legal maneuvering of my New York attorney, we forced our opponents to come to New York and fight us on our home ground.

I had foolishly agreed to perform at El Morocco in New York City on the night before the trial, and this kept me up until five in the morning. At eight-thirty, bleary-eyed and haggard, I was in the chambers of the judge who was to try our case. He pleaded with me to settle the case rather than drag our "dirty linen" before the public.

Half awake and shaking with emotion, I pointed out to the judge that I had done no wrong and that I could not see *paying* anyone to punish me. I had been informed that the judge was going to "give me the works." Moreover, the original lawyer in New York City who had represented my wife had engaged as his assistant counsel a man whose son had married the *daughter of the judge who was to handle our trial*. To make matters worse, my New York attorney, because he had occasionally escorted my wife to dinner on evenings I had been working out of town, was not allowed to represent me. There followed some of the most unbelievable fireworks ever to take place in a courtroom.

I received the happiest shock of my life when this judge gave me a great big ray of hope. During a recess the first morning of the trial as I sat staring moodily out into space, he walked by me and whispered, "I see what they're trying to do to you and I'll crucify them!" This judge has long since passed on to his great reward, and I feel that I am not in any way casting any reflections upon his integrity or honesty as a judge in revealing anything he said or did.

The trial wore on. We were privileged to introduce the recordings of the phone conversations. Today, of course, this would be impossible due to Federal restrictions on the tapping of telephonic conversations. Actually it was almost as difficult in those days but this judge knew, because of something I had told in his private chambers that early morning of the first day of the trial, that I had really tried to make a go of this marriage. He felt he had but one course to pursue.

Unfortunately, the day of the acetate recording had not yet come into being and the tape recorder was many years away. The aluminum disks which had been made (and which could only be played with *wooden* needles) reproduced the voices so badly that it was small wonder that both Fay Webb and her father denied that these were their real voices. However, the verisimilitude of the telephone operators making the various calls to California on the morning I had called her father to come and take her home, was too real to be the work of any expert sound-effects man.

One afternoon near the end of the trial the lawyer whose son had married the judge's daughter, grilled my attorney who had taken my wife out for me. With all the wiles and tricks at his command, he abused and vilified him. This was too much for me. At the end of the trial when the judge was leaving his bench, I glared at the other New York attorney (who had engaged the attorney who had just grilled my representative) with all the malevolence I could.

This man, observing my disgust and anger, stupidly said to me, "Stop acting. You're not in the movies now!" With that I let fly a right which just missed him and suddenly the court was in an uproar. The judge was back at his bench banging the gavel for order and flash bulbs were popping as court officers sought to separate me from my opponent.

Up to this time, my wife's California playboy attorney who had been taking her out had been seated usually outside the rail of the inner sanctum of the court with her father. All three had come East at their own expense. Since a California attorney is usually not allowed to practice in the state of New York (and vice versa), he had been merely a spectator, hoping that the two men they had chosen in New York would bring the case to victory. I had studied his lean, pale features and had hated him with every ounce of gall in my body, as I felt that had he not come into the picture this trial would never have taken place. After I read the Winchell item I imagined that he had probably said to my wife one evening, "Let's bring an action against this jerk husband of yours; he loves the limelight and his career too much to dare to fight us in court. We can accuse him of anything—throw the book at him. Rather than risk damaging his career, he'll kick in for any amount we ask." They failed to reckon with my New England repugnance to paying tribute and submitting to extortion.

Probably the most stupid mistake that Fay Webb could have made was to demand ninety thousand dollars a year. At the time that I met her, she was receiving only one hundred dollars a week from MGM Studios, which was, as I have said, a sop to her father, the Chief of Police of Santa Monica. MGM needed his good will since their studios are on the borders of that city. Even some of the newspapers that previously had given me no quarter as a performer had boiled with indignation as they reported her exorbitant demands for a permanent settlement. One paper in the South headed its editorial on this outrageous ransom, "Let Them Eat Cake."

During the commotion in the courtroom Fay Webb's California attorney, for some unaccountable reason, had moved inside the rail and was sitting at the table next to the New York attorneys representing my wife.

The original New York attorney who had brought the action against me even before I had gone to California to make *George White's Scandals* (the one whom I had just attempted to hit) yelled to the judge who was now banging his gavel angrily for order. "He snuck up behind me, Your Honor. He tried to hit me when I wasn't looking!"

The judge leaned forward and said, "He didn't sneak up behind you and I don't think Mr. Vallee knew that the court was still in session." (The court is in session as long as the judge is still in the courtroom.)

Then followed a most bizarre series of happenings. The judge observed Fay Webb's California attorney seated within the rail. He pointed his finger at the attorney and almost shouted, "I thought I told you to sit outside the railing!" To our amazement he went further and cried, "I understand they call you the Steuer of California. That's a libel on Steuer!"

My wife's attorney turned as white as ten thousand dollars' worth of skimmed milk. He rose from his chair, moved toward the rail, then turned and faced the judge. "I would like to have you in California," he said menacingly.

From the judge then came a statement that of course should have been grounds for a retrial. He quietly answered, "I'll meet you anywhere you say. You name your weapon."

At this point, the original New York attorney representing my wife yelled, "I heard that, Your Honor. I heard that!" The judge (God bless him) very calmly fixed his pince-nez upon his nose and said, "What exactly *did* you hear?" He turned to the bailiff. "Swear this man in." He was duly sworn and the judge eyed him coolly for a moment. "Take the stand, please," he said. "Now, for the record, what did you hear?"

To our great astonishment the lawyer completely lost his nerve and did not enter for the record his challenge to the judge.

To you, dear reader, this may seem commonplace and may not strike you as being so unusual. But let me assure you that, on much less than this technicality of a judge challenging a lawyer to a duel, many a case has been declared a mistrial and assigned to another judge.

It has always been my belief that there is a justice, at least on some occasions, right here on earth and this was a clear case of this phenomenon. Not only did the case continue to its conclusion with this same judge, but he decided in our favor. Back to California at their own expense went my wife, her father, and her California attorney.

Naturally the Supreme Court decision (the trial just described) was appealed and went to the Appellate Division of New York City. It was decided in our favor. A subsequent appeal went to the highest court of the State of New York, the Court of Appeals in Albany. I think here we would have won a resounding victory, but just before the three-man court was to hand down its decision, the Brothers Warner (Harry, Jack, and Albert) asked me to step in to play the lead in a picture which Dick Powell had refused.

I was under contract to Warner Bros. at that time and, being a good soldier, I sent my attorney to California to straighten out my marital situation by a settlement. It was something which I had never wanted to do because I realized that any negotiation would accrue in some portion to the benefit of the attorney who had talked my wife into bringing this thoroughly unjustified action against me. Whatever the amount, it would be paying him for his treachery. It is my down-east nature to rebel not only against waste but to refuse completely and at all costs to be involved in rewarding anyone for a dishonest, diabolical, or cruel action.

I had minded enough that Fay Webb and her father were trying to coerce me but I could not see paying a man (who had enjoyed the companionship, the beauty, and the charm of my wife) for initiating a completely dishonest and unwarranted action.

However small or large a portion he received of the twenty-five thousand dollars is not the point. That's the amount I paid them for no molestation during the making of the picture which Warner Bros. had asked me to do. Of course, he did receive something!

My luck was pretty consistently putrid during that period. Dick Powell decided to make the picture after all and I was left holding the bag for twenty-five grand. My attorney, Hymie Bushel, had failed to make what I would have thought a most logical stipulation—to have Warner Bros. approve the spending of the "no-molestation" money. Hymie didn't even think of asking Warner's for the money, didn't even get his expenses from the studio! Even worse, no portion of this could be charged off as a business expense because, as Warner Bros. so wryly said to me, "*We* didn't marry the girl!"

CHAPTER X

My Life and Times with George White's Scandals

"Oh, You Nasty Man"

TALK ABOUT ECCENTRICS! WHAT QUIRK IN a man's nature could impel him to wear a dark blue suit, a white shirt, and a black bow tie morning, noon, and night? Saturdays, Sundays, and holidays! In the box office, backstage, on the street, at banquets, everywhere! Does this seem a trifle strange to you? Well, such a man was George White, producer of *George White's Scandals* who, to my knowledge, never dressed otherwise. One could only assume that he *slept* in similar attire. This diminutive individual in 1929 was reputed to be worth between three and four million dollars. He was to affect my life very definitely beginning in June, 1931.

Our first formal meeting was typical and I should have sensed the headaches to come. I was summoned to his august presence in May 1929, during my third or fourth week at the New York Paramount. A telephone call had informed me that White wished to see me in his offices at the Apollo Theater stage entrance on Forty-third Street, a few hundred yards from the Paramount. It was quite logical that White would want to see me, for just a few months before I had turned down an offer to appear in Florenz Ziegfeld's production of *Whoopee* at the New Amsterdam Theater. Between shows at the Paramount, I heeded the summons and at the proper moment was ushered into the great man's presence.

For some reason White expressed astonishment at my being there. Somewhat nettled at his attitude of sneering condescension, as though I were a bug under a microscope, I turned on my heel and started to leave. He called me back and asked whether I would be interested in appearing in a *George White's Scandals*.

In my Junior year at Yale, I had witnessed his 1926 *Scandals*, a smash, naturally enough, with the talents of Harry Richman, Frances Williams, and Ann Pennington plus songs written by DeSylva, Brown and Henderson, who gave him "Lucky Day," "Birth of the Blues," and "Black

Bottom." At this show I had been the guest of a wealthy Yale boy who was enamored of one of the McCarthy Sisters, also in the show. I had come away with the feeling that I had seen a very fine production.

Naturally I told White that I would most certainly be interested in appearing in a *George White's Scandals*. Nothing more was said and I left his office. And nothing more happened for a couple of years. Georgie evidently never made snap judgments!

In the spring of 1931 I realized that, although we were hitting forty-thousand-dollar average weekly grosses at the Brooklyn Paramount Theater (monotonously, as a matter of fact), I had pretty well run my course in this medium. Although the Paramount hierarchy seemed to be satisfied with my work, in a few more short months they would realize, as I did, that it was time for a change. We could expect to be dropped unceremoniously from the roster of the Brooklyn production. Therefore, when tentative feelers were sent out by the men of the music-publishing industry that, if I wished, I could be in the next *George White's Scandals* production, I very frankly said that I would be happy to entertain such an offer.

The great White, blue suit, white shirt, black bow tie and all, was persuaded to catch one of our stage shows. That particular week I was doing an impression of Chevalier that registered so strongly with the audience that I was forced to appear for three and four encores. When I finished we had dinner at my favorite hang-out, Manny Wolf's, at Forsythe and Grand in lower Manhattan. This was a fabulous steak house with sawdust on the floor and a long bar where alcoholic stimulants were served as freely as though there were no such thing as Prohibition. It was wide open—no knocking at the entrance, no peeking through little trap doors, no phony passwords. Customers of an evening might be not only the elite of the theatrical world but the Governor of the State of New York, Superior and Supreme Court judges, and leaders in every walk of life. During this dinner we discussed the terms, the date of rehearsal, opening, and in effect practically set the contract.

A few nights later in a small office in the DeSylva, Brown and Henderson Building, Lew Brown and Ray Henderson presented (with Lew Brown singing as only he could) the songs that they had written for the eleventh edition of *George White's Scandals*. Some of these songs have made show-business history—"Life is Just a Bowl of Cherries," "My Song," "The Thrill is Gone," and "This is the Missus." The attitude of everyone present was patronizing as though I were a fledgling who knew little or nothing of show business. To them I was a rank amateur, a dilettante who needed much nurturing and training. Naturally, I was extremely annoyed.

But I bore their patronizing. I wanted a shot at another medium in the field of entertainment.

After Brown and Henderson had auditioned the numbers, White and I left the small room.

"There's one thing I want to ask you, George—"

"Yeah? What is it?"

"Can you work my impression of Maurice Chevalier into the show?"

He snorted. "Rudy, you've got to remember one thing—this is Broadway, not a goddam five-a-day grind at some lousy theater."

"But I killed them at the Paramount with it—three encores. After all, those were *people* in the audience."

"Do me a favor,—just remember you're on Broadway now. This is the big time."

"All right, all right. But—if there *is* a place for the Chevalier bit will you promise me that *I* can do it?"

"Yeah, yeah, sure. If we can fit it in, *you'll* do it."

Two weeks later I secured my release from Paramount Publix. I then married Fay Webb and, during our short honeymoon in Atlantic City, was summoned to my mother's bedside by plane. She rallied from a coma long enough to recognize me and talk with me a short while before she died.

A nightmare of *Scandals* rehearsals then began, lasting from ten in the morning until eight, nine, and sometimes ten o'clock at night. I would sit in the dark expanse of the Apollo Theater for days on end without being asked to say "boo" or sing a chorus or do *anything* for the four weeks of the performer's time that the Actors Equity gave the producer at no cost whatsoever to him. The men all received instructions from White to memorize the lyrics and melody of every song that any other man did in the show. Any male personality who did anything musically in a George White show was ordered to know not only the lyrics and melody of his own songs but those of every other male personality. In the event of a performer's illness any one of the other men could step into the breach at a second's notice.

My part in the show was something that I could have learned (as I did) in a matter of a few hours. I have always memorized melody and lyrics, as I read music, exceedingly rapidly. This was a bit upsetting to Henderson and Brown, who had been accustomed to teaching the average performer his songs by rote. Since I appeared in none of the outstanding sketches, my few entrances and exits and my limited contribution to the show was something that could easily have been accomplished in two days of instruction and rehearsal. All the same, I was forced to sit and sit interminably.

Our opening was to be held in Atlantic City in August of 1931. The last night dress rehearsal in New York took place in the Apollo Theater before leaving for the out-of-town tryout. The final scene took place in a lavish set in which the entire cast was supposedly in a German night club.

Each of the principals was called upon to do a small bit as a reprise of something he or she had done previously in the show.

The comedian of the Eleventh Edition of *George White's Scandals* was Willie Howard, who in my opinion was one of the greatest natural comics the world will ever know. To Willie Howard were given some of the funniest and cleverest sketches anyone could ever hope to have in a musical revue. Even Ray Bolger who probably, even as I, had hoped for a part in some of the comedy sketches, was confined to his own spot in the show and to his dancing. While Bolger had a small part in one sketch with Howard, the skits and blackouts were almost exclusively written for and dedicated to Willie Howard's great talent with an assist from his brother Gene.

But in this German cabaret finale, Willie Howard, after doing a series of impressions of Jessel, Jolson, and Cantor, introduced that great French personality, Maurice Chevalier! After walking offstage, he came back with a straw hat pretending to *be* Chevalier!

Willie Howard's impression was a *caricature* of Chevalier and, although it was well done, it was not a true *impression* of the French personality. I, on the other hand, had studied especially prepared Paramount films of Chevalier doing some of the songs from the picture *Paramount On Parade*. I had played his records morning, noon, and night and studied the motion picture until I knew every nuance, every movement, every gesture, every grimace—everything that went into giving his performance the appeal it had for his audience.

I couldn't believe my eyes. Recalling my conversation with George White the evening of the demonstration of the songs, I looked at Brown and Henderson. Both of them averted their glances. They knew that I was being given a royal double-cross. I was naive enough to believe that one or both of these men would go to White and remind him of his promise to me: that if a Chevalier impression was to be done on the show, it was to be mine!

Neither White nor perhaps anyone else in the entire company was aware of the importance to me of this, my first appearance in a musical revue. I was primarily a radio personality, and I knew that the critics of the press were lying in wait ready to tear me to pieces if I did not acquit myself with something outstandingly different. Of *course*, they expected me to sing a few songs. That was what I was supposed to do. But I realized that unless I did something quite different from what everyone would accept as a matter of course, this show could be the kiss of death for me.

Willie and Eugene Howard had been in several *Scandals* and many musical revues. This was old stuff to them but, to me, it was my first appearance on Broadway in a legitimate theater doing a musical revue.

It was my "make or break" and I knew that so far I had nothing in the show that would in any way distinguish me or bring any huzzahs from the audience or the critics.

Came the opening night in Atlantic City, and the German night-club finale found Willie Howard again doing his caricature of Chevalier.

When the NBC individual who represented me and who had little or nothing to do with my securing the part in this show (but who nevertheless was securing a ten per cent commission for the broadcasting company) visited us in Atlantic City at the first matinee on Wednesday afternoon, he realized as keenly as I did that something had to be done. An appeal to Willie Howard fell on deaf ears. Howard pointed out to me that the impression was great for him. A few days later he reversed himself and sent word that I could do my Chevalier impression: he would relinquish it. We had previously appealed to White who ignored the fact that he had promised me that I would do it.

"Dammit, Rudy—Willie Howard is too important to me and the show," he said, with the implication that I was not in the least to be reckoned with. "I can't ask him to drop the Chevalier bit. That's all there is to it."

It was fortunate for me that I was given the opportunity to do this bit of mimicry. It turned out to be the only thing that brought me any real praise, not only in New York City but on the road. With no undue false modesty, it was one of the production's highlights and achieved such results as "stopping the show" for sometimes as long as forty to fifty seconds, which (if you've ever timed it with your watch) is a long time.

Our *Scandals* then went to Newark for another try-out where Ethel Merman joined our cast. Our little epic opened in New York on September 14, 1931, and it proceeded to run until February when it went on the road.

George White will probably always feel that I brought his New York run to a close but even I could ascertain from *Variety's* weekly list of grosses that it was time for us to get out on the road and make some real money. We were in the trough of Depression and White was just hidebound enough by the tradition of musical revues to believe that I could not be left out of the production for two weeks without the necessity of closing it.

"George, you've got to give me two weeks off," I pleaded. "I hate to say this but I'm about to crack up."

"What the hell's the matter with you?"

"Oh, I don't know—the grind, the rat race and, of course, there's Fay. She's been on the Coast for over three months."

"I hate to give you the show-must-go-on routine but do you realize I'll have to close it if you leave? Put all those kids out of work."

"You don't have to close the show. If it's okay with the Pennsylvania and my radio sponsor for me to take a couple of weeks off, why can't you see it the same way? How about a replacement—how about Morton Downey?"

"Nah!"

"All right—how about Bing Crosby? He'd be great."

"Now come on, Rudy! He wouldn't mean a damn thing to my show. Look, I don't want to argue with you—take your two weeks. I'll close the show and we'll reopen in Boston when you get back."

I knew Crosby was very hot on records and radio at the time. He'd probably be so popular in the *Scandals* that White wouldn't care if I *ever* returned. But White would have none of it.

He wasn't the only one who missed the boat on Crosby. I once worked up an impression of Crosby that was so believable it fooled one of the members of his original trio. He happened to hear me do it (while his back was turned to the stage) at the Pennsylvania Grill one night. Later on he asked me, "Where'd Bing go?" This number got tremendous applause at the New York Paramount but Borris Morros, much later the "American-Russian" spy, who was the dictator of shows at the Paramounts at the time, asked me to drop it.

"Bing's all washed up," he said with great finality.

"You and I should make what Crosby will earn in the next ten years," I answered. That was 1931. Now, some thirty or so years later, Crosby is old Fort Knox itself.

And so, the *Scandals* closed. I went to California, flying in an old tri-motored Ford plane, chatting with Will Rogers who got on at Amarillo, Texas. Although I wired Fay Webb at every place along the way where telegrams could be sent, mine was the agony of watching Will Rogers greeted warmly by his family while I stood alone at the airport and waited one hour for the arrival of my wife.

I rejoined the show in Boston where we played a fortnight, grossing fifty thousand dollars each week. Then we embarked on a tour of major cities and occasional one-night stands throughout the country. White, whose original interest in me had been because of my radio reputation, realized that if he could secure an occasional armory or large auditorium (sometimes with extra wooden seats to take care of the thousands who turned out to see a personality they had come to know through radio) he would achieve financial grosses unknown to touring musical revues. We finally reached Chicago where the sponsors of my program informed me that, if we went farther, I would have to resign from the radio show. Although I carried eight key men with me, the difficulty of finding additional good musicians in towns such as Canton, Ohio, and often even in larger cities was seriously affecting the quality of our broadcasts. I informed White that I could not go farther than Chicago. Evidently he had in mind to tour the production to California, maybe staying out for as long as three-quarters of the year, milking every town and hamlet that could possibly play the *Scandals*. I had no choice in the matter. My radio show was at stake. The Eleventh Edition of the *Scandals*, therefore, folded in Chicago in the spring of 1932.

Those were bleak days.

It was a time FDR was campaigning for the Presidency and talking about that "forgotten man." He spoke very well and got the job. The Depression began to look as if it was booked for a long run—economics forced the invention of the double feature which later led to "Bank Night" and free dishes at the movies. And there were some great pictures too: *Grand Hotel*, *The Champ*, with Jackie Cooper, *Scarface*, and the musical extravaganza, *Forty-second Street* with Ginger Rogers in a bit role.

And so while Roosevelt was trying to get elected, I was campaigning my way back to New York. Willie and Eugene Howard, Ray Bolger, I and others from the defunct Eleventh *Scandals* played the Paramount Publix Theaters—and that wasn't a bad talent package now that I think of it. Back in the land of the rat race for a few weeks and then to a tour of one-nighters from which I returned to New York each Thursday for the Fleischmann show.

On these tours I realized I needed a girl singer badly and my thoughts turned to Alice Faye. I had come to know her and like her immensely during the *Scandals* run. She was a cute blond lovely in the chorus, very friendly, with a smile warm enough to melt the heart of an Eskimo. In the Atlantic City *Scandals* tryout in 1931 one of the semi-principals, a girl with a big song that stopped the show opening night, developed laryngitis. I suggested Alice as a replacement but George White turned her down.

Oddly enough I had never really heard her sing professionally. The only times I had seen her perform were in those impromptu numbers she would do for kicks at little parties the *Scandals* company enjoyed from time to time after rehearsals. Her unique way of handling a song stuck with me, however—I know she had great authority and physical appeal. So she joined me on the grand tour in Harrisburg, Pennsylvania, and the first night, this ex-chorine was the smash I thought she would be. Next stop: a featured personality role on my Thursday broadcasts.

It wasn't long after she came on the show that the papers were served me asking that my separation agreement with Fay Webb be set aside on the grounds of duress and fraud.

You know the results of this play if you were paying attention a few pages back. Alice was as fiercely loyal as a mother rhinoceros at bay with brood. One of my favorite memories of Alice is of a time in Island Pond, Vermont, my birthplace, back in '33. I forget just what the cause but an altercation concerning me was taking place on the dance floor. Alice took sides rather heatedly and it required a strong Canadian lumberjack to hold her back from the fray. Picture it—there was this huge, six-foot Canuck holding my diminutive vocalist a few feet in the air as she kicked away at his shins to escape. The more he laughed at her struggles, the madder she got. Fortunately, reason returned to the dissidents and the dance continued peacefully.

Alice was still with my company in 1934 at the Hollywood Restaurant. Situated at Forty-eighth Street and Broadway, this ornate club was one of the most successful of that day. Prohibition had just been wiped from the Constitutional Amendment slate and night life was wilder than ever. In addition, the Veterans' Bonus was passed, pumping a lot of money into circulation with the result that the New York scene began to resemble Mardi Gras and Las Vegas combined. Alice was an unqualified smash, night after night.

At this juncture Wee Georgie White proposed my appearance in a movie of the *Scandals*. As I have said, I felt that I must do something to atone for *The Vagabond Lover* so I indicated my willingness even though Fay Webb's attorneys were waiting to pounce.

"Just name any figure you want, Rudy," White said at the outset. "I want you to make some money. After all, Fox Studios has all the loot in the world."

Then gentle Georgie reversed his tactics. "They've got me buying the talent now," he whined. "Honest to God, all I can offer you is twenty-five hundred a week for four weeks work. Ten grand."

I made a few mental calculations. "For God's sake, George," I said, "it will cost me nearly that to move my broadcasts out there! Plus the fact I'll have to give up the Hollywood Restaurant job and theater dates. After all, I can't underwrite the picture!" The disastrous première of *The Vagabond Lover* crept back into my mind. After all, a man has to try to make retribution for certain dastardly crimes. "Okay, George. You've got me; I'll do the picture."

Some time before, I had tried to sell White on using Alice Faye in this production. He'd let me persuade him to catch her performance with me at Loew's Theater in the Bronx but he had been noncommittal. After he'd gone to the Coast to prepare the picture, he suddenly wired me he had secured a special song for her in the picture. Just coincidentally, the song title sums up my estimation of George White—"Oh, You Nasty Man."

At the time, I had formed an agency to handle talent, and as Alice was one of our artists, we signed a satisfactory picture contract for her and we all entrained for Hollywood. When Lillian Harvey resigned her role, Alice's "rushes" doing "Oh, You Nasty Man" had already been viewed by the Fox brass and were adjudged sensational. She got the lead and became a reigning star for years. Later on, she decided to forgo a full-time screen career to be the wife of Phil Harris.

But George was a cutie and never hesitated to *use* anyone to further his aims. During the filming he arranged to have me stranded for a very long time atop a high pillar on the set from which the ladder had been removed. It got huge headlines and a barrel of publicity which helped the picture's grosses. As White got a percentage, my ridiculous plight made money for him. As for me, the picture cost me about seventy-five thousand dollars in legal fees, transportation, etc. Wouldn't you think this would have cured me of this small-time Svengali White? Some of us never learn!

So this blue-suited postman rang for the third time. White asked me to play a part in the Twelfth Edition of *George White's Scandals* in 1936 but after looking over the songs and the general outline of the show, I felt that, to put it as charitably as possible, it was not going to be a very outstanding production. Even though Willie and Eugene Howard were again to be in it, that little intuitive voice that had guided me pretty well up to this date said "Stay out of it." Cliff "Ukulele Ike" Edwards was assigned the part that I refused and, when I caught the show in Newark, I was greeted by shouts of "Bow Wow!" from Bert Lahr, Willie Howard, and Cliff Edwards when I visited their dressing rooms. These animal-like cries were uttered to indicate to me that the show was a "dog"! As I watched the show unfold, I realized only too well that it was a veritable bestiary—it was not only a dog, it was a turkey.

Gentle reader, have you sensed in the few preceding paragraphs that I am not seeking a job as executive secretary of the George White Fan Club? If so, your surmise is a well-founded one.

I am not deprecating George as a showman because his average of successes is pretty damn' good. Nevertheless, I would like to take this opportunity (and who's going to stop me—after all, it's my book) to question his judgment on one hand, his taste on another. And, while we're on a bill of particulars, if you feel my case is baseless, please write me care of my publisher.

I question his judgment on the grounds that he bluntly rejected the idea of Bing Crosby as my replacement in the Eleventh *Scandals*. (The term Eleventh *Scandals* sounds like a regiment in the French Foreign Legion!) One hundred and fifty million or so Americans can't be wrong.

In impugning his taste, I have to recall a very black moment in my life which still leaves me full of remembered rancor—I must confess I hold onto a grudge the way a snapping turtle holds onto a fish.

It was a sordid happenstance in the 1931 *Scandals*. My mother had died two weeks before the *Scandals* rehearsals. When we arrived at Atlantic City, the composers Brown and Henderson were still trying to put over a song which they felt was one of their best. It bore the title "If I Thought I Could Live Without You, I'd Die." Ethel Barrymore Colt sang it to a baby in a cradle. There were several other renditions of the number by other members of the cast. One of the most ridiculous was Willie Howard's rendition. At that time he was at least sixty years of age out onstage with a black, shiny wig. He sang it to a woman with graying hair, obviously supposed to be his mother. Before the second-week matinee began, I was informed by the stage manager that Mr. White had sent an order for me to sing the song in place of Willie Howard.

I dispatched the stage manager to point out to White that the audience (made up mostly of women) would resent my apparent attempt to capitalize on the death of my mother by singing a song to a woman who was supposed to represent her. I pointed out that it would not only be embarrassing to me but it would cause resentment by the public. Most certainly they would feel that this was playing a bit too obviously on their sympathetic potential.

The stage manager returned to inform me curtly that White said "do the song"! Always, like a good soldier, I obey orders even when I know they are stupid or wrong! When I was halfway through the song I could feel the general air of shock, astonishment, resentment, and indignation from many sections of the audience. Any performer can sense those things in a moment. No sooner had I come off the stage after singing the song than White rushed backstage to apologize, saying that he hadn't realized, he didn't think! This, believe it or not, after I had taken particular pains to explain to him what would obviously happen were I to do it!

After watching, with a certain amount of visceral pain, the opening night of this "turkey" in Jersey, I moved to Pittsburgh with my band and company of entertainers to play the Stanley Theater.

About one in the morning the phone jingled in my hotel room. "Rudy?" a metallic voice said. "This is George."

I had just dropped off to sleep and nothing registered very well. "George?" I mumbled. "George—"

"George White, goddammit! The show's in trouble. Bad trouble. We're in Boston and business stinks!"

"I—ah—I'm sorry to hear that, George," was about all I could muster. I was still half asleep.

"Rudy, you gotta save the show. It's a good show and all we need is a big commercial name to type it. Will you do it?"

"Now come on, George. First of all, I don't think it's such a hot show and, besides, I'm involved with a hell of a lot of theater bookings. I just can't make it. Like to help you and all that. But you know how it is." I wanted to get back to sleep. I was bushed. So he gave up and hung up.

But George White never gave up, never took no for an answer. First thing I knew he flew down to Pittsburgh and bent my ear until four in the morning.

"It's not for me so much," he pleaded. "Think of those fifty, sixty kids'll be thrown out of work. Would you want *that* on your conscience?"

This got to me. Maybe I felt guilty having such an easy time all during the Depression. I don't know. Maybe White is the greatest salesman since the apple peddler in the Garden of Eden. Another possibility: as I look back through the pages of this book I am faced with the possibility that I may well be one of the great, all-time pushovers, a patsy *par excellence*.

So I managed to cancel the rest of my tour, learned the songs, the routines and agreed to join the show in Washington in a few days. I made one proviso with White. I wanted to do an impression of Fred Allen in the show. (Ever since I had first seen him at that little theater in Connecticut in 1926 I had admired his style. I had tried out this Allen impression at the Brooklyn Paramount and the Hollywood Restaurant with great success.) White agreed to this demand.

"By the way, George," I said, remembering the Maurice Chevalier hassle, "do you mind putting it in writing?"

With this understanding signed, sealed, and delivered, I joined the company for the opening night in Washington. Just a few minutes before curtain time I was told that I was *not* to do the Allen impression! As I write this sentence so many years later I can still burn a little at White's perfidy. But the crowning act was still to come!

Again I obeyed orders but I was so disgusted that I failed to show up in the finale, causing much comment in the press. All the same, I did do the impression beginning the second night in Washington and we moved on to New York. After the down-beat opening-night reviews and with a few more performances under our belt, it became obvious that neither my presence, the presence of even the fabulous Bing Crosby, or anyone else for that matter, could save this doomed production.

Then my attorney phoned me with some very singular news. "White wants you out of the show," he said in a voice full of disbelief.

"Out of the show?" I asked incredulously. "Has he finally gone completely out of his mind? But why on earth—"

"He's evidently trying to cut the pay roll to keep the show running."

"This is just great—after I gave up those theater bookings. They would have paid me three times what I'm getting from White. And I can't win —suppose the show maintains its gross without me—or, by some fluke, does better business. *That* sure as hell won't help my career any!" I seethed in silence for a moment.

"Rudy—are you still there?"

"Yes—I'm trying to cool down enough to think. I'll tell you what—you tell our mutual friend Mr. White *I'll take a cut* if he will ask me to *privately*."

Came the evening of the fracas. It was March 17 and I came to the theater from the annual dinner of the Friendly Sons of St. Patrick.

With no notice White again sent me a message not to do the Allen impression. As I saw him scurrying about backstage in his blue suit with a green carnation in his lapel I thought, "Oh, God! How can I be so goddamned stupid as to have gotten involved with this character again!"

After the performance, I started for my dressing room only to be stopped by White's arrogant two-fingered whistle which was always his signal for us to come running. The rest of the principals clustered around him as he asked several of them if they would take a cut. As I started to go to my dressing room, he yelled at me to come back and then asked me if I would take a cut. I was furious that he had not deigned to ask me privately. I tried to remain calm. "You've made the profits," I said. "Why not take the losses?"

Then to my amazement he said, "I lost enough money with you on the tour of 1932."

Recalling the gymnasiums and auditoriums in which we worked, with no dressing rooms, the large audiences and fabulous grosses for those days and the critics' reviews which stated that the audiences had turned out mainly to see the radio personality, I felt that this was too much. I was no longer at all calm. "You little ————, you know very well that is a goddam lie!" I was in tails and I had my hands in my pockets.

White glanced up at some of the chorus girls watching the scene from outside their dressing rooms. In the manner of a prize fighter he approached me, with a smile on his face. I thought he was only clowning. Without any warning I felt a stinging blow on the bridge of my nose and realized too late that he had struck me. Before I could get my hands out of my pockets, the stagehands had separated us and the fracas was over.

I was barred from the theater pending a hearing before the American Arbitration Society. After due deliberation, they ordered White to reinstate me in the show. White had threatened that if he was ordered to do so he would close the show. Rather than see the members of the cast suffer, I did not return. Cliff Edwards went back into my part—the same Cliff Edwards who, when I asked him if he would mind my stepping into the show, had said that it was perfectly agreeable with him. (I later learned that he often lurked in the wings cursing and reviling me as I portrayed the role he had left; he should have realized the only reason I stepped into the show was to try to save it and keep everyone working.) His resentment further manifested itself as he testified against me at the arbitration proceedings. Edwards returned to the part but his triumph was short-lived. The show folded one week later, as it should have done months earlier, leaving me sadder but wiser.

CHAPTER XI

Songs Can Be Dangerous

"We are poor little lambs ..."

To a SINGING ENTERTAINER, A SONG IS not only his medium, his vehicle; it is actually his lifeblood. As I write I realize even more fully than before how my own career has in a way been strung along on songs.

The songs, the popular tunes of a nation are willy-nilly its quintessence. They are the sounds of today and the memories of a sweet, redolent yesterday—they are the bourgeois leitmotifs, the sound tracks of which a sizable part of our lives are made. Intellectuals brand them as shoddy and ephemeral, not comparable to, say, Mozart or Ravel. God knows they are right—I don't suppose for a moment that "Mairzy Doats" or "Open the Door, Richard" will survive this century, while at that time Wolfgang and Maurice will most certainly still be swinging. But that's not really the point. Although Mozart and Ravel are huge stones in the edifice of culture (if I may get a bit flowery), may I please plead that the "pop" tunes are at least a part of the mortar. I will venture to say that most of our love affairs—the first time you met *that* person or had a big date or a great evening, etc.,—are susceptible of blessed recall upon application of some one special tune. I speak from experience. I've had this musical magic as part of my own life—and who knows how many times I've applied it to others as I performed.

A great singer without the right song is as nothing; a mediocre vocalist with a great song may well be an overnight star. Such is the power of "material." But you can have great material and still fail if few get to hear you. We were being heard from a solid-gold podium called radio and we caused a helluva lot of consternation in tin-pan alley.

When we first clicked on radio from the Heigh-Ho, song-plugging was quite a different thing from what it is now. A song-plugger was and is an employee of a publisher whose mission is to inveigle an artist into performing the publisher's songs. It's as simple as that. Now the *ways* they go about this inveiglement are something else again: that is a book in itself and, I'll wager, a very juicy one.

115

At any rate the methods of plugging back in the twenties and early thirties were primitive indeed. The song-plugger would lure the night-club, theater, or dance-band performer in various ways to his office along Broadway for a "demonstration." The "office" was a tiny cubicle hardly large enough to swing a cat in or even to swing a piccolo, for that matter. The furniture consisted of a piano and two or three seats.

The plugger had to play and sing the latest songs on which his firm was "working"—whether he could play or sing adequately or not.

After a chorus or two the demonstrator would pivot around on the stool and eye the unfortunate victim. "Is that great or is that *great!* Work on it—just give it a nudge, you got another 'Stardust'!"

"Sounds possible," the poor listener would say embarrassedly. "I'll try to include it in my repertoire."

Obviously this was not putting the best foot forward. Invariably the demonstrator's voice left much to be desired, the tempo was rarely suited to the melody or lyrics, and the clanky piano that had never felt the hands of a tuner did little justice to whatever melodic beauty or harmonic values the number may have had. You had to have an ear and imagination in spades to pick them in those days, to visualize your own orchestration and interpretation of the piece. But even by this hit-or-miss method, songs were somehow publicized and the music business throve, particularly with the leading publishers.

Then a mystifying thing happened. The jobbers (sheet-music whole-salers, so to speak) reported to the publishers an unusual number of calls for specific songs from the girls behind the music counters in the five-and-ten-cent stores in New York City, Pennsylvania, and New Jersey. What flabbergasted the jobbers and publishers was the fact that neither group had ever *heard* of the song! There was only one clue to the enigma; the five-and-ten girls reported that their customers said the songs were being broadcast by a performer called Rudy Vallee from an exclusive club on the East Side of New York City!

Now the songs the buyers were clamoring for were perfectly good tunes. I picked them because I happened to like them and for no other reason. However, none of them happened to be the property of the "big" publishers. Hence their consternation.

I, of course, knew nothing of this phenomenon at the time. All the same, as representatives of the leading publishers bribed their way past our mendacious *maitre d'* at the Heigh-Ho (who looked down his nose at their lack of formal attire) to come backstage to see me, I became acutely aware that we had started something. These pluggers were also aware that we possessed some magic power that enabled us to interest listeners in almost any song we played—and we had a radio outlet. Bless Guglielmo Marconi!

As the song-plugging pace quickened, we were visited by Jack Robbins, who was to become one of the most powerful of all publishers. It was during a Saturday afternoon tea dance, I remember, and with him was an English publisher who had brought him a tune, "If I Had You." They gave us copies and sat there as we made our broadcast. The direct approach! After this I suddenly found myself being romanced by three or four representatives of tin-pan alley, each with his own folio of assorted tunes his company was "working on."

It was during this period that Ted Collins came to me with an offer to make a series of low-priced recordings to be sold through the ten-cent stores. We were permitted to record anything we wished in his studios which were a subsidiary of Columbia Phonograph Company. After the session, Ted took me to a restaurant and I could tell that he had something on his mind. I had the feeling that he thought I and my band had great potential and was considering giving up the record business to manage us. His genius in this area was evidenced later on by his masterful building of Kate Smith to stardom. I have often thought that having him as an advisor would have saved me from much of the grief and heartache that I was to know. But, alas, for some unaccountable reason it did not quite come to pass.

Another important part of the Rudy Vallee "sound track" was written by Charles Henderson, a Harvard lad, a pianist with whom I had played many dances in and around Boston in the fall of '27. He was in town with the Hasty Pudding Show and dropped by the Heigh-Ho that evening.

"Why don't you sit in for a few numbers?" I asked him.

"Why not, Rudy—it'll be like old times." He worked a few numbers with the band and then I invited him to ad-lib on the piano. The first thing he played was a lovely minor melody that immediately struck my fancy.

"Where did you get that one, Charlie?" I asked. "It's a beauty."

"Oh, it's something I've been fooling around with lately. Do you really like it?"

"Do I like it! Listen, will you write it out for us? We'd like to add it to our book and keep on playing it."

He set the melody down for us and the band liked it as well as I. Charlie called it, oddly enough, "Slavia," which seemed a rather harsh name for such a gorgeous tune.

We made a night of it, playing, and rehashing the preposterous things that had happened to us when we were in the band together.

"Oh, by the way," I said, "remember that society wedding we played in Boston and this good-looking fellow played a piano solo while the band was taking a break?"

"Oh, yes. It was that wedding-reception affair. I remember."

"Well, that thing he played has been haunting me ever since. Somebody said it was an Amherst prom song or something. But I can't quite remember how it goes."

Henderson had a terrific memory and proceeded to write out the melody *and* lyrics so we could put the song in our books!

After Charlie's departure for Boston we continued to program "Slavia" and our patrons loved it. One night I decided to write some lyrics and give it a title. I have never possessed nor pretended to possess any melodic creativity but I have always been fairly adept with words. First of all, I sought a two-word title in which the high note would have a double "E" sound, that being a phonetic which facilitates singing such a note. The title "Deep Night" popped into my mind as I pictured a couple out in the garden deep in the throes of passionate amour on a lovely moonlit night. I developed this theme and it became our first Victor recording.

The "Amherst prom song" also became a favorite of our listeners and dancers and we played it frequently. Suddenly, there came a letter from a lawyer asking that I come to see him about that song. It happened that he was a Negro and he informed me that he represented an Amherst student who had written the tune back in '24 but who had never been able to place it with a publisher. This jibed exactly with what Charlie Henderson had told us.

"Mr. Vallee," the colored attorney said, "if you are able to get the song published, I am empowered to offer you fifty per cent of the royalties."

This sounded like a very good deal to me and I was quite interested. I knew from the warm reception it had whenever we programmed it that the song had excellent possibilities. However, about this time Mills Music, one of the major publishers, had a song called "Girl of My Dreams, I Love You." It had become tremendously popular and had been recorded for Victor by Blue Steele and his orchestra. "Our" song was called "I Love You, I Love You, I Love You, You Are the Girl of My Dreams." Since it was not published, the girl at the sheet-music counter would always substitute the Mills Music song even though the customer was asking for "our" song, having heard it in the club or on the air. Mills suggested we hold back our song until the fall of 1928 at which time they assured me their sheet music would have run its sales course and be taken off the counters. Strangely enough he did not seek the publishing rights to "our" song but the request made sense and I removed it from our broadcast list and ceased to do it.

That fall (1928) after we had returned from a summer engagement at the Milton Point Casino, I happened to visit the office of Robbins Music which was fast becoming one of the leading publishers. I spoke to one of their professional managers (that's a ritzy title meaning song-plugger), Jack Bregman, who had heard we had many unpublished songs in our book.

I mentioned some of the tunes we had and when I came to the "Amherst item" he became quite excited. He took me to his office. It was an astonishing coincidence! There sat the late Leo Reisman, the orchestra leader, placing a phone call to the Amherst bookstore in Massachusetts, trying to track down that particular number!

"Cancel the call, Leo," I said. "I've got the whole story here." The colored attorney had given me the copyright card of his Amherst client who had registered the song with the Library of Congress in Washington. Proudly I pulled the document from my pocket.

"Well, I'll be damned," Leo exclaimed, hanging up the phone. "I wish I had a nickel for every time I've played that number in Boston."

"I wish *I* had a nickel for every time I've done it here in New York," I replied.

"It's one helluva song," muttered Bregman thoughtfully.

"You know, every band leader in Boston claims *he* wrote it," continued Reisman. "I played it for Jack Robbins the other night at the Waldorf and he liked it so much he's been trying to get the rights to it ever since. That's why I was calling Amherst. And now *you* walk in with an ace up your sleeve!"

"There's enough here for everybody," Bregman said. "We'll cut the royalties up between the composer, Reisman and you."

"We'll put a picture of you and Leo on the cover of the sheet music. We'll bill it as 'Words and music by Rudy Vallee, Leo Reisman and the guy from Amherst.'"

As Reisman and I left for the subway we were walking on air. He suddenly turned to me and asked, "How much is one hundred thousand times a cent?" I roared with laughter. Already he was counting his royalties!

Of course, Reisman and I redoubled our efforts to popularize the song with our bands. Then right out of the blue complications set in, to put it mildly! Bert Lowe who was leading an orchestra in Boston (he was one of the many who took bows for the song's composition) had somehow unearthed a sheet-music copy of it published in 1922! He had located the two young fellows who had published it that year, had gotten the rights and taken the tune to Shapiro-Bernstein, a rival publishing firm. This outfit had notified Robbins Music that Robbins had no legal title to the number.

Robbins lost all interest in the song because it was considered too difficult to fight the counterclaim. Even though it was quite possible that "our" Amherst boy might have written the song previous to the 1922 publication that Bert Lowe had discovered, *common-law* proof would have to be found requiring many witnesses as to the exact time and date of composition. The song went on to become a smash hit, selling over a million copies of sheet music and God knows how many records—but Reisman and I were left out in the cold! He had figured out his royalties a little prematurely.

I engaged a colored attorney to fight the case but he died before it came to trial and my five-hundred-dollar retainer went down the drain. Shapiro-Bernstein wanted no hard feelings between us. After all, they wanted me to plug their songs. In an effort to mollify me they had a special song written called "Heigh-ho, Everybody, Heigh-ho" but I knew in advance it was a real "dog" and couldn't be given away. I, of course, could hold no grudge against Shapiro-Bernstein but it was unfortunate that Reisman and I, who had really started the song on its way, were unable to share in its profits. Songs can be dangerous—they can blow right up in your face!

Another case in point. This explosive musical episode began in the fall of '27 when I was playing with the Yale Collegians in Indianapolis. I heard a local band play a tune which intrigued me greatly. Charlie Davis, the band leader, refused to give me the words and music at the time.

We now modulate to the summer of '28 when we were appearing at the Milton Point Casino. One evening after our band chores were over, I met two lovely girl twins who were going to Purdue University. They asked me if I knew the "Vagabond Lover" song and proceeded to sing me the melody and lyrics of the same item Charlie Davis had refused me! I jotted it all down and began to broadcast it from the Heigh-Ho.

As we neared the New Year of '29 our popularity was increasing by leaps and bounds. The publishing firm, Leo Feist ("You can't go wrong with a Feist song"), began to romance me. They put me on a weekly retainer as they had previously done with Guy Lombardo, feeling that our good will and intuition in picking hits was worth it. Further, they agreed to publish any song I would suggest to them.

I gave them "I'm Just a Vagabond Lover" and there is no doubt in my mind that Feist took it merely out of politeness; still the entire verse was written by me (melody and lyric) as well as about forty per cent of the changes in the chorus. To their astonishment it sold nearly seven hundred thousand in sheet music and a tremendous number of records even though we were the only band that actually ever gave it a "ride."

It was then decided that I was to make an RKO picture and it was to be called *The Vagabond Lover*. This Feist publication would be the "title song."

I had been disturbed by several letters from various parts of the country from individuals who protested the fact that I called it *my* song. In a few cases the letter writers had claimed they had written the song themselves. There was one epistle containing a fantastic tale. It seems that the writer (from 'way out West) had discovered in the musty old trunk of a cowboy friend a copy of this ill-starred composition.

It was while appearing at the Palace Theater that one Sunday morning I wrote the complete verse and melody for the verse, as well as reconstructing the lyrics of the chorus to a considerable extent. Frankly, I was quite perturbed by the letter I had received from Chicago written by the young man who had taken out the Library of Congress registration in 1927. You see, the song was definitely a sensitive and esthetically appealing one with a high quality of melody and lyric. And yet the Chicago letter was couched in the "dese-dem-and-dose" idiom! However, he had the copyright card and I couldn't argue beyond that.

I brought the young man to New York and gave him the lion's share of the $1500 advance which Feist gave us on the song, which was now really beginning to click. We had recorded it for Victor and were plugging it for all we were worth on the stage, in the club, and on the air. Nevertheless, I was uneasy about it and I wasn't greatly surprised when suddenly a legal action was brought by a Chicago attorney named Brown who claimed to be the true author of it.

Although Brown in his original action sought to tie up the Victor company, Leo Feist, and me as well as our Chicago "author-composer," he was persuaded to leave the rest of us alone so that the song could make as much money as possible for whomever eventually would be determined the rightful copyright owner.

There is a clause in all publishing contracts which states that, in the event of litigation, the composers and authors will bear all costs. To send a lawyer to Chicago to fight the case cost me nearly two thousand dollars but there was never any question about my part in the composition of the song. The Chicago court found in favor of the Chicago attorney; the fantastic story concocted by my "dese-dem-and-dose" friend as to how he came to write the tune was discredited. I had been hooked beautifully and all the work I had put in on the song brought me at least something— after deducting the cost of sending a lawyer to Chicago, I still cleared four or five thousand.

I recall the headline in *Zit's Weekly*, a show-business publication, which branded me (in red ink, mind you) rather unjustly, I thought...

RUDY VALLEE
CALLED SONG PIRATE!

By this time I was being besieged by the leading publishers in New York to introduce their songs. To be perfectly frank, they offered me what has in recent years become a dirty word—"payola," or a "cut-in," for my part in bringing a tune to public attention. In a way I can understand why certain groups may frown on this practice but in a sense I feel that payola is justifiable. Nuts! I've said it and I'm glad! After all, without an entertainer "working" on it, a song very often languishes unheard on the shelf. Throughout the years Jolson, Cantor, Harry Richman, Sophie Tucker, Gene Austin (and Vallee) have been "cut in" on songs they have made into hits.

I would venture to say that Gene Austin who has written many songs made more money from royalties on numbers he had little or no part in composing than he did from his Victor recording payments which, as you know, were sizable. His "cut" from some of the tunes he "made" in '25 and '26 when he was the Number One crooner must have run to hundreds of thousands of dollars. In my opinion he was the first very popular *natural* singer or crooner and he handsomely deserved any payola he received. At Christmas time, I was told it was not unusual for a publisher for whom Austin had made hundreds of thousands of dollars to furnish and redecorate his apartment or give him a new automobile—this in addition to a fat check for royalties on a song Gene had made famous through his magical artistry.

It was my privilege to introduce such songs as "I Kiss Your Hand, Madame," "Miss You," "If I Had You," and "Honey." This last number had lain on the shelf for a long time gathering dust but when we gave it a ride it sold over a million copies and launched the career of Dick Whiting—yet I was not cut in and received not one penny. In spite of the fact that his "Japanese Sandman" had given him some stature years before, it was "Honey" that made him a great success as a popular composer. In this period we also launched "Coquette," "Marie," and "Lover Come Back to Me" on records.

As I believe I have mentioned before, the Will Osborne band played the Villa Venice upstairs over the Villa Vallee and we would steer the overflow crowds up there. I would alternately "front" each band from time to time of an evening. As I would come up I often noticed them playing a beautiful melody which was unfamiliar to me. Osborne told me it had been written by his pianist, Paul Denniker, and a colored lad named Andy Razaf, the latter the collaborator with "Fats" Waller on the master-pieces, "Honeysuckle Rose" and "Ain't Misbehavin'." Again, it was a number that had merely been occupying space on the shelf of a small publisher. By coincidence, the publisher was my old friend Joe Davis who had arranged for me to meet Rudy Wiedoeft. I recommended that he really get after the song and promised that I would record it. It caught on and sold nearly a million copies. It was the now-famous standard, "Sposin'."

There was one beaut on which I turned down a cut-in offer. It was written by a young Harvard boy, a brilliant pianist who insisted on sitting in with us when we were playing the Westchester Biltmore. Later on the chap thoroughly mastered the subject of music to the extent that he became musical director for MGM and had much to do with many an

Academy Award-winning production. He, Johnny Green, had written this song but, when I studied the lyric, I felt it a little too sensual and physical for me to introduce over the air. It remained for Leo Reisman to make the Victor record of it, featuring his great pianist Eddy Duchin, and the song is still associated with Maestro Reisman. Perhaps I was right in turning it down but, looking back, I realize I passed up a nice annuity in the lovely "Body and Soul."

Al Dubin, a top song writer of the day, brought me the tune, "I'm Dancing With Tears in My Eyes," and permitted me to broadcast it first. Together with Guy Lombardo I had first recording rights to Walter Donaldson's wonderful "You're Driving Me Crazy" and the number did quite well. I gave a lot of tunes the "full treatment" in those days and had successes as well as the inevitable "bombs" now and then.

Perhaps the most unusual and uncomposer-like individual I ever met was Herman Hupfeld, he of the robust frame and florid, Germanic features. I was to bring him very good luck on three of his tunes. The first was "As Time Goes By" which I recorded in 1931. Unfortunately I chose a key much too high for my voice which was already tired from overwork. The song originated in a Broadway show called *Everybody's Welcome* starring Frances Williams. It was not a success and our record also proved unpopular. Nevertheless, by a strange fluke, the number was included in the film *Casablanca* (with Humphrey Bogart and Ingrid Bergman) and became an overnight hit in the early forties. As the American Federation of Musicians was on strike against the recording companies, no new records were being made. Therefore, Victor dug my disk out of the files and the reissue sold beautifully even though I detest my rendition of it.

As a footnote to this composition, I am always reminded of a very lovely lady each time I hear it. You see I have my own leitmotifs just as anyone else. In 1932 when I was in Chicago with *George White's Scandals* I watched a condensed version of *Everybody's Welcome* at the Chicago Theater and I was entranced by the beauty and singing of a pert young creature who did the song so well. I tried to meet her only to find she had to rush for a train to get to the next city where the production was to play.

To me, here was true greatness, real star-quality. In addition she had great romantic appeal for me and this was another reason I wished to be introduced. (By this time my marriage to Fay Webb was definitely on the rocks.) Frankly, I think she was a bit frightened by the fact that I was married but maybe she *did* have to catch a train. This saucy-nosed lovely was billed as Harriet Lake and I'll never forget the way she handled "As Time Goes By." I knew she had "it" unmistakably and I was not too surprised when, as Ann Sothern, she achieved stardom in a motion picture called *Let's Fall in Love.*

The second Hupfeld "good-luck" opus was "When Yuba Plays the Rumba on the Tuba." The intricate music and wacky words were both those of dear old Herman himself. Walter O'Keefe did it first in *The Third Little Show* but I must blushingly state that this unique song is still associated with me due to a record I made of it as well as the air play I gave it. The record never was a big seller but it is rare to find anyone of that generation who does not remember it. It was different and just insane enough to catch favor in the wild, early Depression years of the early thirties.

Hupfeld was not a man who could write a simple, popular song the way, say, Irving Berlin does so masterfully. Most of his output had just a touch of the offbeat about them. Oh, he was a character with a mind of his own. He was to give me the most fantastic example of a contradictory song writer I had ever known. That, dear reader, is saying quite a lot, believe me.

We were in Rubinoff's dressing room at the Paramount Theater, Dave and I and Hupfeld. It was the typical plain dressing room and the three of us plus the piano were straining the seams of the cubicle. (Dressing rooms—the bane of the performer's existence! Maybe there are Elysian dressing rooms in that Great Backstage Up There! Until then, we must suffer.)

Anyway, Herman was, to put it as delicately as possible, somewhat inebriated and resultantly having a ball. He was all over the keyboard, demonstrating and selling Rubinoff his publisher's latest product.

After a number of these ploys, Hupfeld unaccountably began playing a melody from out of nowhere that caught me up short. He just sort of *wandered* into it!

"Herman, for God's sake! What is *that*?" I exclaimed.

"Oh, that," he answered, almost embarrassed. "I didn't *think* you'd like it."

"Like it!" I almost yelled. "It's marvelous. Have you got the words and music here?"

"You're kidding me, Rudy," he said rather sadly and thickly. He was reproachful, in the way a person who has been drinking is quick to take offense. "This is just a goddam nothing tune I wrote once for a musical."

"I am not kidding, Herman. It's a great song."

"Rudy, please do me a favor. Don't program it. It's one of the worst things I ever did. You're wasting your time. Please forget it. You want something *really* good, just listen to this—"

Then he went into another pop which I have long since forgotten—and so on far into the night. The next day I called the publisher.

"I know, I know. Herman told me," he said resignedly. "Look, Rudy, will you please lay off this tune. We've got—"

"Never mind what you've got. I want this one," I said firmly. "If you get me an orchestration of it, I'll feature it at the Atlantic City Steel Pier next week. Okay?"

"Okay," he muttered. "I still think you're crazy."

The publisher brought the arrangement down to me at the Pier during one of the intermissions and we programmed it quietly with no announcement, no fanfare at all. We played it, I did several vocal choruses and, by God, the audience broke into applause—something they had done for no other number all afternoon. I was convinced more than ever that this was a sleeper.

The following Thursday I scheduled it for the Fleischmann show but I hit a snag. A few minutes before air time a representative of the NBC "censor department" approached me.

"Rudy—about that closing number," he said ominously. "Either you take out the word 'bed' or we can't use it."

"Jesus Christ," I said as calmly as I could, "this is a helluva time to tell me. We're ready to go on the air."

"Now don't get excited," he replied soothingly. "It's just that word 'bed.' This is a family show, Rudy."

"It stays in," I almost shouted. "You've got to have a dirty mind to make something out of that in the context of what is really a sweet, sincere song."

"I didn't make the rules, Rudy!"

You don't fight City Hall or a network with only minutes to spare before a show goes on. I made a change from "bed" to "sleep" and the song still worked. It was a song that I and countless others, I am certain, still cherish, so apropos of the Depression times was its lyric and its mood.

"Rudy, if that song does *anything* for you," Hupfeld had said when he saw I was really going through with it, "I'll get you champagne for Christmas."

This charming ditty went for several hundred thousand records and sheet music!

In 1951 I was appearing at the Roosevelt Grill in New York City and had occasion to talk to the composer shortly before his death. "I never got all that champagne you promised me, Herman!" I kidded.

A few days later I received a magnum of champagne with a note of thanks for helping put over "Let's Put Out the Lights and Go to Sleep."

The sounds of my time and the grist for my mill were songs and songs and more songs. I have most of the records but I don't really need them— I can conjure up a mental playback whenever I want to. There were two million-copy items (records and sheet music) I introduced and still remember with pleasure: "Springtime in the Rockies" and "When Your Hair Has Turned to Silver." I popularized a song that was to launch the great Johnny Mercer. I was the first to give it a Negro dialect interpretation which was later adopted so aptly by Ben Bernie. It was "Lazy-bones" and it's still a standard.

And, yes, I booted a few, dammit! Just as Leo Reisman counted the profits he didn't get on the "Amherst prom song," sometimes I find myself adding up the royalties on hits I missed.

Once, it must have been about 1930, Georgie Joy came over to plug a tune for me while I was playing the Brooklyn Paramount. He caught me as I was coming offstage and I was upset and fuming about something that had gone amiss. After listening to a couple of choruses in my dressing room, I practically threw him out bodily; I also threw out a check for ten thousand dollars simultaneously since the Lombardos introduced "Swinging in a Hammock" and it was reputedly a million-copy smash. I was offered "Just a Gigolo" also but felt embarrassed to do the lyric. It was given instead to Vincent Lopez for introduction; I hope he had a cut-in on it for it must have made a bundle.

Near the end of the summer of '31 after a stint one evening on the Pennsylvania Roof, Jack Robbins and Jimmy McHugh came by with a bunch of English records they had just received. After a bite to eat we repaired to my apartment for a listening session.

One recording stood head and shoulders over the rest; great melody and lyrics, wonderfully recorded and possessing remarkable piano styling. The leader was an unknown (at least to us) Englishman named Ray Noble who was nonetheless very important to the English Victor company due to his unusual way of balancing instruments and his own unorthodox recording technique. I liked the song so well I promised Robbins I would make a few changes and it would become my theme song from the Pennsylvania Grill in the fall and I would program it on the first Thursday Fleischmann show. Between the Thursday we introduced it and the following Saturday afternoon over ten thousand copies of "Goodnight, Sweetheart" were sold, a pretty fantastic achievement for that, or any, day. Years later, in the late thirties, this hit was revived in the movies when I sang it as the character John D. Hackensacker III in *The Palm Beach Story*.

For some reason Victor gave the assignment to record the tune to Wayne King and I was so furious that I broke my contract with them, only to resume the affiliation a few years later.

You would think that, enchanted as I was with Ray Noble's composing prowess, I would have welcomed an opportunity to present his next song. Oh, no! The publisher brought me "The Very Thought of You" and I turned it down. To make this lapse in judgment even more harrowing, Warner Brothers made a movie using the song's title and played the tune throughout—every time I heard it I experienced considerable anguish at the thought I had booted it badly.

While we're on the subject of "hits I missed," I must blush to tell you

I turned my back on that perennial gold mine known as "Isle of Capri"; that was, conservatively speaking, many thousands of dollars that never graced the Vallee coffers. In all fairness to myself, I did pick Noble's "By the Fireside" which, while no "Goodnight, Sweetheart," had a very, very respectable sheet-music and record sale. For the record, any song that bears my name embodies changes I have made in both melody and lyrics—changes enough to justify the appearance of the name "Vallee" on the sheet music cover.

The year 1936 was very good to me in finding songs that were to be associated with me and endure through the years as a sort of trade-mark. It was the year Social Security went into effect, and the year Lindbergh went to Germany at Goering's invitation to inspect that nation's aviation achievements. When Lindy returned he warned the nation of the potentialities of German air power but no one paid much attention. That same year Bruno Hauptmann was electrocuted for the kidnaping of the Lindbergh child. This was the period when Broadway was graced by the Rodgers and Hart masterpiece, *On Your Toes*, and the motion-picture scene had such epics as *Anthony Adverse, The Great Ziegfeld, Mr. Deeds Goes to Town*, and Chaplin's *Modern Times*. It was an historical moment in politics, too, as FDR battled Alf Landon for the Presidency. *The Literary Digest*, you may remember, was a great magazine for straw votes on elections—the political counterpart, in a way, of the radio and TV rating systems of today. This respected magazine, it seems, predicted a landslide by Landon and copies of it are now collectors' items. Roosevelt carried every state except Maine and Vermont. At the same time, European sabers were rattling as Hitler moved into the Rhineland, Mussolini mopped up in Ethiopia, and the Spanish Civil War burst into flame.

Back in the States, though, we were at peace and making some progress at digging ourselves out of the rubble of the Depression. John Royal, a vice-president of NBC, returned from a trip to Europe and gave me a recording and the sheet music of a song. It had originated in Corsica where the language is a composite of French and Italian.

"All I know is that it's the rage of Paris," he said. "Why don't you look it over? It might make sense for you."

"John, if you've brought it back it must have something." I knew he was a good showman with years of experience dating back to his management of the Palace Theater in Cleveland. I looked it over and played the record. "The record doesn't do much for it," I said, "but there's definitely something there. I'll work up some English lyrics and get an arrangement made."

I began to plug it on the Fleischmann Hour every three or four weeks in '36 and '37 and eventually, as all good things must, it began to attract attention. As it started to click and the music stores began to get calls for it, the American publishers looked through their files to see if they, by any chance, happened to have it. M. Witmark and Sons found they had had it for years, and commissioned me for the English lyrics. I remember hearing on the radio with great satisfaction in the fall of '38, as I drove through the sweet-smelling orange groves of Santa Barbara, California, the mellow strains of "Vieni, Vieni" as *Number One* on "The Lucky Strike Hit Parade."

It was in '36 that I introduced "The Whiffenpoof Song" to the national radio audience. As an undergrad I had naturally heard it sung on the Yale campus by a select body of men who had formed a sort of singing and drinking society called The Whiffenpoofs which included some of the best voices at the school. I was never a Whiffenpoof and never received an invitation to join. It would have been impossible anyway as I was busy blowing my sax all over the area to put myself through school. All the same, it was a great song and remained in my memory even after I left New Haven.

The remnants of the haunting melody were brought to the forefront of my consciousness quite forcibly while I was appearing one afternoon on a special NBC radio show in 1936 called "Yale Around the World." It featured such divertissments as a radio pickup of the voice of alumnus Henry Luce, the *Time-Life* man, from his birthplace in China. In New New York I broadcast with Professor Phelps, Stanleigh P. Friedman, who composed three traditional songs for Yale ("Whoop It Up," "Glory For Yale," and "Sons of Eli"), and another of my classmates, Ben Cutler, football and hockey player, trombone and tenor sax-playing dilettante, who sang "The Whiffenpoof Song" since he had been a member of that select organization. It was sufficient to revive the memory of this great song and I programmed it the following Thursday and recorded it soon after for Victor's "Bluebird" label.

I was subsequently asked by a representative of Miller Music, Inc. to assist in the publication of the song, which I did, although steadfastly refusing to have my picture on the sheet-music cover since I knew this might not be acceptable to Yale men. I did help in designing the cover, however, made some changes in the harmony, and then wrote the alumni registrar of the university for a list of members who might wish to purchase copies. I figured they and their daughters might be able to play it more easily than the old-fashioned, four-part vocal arrangement which had appeared in the Yale song book for years.

A very nasty letter from the alumni secretary was the reward for my pains. It stated that he regarded the publication of the song for commercial reasons "reprehensible" and the alumni list was refused me! I replied that I wished in no way to enrich myself and that I would gladly turn over my royalties to the Yale alumni fund. This composition had such a poignancy and beauty, I continued, that it should become the property of music lovers all over the world.

Another cold letter was received and another refusal. There was nothing

I could do, as the song was already published. Miller Music, through much effort and expense, had secured the rights from the Rudyard Kipling Estate for use of the lyrics which had been adapted from one of Kipling's poems, "Gentlemen-Rankers." The other three composers and authors (one of whom was not even a Yale man) were to receive royalties and I assume they kept them, as they had every right to do.

Through the years I continued to do the song and, as its popularity increased, Miller sold several hundred thousand copies of sheet music, and my Bluebird recording, among others, flourished. My first two royalty checks were donated to the alumni fund with no thanks or even acknowledgement. I learned I was the butt of many jokes among some of the pin-brained undergraduates and some of the die-hard alumni because I had simply assisted in bringing this great song to the attention of the public. I decided future royalties would go instead to another of my favorite charities—Rudy Vallee!

Of the countless songs I was involved with there is one which is as closely associated with me as "The Stars and Stripes Forever" is with John Philip Sousa. It is, of course, the University of Maine "Stein Song." Its history of conception, introduction, and credit for popularization combined with "man's inhumanity to man" and lack of appreciation for composition are quite unparalleled in the chronicle of popular tunes.

The "Stein Song" had its beginnings as a march called "Opie" written by a German bass player named Emil Fenstad in 1901 and published by Carl Fischer, a band-instrument house and publisher of band music. Then, in 1904, two University of Maine freshmen decided to enter a contest designed to find a prize-winning Maine song. The competing songs were to be introduced and the winner chosen at a campus minstrel show.

One of these students was Adelbert Sprague who was later to become Professor of Music at the university as his father was before him. He knew of the march "Opie" and extracted a portion of its melody and gave it to his collaborator-roommate, Lincoln Colcord, who was later to become a famous author and authority on Japan. In thirty minutes Colcord completed the lyrics which I still consider among the finest of their type and which so perfectly mate with Fenstad's melody. The song was an instant hit at the minstrel show but there was some reluctance about using it as *the* Maine song. You see, it was quite obviously a drinking song and yet the sovereign state of Maine was still one of the last bastions of Prohibition, as dry as the Sahara and quite unlike its very damp neighbor, Massachusetts.

It was left for the president of the university to solve the problem. Returning from a weekend spree in Massachusetts, he resolved the matter once and for all. "In my opinion we should adopt the song," he announced in a brilliant piece of creative obfuscation. "After all, one may also raise steins containing milk or water!"

So it was thus made official and in the ensuing years it was sung by the student bodies, usually in a very uninspired manner. When I attended the university, 1921-22, these rather listless renditions did not cause the song to hit me with much of an impact. Yet somehow the melody and lyric continued to haunt me through the years after I left the university.

In the fall of '30 I decided to emulate in a small way on my radio program Fred Waring's presentations of the various marching songs of colleges which his audiences seemed to welcome. Naturally, one of the first I thought of was the "Stein Song" and I wrote Sprague at the University for a copy. For years the firm of Carl Fischer had been printing a supply to be sold at the University of Maine bookstore but I don't suppose over twenty or thirty copies were sold in any given semester.

Sprague dispatched the sheet music to me but tragically neglected to inform me that at that precise moment he was negotiating with Carl Fischer for the rights to publish the "Stein Song" there on the campus. He wished to buy the copper engraving plates which Fischer had been using for printing and, for a nominal sum, I am sure he could have secured the rights to that portion of "Opie" used in the song. I wish to God he had mentioned this—had he done so I might have waited until negotiations were completed one way or another. In that way, the royalties accruing to the university might well have built some fine edifice for the campus. Alas, it didn't happen that way at all.

Came the next Thursday's broadcast. We did the "Stein Song" as part of it and made our weary way from the Brooklyn Paramount stage to our other job at the Villa Vallee, and began our "swing shift" which lasted until four A.M.

As usual, there were a number of song-pluggers lined up along the wall to give me the big hello, to thank me for doing one of their tunes or beseech me to give one of their new gems a "ride real soon." However, on this evening, this post-"Stein Song" evening, the lot of them behaved rather strangely. After all kinds of eyewash, palaver, and circumlocution, they came down, to a man, to the basic question:

"Who published the college song you did this evening?"

This strange fixation of these promoters coupled with an unprecedented number of wires from Fleischmann listeners made it obvious that the Colcord-Fenstad opus might well prove to be the most popular song I had ever introduced.

Other than the purchase of a saxophone, I had never had any dealings with the Fischer people but I got in touch with them immediately to report the potential I felt the song had. I spoke to one of the executives, Walter Fischer, who agreed to send an emissary to discuss the matter.

The next day I had switched to the New York Paramount when between shows I was confronted by a rather cold-blooded minion from Fischer's establishment with a somewhat Prussian mien. He constantly looked as if he had just finished shouting "*Dumkopf!*"

He had just witnessed our performance wherein we were required to do three encores of the "Stein Song." "Well, Mr. Vallee," he said deadpan, probably playing it very cool, "what do you propose we should do about this number?"

I just looked at him incredulously for a moment. "Did you see what happened to the audience out there just then when we played it?" I exclaimed. "You've got the goddamnedest hit in years!"

"So?"

"My good man," I said as dispassionately as I could at the time, "all you've got to do is put out popular sheet music on it and sit back and watch it go!"

"But, Mr. Vallee, suppose it does *not* go. We will be out of pocket over two hundred dollars."

It was difficult to get through to this man. "I tell you what I'll do," I said. "You go ahead and I promise to buy up any copies you get stuck with. Fair enough?"

"Done. Now what sort of a royalty arrangement shall we make with you?"

"I've made legitimate changes in the song which I believe add to its commercial value—I think one-third of the composer-author royalties would be agreeable." I assumed, of course, that Colcord and Fenstad had contracts with Fischer.

This was agreed upon and the first batch of copies printed were sold in the course of the first day. I didn't have to buy up any overstock! The record we made in '30, which I have always thought very poor, sold tremendously even though the recording industry was going into a monumental slump. The "Stein Song" swept the world before it and was published in just about every country that harbored a printing press. It made the University of Maine known world-wide and I am told the attendance there the following fall increased considerably.

Then the bomb dropped. Lincoln Colcord called me from Maine with alarming news. "Rudy, you better brace yourself. You're going to get clobbered. One of the newspapers is going to publish a story about the 'Stein Song.' You're going to be the 'heavy.' You know—you're getting royalties and I'm not."

"Lincoln, for God's sake! You mean you're not getting paid?"

"Hell no. I don't have any contract. On top of that, the publisher just offered me five hundred bucks!"

"That's ridiculous, Lincoln. Look—you get down here as fast as you can. I'm going to set up a meeting with the publishers and we'll get this straightened out!"

A council of war was set up which included an impartial arbitrator. We found that Colcord had never given the university any right to use his lyrics. After all, it is rare indeed when an undergraduate demands a contract for a school song from his Alma Mater! This left Carl Fischer holding a most embarrassing bag with no legal right to Colcord's lyrics. The copies they had sold had in a sense been unauthorized copies!

In legal ruling on such matters where a man's melody or lyric is used without contractual consent, a judge has no alternative but to give him all or any rightful part of the royalties that he may demand. Realizing that Colcord could secure the entire amount the song had earned for the publishers, they asked him what he wanted. Before I could stop him he settled for $3000, although royalties at that time would have amounted to at least six or seven thousand dollars.

There is a sad postscript to this story. The song probably earned in the neighborhood of a quarter of a million dollars (as the publisher's share) for Carl Fischer which would have paid for a gymnasium (then a-building) for the university's campus. This bonanza Fischer practically stumbled over because it was hardly necessary to spend a single dollar for plugging or promotion. The Fischer organization was hardly aware they had it in their catalogue! The song was so inherently great all we had to do was give it an up-to-date arrangement and it took off like a rocket. Every band and singer had to program it by popular demand whether they liked it or not. Although I donated a share of my royalties to the gymnasium fund, I have always regretted that it was not possible for the university to have owned the song completely.

I don't think there is any question in the minds of those who remember the 1930 introduction of the "Stein Song" that I not only introduced it but popularized it and was definitely associated with it. Even today, more than thirty years later, the drama critics have recalled it when reviewing the musical *How to Succeed in Business Without Really Trying.* The mock college marching song, "Grand Old Ivy," which I do in the show, they have dubbed an echo of the venerable "Stein Song."

Be that as it may, the NBC lawyer who presided at the meeting wherein Colcord received his utmost due decided to take a great big bow for the discovery and popularization of this composition! This NBC executive gave the press a fantastic story, something to the effect that "in an effort to test the power of radio it was decided to choose a song very unlikely to be popular"—willy-nilly a college marching song in 6/8 time was pulled out of the dank and musty files of Fischer's march catalogue— and, in a most clever coup, the song was given to Rudy Vallee since he had gone to the University of Maine! In retrospect it is a rather droll fiction but at the time I was fuming. That any individual or group of individuals could have been so vainglorious as to hand the public such a crock of self-seeking malarky was beyond comprehension. Fortunately, I doubt that anyone who read the story gave it much heed.

And so it went, down through the years: the joyful songs and the sad songs, the smashes and the bombs. There were the sweet, lively hits from the Broadway musicals and the sometimes overblown ballads from the movies. My God, how many man-hours did we put in on the stand grinding out the trivia (and an occasional minor masterpiece) of the day....

A drunk yells out from the night-club floor to sing the "Sow Song"! Ironic! By many it's associated with me but I never sang it. Cyril Smith was the vocalist when we recorded it for Victor. He was managed by me and my pianist wrote the melody. But I still get requests. . . .

I am riding in a cab in New York in 1938. On the radio a record is playing and on it I hear myself singing (and laughing) "The Drunkard Song." At the end of the rendition the station's disk jockey asks rhetorically, "What caused you to break up, Rudy?" Well, in 1935, I had been asked to make this record, at a time when I was as close to a nervous breakdown as I'll ever be. The lyrics struck me as so hysterically ludicrous that I broke up constantly throughout the session. The recording engineers finally decided to let the machines roll and take what they could get. The boys in the band caught on and began to make crazy faces and bizarre interpolations on their instruments which abetted the general hysteria. I believe most listeners adduced that I was a trifle tight but, so help me, these are the facts. . . .

I am dancing in 1925 to the dulcet strains of Jack Hylton at the Piccadilly Hotel in London. I hear a tune which is to become closer to me than all the others. I program it as a theme on radio from '29 to '39 and from '40 to '47. Its lyrics say so eloquently and yet simply that "We are here to perform for you." I never receive a penny in royalties for it but "My Time is Your Time" is, in so many wonderful ways, "my" song....

And so on and so on, song after song. A bandleader, a crooner, a dispenser of trivia. Perhaps. But, God, I had a lovely time of it and I like to think my listeners shared that lovely time.

CHAPTER XII

Hand Me Down My Crystal Ball

"When the Pussywillow Whispers to the Catnip"

I SEEM ALWAYS TO HAVE HAD A FACILITY for sensing the talent potential in a person and the possible appeal a song might have for an audience. Now I am not going to tell you that I hear a little bell ring at the moment when I am confronted with a performer of genius but, goddamit, *something* happens.

Someone has said that if I had put under my management every person who made that "something" happen within me, I would have a stable of paragons equal to that of the large talent agencies of today.

"My God, Rudy," a friend once remarked, "if you had only signed Edgar Bergen and collected a percentage down through the years you would have made a fortune."

"There's only one thing wrong with that statement," I answered. "I regret to say that I had nothing to do with bringing Bergen on the show. As a matter of fact, if he had listened to me and used Mortimer Snerd, the country-bumpkin effigy, instead of Charlie McCarthy, he might not have made it as easily." I sensed Bergen was a tremendous talent but my advice was something less than Olympian.

As a matter of fact, it would have been impossible to put under contract many of these individuals whom it has been my privilege to guide and help, because it is always difficult for one performer to manage another. It's like one heavyweight boxer handling another heavyweight— it just doesn't work very smoothly. Moreover, once an artist is signed with you it is difficult to keep him. They generally feel their success would have come anyway without your help and, as most agents know, there is little gratitude from the temperamental client.

This intuition, this "something," first manifested itself when at the age of fifteen I would pick out a record in my father's drugstore that seemed to "have it" and begin to give it a "ride." I would plug the number on the phonograph and dispose of large numbers of it as the customers seemed to agree with my choice.

When I was first a "bit player" on saxophone in various rather undistinguished dance bands, the leaders generally took my advice on what songs to program during the course of an evening. I built something of a reputation for picking out a group of tunes that would make a well-balanced, crowd-pleasing sequence. And when I was in London at the Savoy I stumbled upon some real "pop" classics which I brought back with me and which became million-copy sellers.

Now it can be told; the story is out—*I Discovered Rudolph Valentino!* Here's how it happened. I was watching a motion picture in Portland, Maine. It was *The Four Horsemen of the Apocalypse* and featured (not starred) a dark gentleman who wore a Gaucho outfit and tangoed beautifully. I was intrigued by his star quality, and that "something" happened. In a few years I was not surprised to find him becoming the idol of the feminine hearts of America in *The Sheik*. I felt a little smug in having discovered him. The only thing that detracted from my smugness was the fact that a few million other movie fans had discovered him at the same time.

All right—so I *respond* to greatness. What's so bad about that? One evening we Yale Collegians were playing on the same bill with Fred Allen who preceded us, in New Britain, Connecticut. Sting! I got the message quick—here was the sound of genius. I listened attentively to every joke he uttered, and realized that here was cerebral humor fit for the gods—and people too. He was a vaudevillian at the time (in '26) but I could have easily predicted then that he would be a sensation if he found the proper medium. He found it—the one I found—radio! I was so enamored that while waiting on the stage in the dark I memorized his whole act and did the impression through the later years. There'll never be another like him.

My first real perception of completely undiscovered greatness was in the fall of '26, during the December vacation, when I came down from New Haven to spend a night in New York. I had a date with a luscious Shubert chorus girl and we wound up at a club on Fifty-second Street called the High Hat. During the show a young lady from Philadelphia, a friend of one of the performers, was induced to do a couple of numbers. To me her style and delivery were so fresh and unique that I told my friends at Yale to be sure to catch her when she appeared the following fall in New Haven with a Shubert show. She must not have been very well presented because my buddies who caught her seemed to think I had given them a bum steer. Once when I picked my Shubert chorine up at her hotel, her room was crowded with the gals from the chorus having a snack and this great stylist happened to be among them. I told her straightforwardly how much I loved her bit at the *High Hat* and the rest of the girls, including my date, looked at me as though I had taken leave of my senses. A few years later the *boop-boop-a-doop* style was sweeping the country and this young character, Helen Kane, was its delightful purveyor.

The first time I had the opportunity to guide and help a talented personality came after we, the Connecticut Yankees and I, had arrived and were playing the New York Paramount. The doorman informed me a young man who had come all the way from Baltimore (I recall I was told he had walked!) was outside to play the harmonica for me. I needed to hear him on only one composition to know that here was a most sensitive and gifted artist. Without hesitation I sent him to the producers of the various Paramount stage shows and was overjoyed to find him a few weeks later earning five hundred dollars a week as one of the outstanding features of a Balaban and Katz presentation. Of course, this man was Larry Adler and I don't suppose a greater harmonica virtuoso ever lived. I wanted him desperately for the Villa Vallee as a regular performer but the owner couldn't see it!

In 1929 I appeared in a film short, one of the early experiments in three-dimensional films. The cast was made up of unknowns plus a few vaudeville and musical-comedy performers in and about New York. I'll never forget the appearance of a rather thin, angular, flapperish-appearing girl who had a very small part in the proceedings. Out of the twenty or thirty persons in the cast I marked her for a great future. I still have this short in my film collection and take great delight in projecting it and asking friends if they recognize this young lady. They never do even though it is the glamorous, Academy Award-winning Ginger Rogers. The night of Ginger's triumph in *Girl Crazy* we spent dancing at the Central Park Casino. Had I not been set on the idea of marriage to Fay Webb, I feel that our casual evening might have developed into something much more serious.

Then there were these two violinists. One I spotted in the string section of the large Paramount Theater orchestra and hired to lead one of the orchestras we were supplying for debutante and other society functions around New York. After several years of this work, he went out fronting his own band with my blessing and even today the name Richard Himber is in the fond recollection of a host of listeners and dancers as a great band leader of taste and originality.

The other fiddler was enormously gifted as a soloist, conductor, and arranger. For years he had beaten his brains out in the pits of theaters and, while he gave great pleasure to multitudes, no one seemed to recognize that here was a great star in the rough, so to speak, just waiting to be mined by some manager or promoter.

"Rudy, I'm getting fed up with pit work," he said to me one day in that quaint Russian accent of his. "You're making it big in radio—maybe there's a place there for me too, no?"

"I'd never thought about it," I said. "Maybe there is a place for you in radio."

"Just get me an audition with your network boys—I'll kill them!"

They turned out to be *nyetwork* boys! After several weeks of hemming and hawing after the audition, we got a big *no*—they "saw" nothing in him.

After I had been on the air for Fleischmann a few months, the sponsor, Standard Brands, asked me to do still another show for another of their products, Chase and Sanborn Coffee. I declined the honor because I felt I could not do justice to two shows; could not, as it were, serve two masters. Nevertheless, Standard Brands pressed me for suggestions for talent on the new coffee show and I asked for a few days to think about it.

As I watched my violinist friend do his overture at the Brooklyn Paramount (I was in the wings waiting to go on with the Connecticut Yankees) I suddenly realized here was the perfect man for my sponsor's Sunday night show! First of all, he had an exotic, intriguing, long-hairish name—Rubinoff, and he played the violin in a serious musical way as well as, when necessary, with humorous effects. But above all he could mix orchestral colors as no one else could. There are few men who can conduct an orchestra to perfection (especially in light popular music or selections from operettas) and deliver the dynamic effects Rubinoff could in his fabulous overtures.

I arranged for my sponsor's executives and the ad agency's representatives, all of them cold-blooded Yankee businessmen, to catch Rubinoff's one o'clock show. The timing was calculated—at that hour the audience was predominantly female, a gender that always found Dave delightful. As it happened, the maestro had an unusually fine overture that week, one in which he took a popular tune and played it the way it might be interpreted in various countries around the world. The big shots were captivated.

Next the network brass had to be sold and a closed-circuit broadcast was arranged so an audition could be "piped" into the offices of the NBC executives on Fifth Avenue. As a theme song I suggested to Dave that he use the lovely melody, "Give Me a Moment Please," from the motion picture *Monte Carlo*. Further, I aided him in selecting the numbers he would use for the audition, which was a success.

A one-year contract was negotiated and I helped arrange the fee. Irving Berlin's secretary, Benny Bloom, saw me on the street. "Rudy, I understand Rubinoff's gonna land the Chase and Sanborn show."

"That's right," I said.

"Why don't you be smart? Form an agency. Handle Rubinoff and take a commission."

"Benny, I can't take commission from a man when I'm earning four or five thousand a week myself."

"All right. I understand. But let me handle it. . ."

"No," I said. "I just can't bring myself to do it."

My reward was the satisfaction of having a part in bringing this fine entertainer to radio. On his first network show I appeared to introduce him to this, his first radio audience. I told how Victor Herbert had brought him to America and in a few succinct words tried to sell him to these new listeners.

Later on, when coffee sales began to slump and the show's rating weakened, Rubinoff was tempted to leave the show but I persuaded him to stay.

"Hang on, Dave," I adjured him. "The fans you make among the radio listeners will come to see you in droves when you make personal-appearance tours. I know. It happened to me."

When Eddie Cantor joined the show and the rating climbed tremendously, Rubinoff's salary increased until he was making more money than I was on my own broadcast!

Ironically, before Dave began his radio series, I received a call from the character who managed me for the network. "I hear this Rubinoff is a very hot property," he said breathlessly. "How's about putting me in touch so we can handle the deal?"

"Sorry, old boy," I answered, trying to keep the gloating out of my voice. "You had your chance. Remember when you said he had nothing for you? I'm not going to let you get on the bandwagon now that it's already rolling!"

There was also, as I have said, a lovely young lady by the name of Alice Faye, she of the warm smile, the lovely blond tresses, the pert, frank, and open face. The moment I first heard her clowning and singing at one of the cast parties thrown by the *George White's Scandals* (she was a mere chorus girl at the time!) I knew her instinctive gift for handling light rhythmic songs combined with tremendous physical appeal would carry her far. I never thought of her as a fine actress but later on Zanuck and the Fox Studios, by giving her the right roles and guiding her in that direction, brought out these other facets of her personality.

I still delight in kidding a top executive who said I was wasting the comparatively modest amount of money I paid Alice each week to sing on the Fleischmann Hour.

"Don't worry about it," I told him. "Mark my words. Some day you will be offering her five thousand a week and she'll spit in your eye."

So help me, this same executive later tried to sign her for that exact figure for a shoe-polish manufacturer's weekly broadcast and she turned him down!

One night in '32 I was really down in the dumps as I returned to my apartment from performances at the Pennsylvania Hotel and in the *Scandals*. The apartment was agonizingly empty since my wife Fay was at that time preferring California to New York.

I turned on the radio and my spirits rose somewhat at hearing the strains of "Violets," my SAE fraternity song. It was the theme used by Herbie Fields and his orchestra broadcasting from some hotel in Denver. My morale improved much more as I heard the band vocalist sing "I've Got an Evening for Sale"; while she was not an exceedingly gifted singer her vocal quality was so different, so compelling that I immediately dispatched a wire to Fields thanking him for "Violets" and complimenting the girl singer's rendition.

It must have been about three years later—I was watching the rest of the show waiting for my introduction—when I felt a tap on the shoulder. I turned and was confronted with a handsome gentleman who gave me the SAE grip. He introduced himself as Herbie Fields and then presented me to a lovely, dark-haired girl who was with him. For some reason he neglected to tell me at the time that she was his wife but he did make a gift of her to me to guide and manage with no strings attached. Of course, she was the singer I had so admired on the broadcast long ago, Dorothy Lamour.

I invited her to my office and made plans to present her in some smart New York supper club. I knew El Morocco needed something to stimulate business and, since they did not present personalities, I felt she might inaugurate a new policy. John Perona, the club's owner, happened to use the same attorney that I did and in the past had sought my advice on public-address systems and on which bands to use in his room. He was enthusiastic and agreed to try Dottie if I would consent to introduce her to the audience. I agreed. She did several numbers from the musical *Anything Goes* and the listeners seemed to like her but Perona was very noncommittal.

"Very well," I thought. "If Yale doesn't want her, maybe Harvard will!" I took her to Sherman Billingsley at the Stork Club and he instantly agreed to use her, and there she remained for eight weeks.

By this time one of my aides had arranged for her to begin a sustaining (unsponsored) show on the network. A Paramount scout heard her and we let Dottie make her own deal with the studio where, as the Sarong Girl, she traveled many "roads" with the Messrs. Hope and Crosby. Of all the personalities it has been my good fortune to help, I believe Dorothy Lamour is the most grateful and appreciative. I have a feeling that if I ever really needed her help I would only have to ask it of her.

In the summer of 1934 I was driving through the night from a dance date at Wilkes-Barre, Pennsylvania, on the way back to New York for a Thursday rehearsal and broadcast. Over the radio I heard an announcer's voice which *Time* Magazine later described as sounding like "a bunch of frogs in a shoe-box." It emanated from a small station in Alexandria, Virginia. At that time disk jockeys *per se* were practically unknown but this individual was spinning platters and, in between, sounding off

in his inimitable relaxed and folksy way. I was so taken by his unorthodox approach that when I reached New York, tired and dusty as I was,
I took the trouble to send him a wire (see picture No. 20)

Of course, Arthur has become the greatest money-maker for CBS
in that network's history. At the time I was first exposed to this man's
"audio-charm" I tried to convince John Reber (the same radio executive
who worried about my paying Alice Faye!) that Godfrey was right for
our show. No dice. I don't know why I never needled him about it. He
probably forgot the incident, anyway, the way he had probably forgotten
turning down Fred Allen for our broadcasts over my vehement urging.

"Allen is finishing up his series for that starch company," I pleaded.
"He will be great for our show! There's nobody around like him."

"You're wrong, Rudy," he said pontifically. "Allen is too special
for the masses."

Later on this man had to eat those words when he chose Allen for the
Chase and Sanborn Show over which Fred presided for a long, long time!

One evening I was to hear a torrent of unusual sounds coming from
the speakers on the stage I had just left after playing a benefit. I rushed
back to watch an amazing, almost bewildering, series of impressions done
by a very young, dark-haired boy. They were performed with such perfection that I stood transfixed. I was so engrossed that I did not realize
that Harry Hershfield, the famous columnist and raconteur, who was
running the benefit, was watching me for my reaction.

"You look interested, Rudy," he muttered at my elbow.

I turned to him. "Where on earth did you get this kid, Harry! He's
terrific! Maybe I can do something for him."

"Why the hell do you think I put him on the show? I *want* you to
take him under your wing."

Al Bernie was only fourteen years of age at the time and technically I
was violating the law—but I presented him anyway at the Hollywood
Restaurant as part of our company. Three weeks later he was on his
way with his mother and father to play a Chicago theater at three hundred and fifty a week plus fares for the family.

This talented youngster became a part of our company and shared the
headaches and heartaches and the fun through the years of one-nighters,
theaters, the Astor Roof, the Cocoanut Grove, and the summer vacations
at my lodge in Maine. He was always straying from his great impressions
of famous people and trying to do straight comedy, a transition I tried to
discourage. Nevertheless, today he plays the Copacabana, the country's
leading theaters as well as the Las Vegas oases, and other top night spots.
Perhaps he has never equaled the acclaim of say, a Joe E. Lewis, but I am
happy to say he is doing very, very well!

Do you remember Earlyne Schools, gentle reader? Do you remember
Victoria Schools? George Abbott changed the "Earlyne" to "Victoria"

when he directed her in *Best Foot Forward*, the wonderful Rodgers and Hart musical. There's a good chance you don't remember her—she was around only a tragically short time at the height of her artistry. But if you were lucky enough to hear her truly at her very best, then unquestionably you will always recall her with pleasure. She was certainly one of my most amazing protegées.

I first encountered her at the home of a famous jeweler in New York City. Richard Rodgers was playing the piano and she was singing his "Blue Moon," first in one octave then suddenly soaring an octave higher in a voice that was extraordinary in its purity and beauty. Then she sang "Will You Remember" from Sigmund Romberg's *Maytime* and my throat tightened with emotion—here was a veritable Jenny Lind.

Although Sam Goldwyn was later to put her under contract, it was my privilege to present her at the Astor Roof with us that summer as well as feature her on our broadcasts. During the years I managed her I secured her a screen test at Warner Brothers and saw her triumph in the aforementioned *Best Foot Forward*. Sigmund Romberg himself took her on tour with his orchestra.

Earlyne was possessed of a strange, introverted personality. She was given to dark moods and periods of despondency. We must assume that one of these fits of melancholy was too much for her. She must have found herself so deep in the quicksands of gloom that she was unable to fight her way out, for she took her own life. Thus were millions of people deprived of the chance to savor the voice of this Jenny Lind of another day. Thank God for the chances I had!

You talk about characters! I worked with one I'll put up against the most outlandish you can nominate. He was from Niles, Michigan. I do not know whether his birthplace is significant, having never met anyone else from Niles—for all I know everybody in Niles may be a character! At any rate, we picked him up in Washington during one of our tours. He was playing a Chinese restaurant and it was quite an act. The corniest line of jokes you ever heard opened the bit—then he would play drums, piano, and trumpet *simultaneously*. He billed himself, appropriately enough, as Vic Hyde, "The One-Man Band." Like Larry Adler, Vic enjoyed his greatest successes in England, playing all the spots from posh night clubs to that pinnacle of British entertainment achievement, the Palladium.

To us he was a loyal though eccentric character. Every year he sought to increase the number of trumpets he could play at the same time. Once at my lodge in Maine he conceived a brilliant idea. He had a trumpet made which was exceptionally long. With this bizarre instrument in tow he swam to the middle of the lake, submerged until only the bell of the horn protruded above water and played a solo! Well, it takes all kinds. I only hope that music historians will mark well this epic accomplishment in the annals of man's creativity. Somebody should write a book about *him*! In the event they do, I append another Hyde anecdote for the prospective author's edification. . . .

While Vic and the rest of us were playing the Astor Roof one time, the doctor discovered that the one-man band would have to be a one-lung man for a while. One of his lungs was tubercular and had to be deflated in order to heal. Naturally, I told Vic it would not be necessary to perform during this period. But no! He insisted on working every show. It's tough enough to play one trumpet with two lungs but by this time this virtuoso by use of a specially designed mouthpiece had made his dream come true—he was playing four trumpets at once *with one lung*! Oh, yes—I almost forgot—as he played the trumpets he did a tap dance. When we went on tour shortly thereafter Hyde would drive all night to our next booking and appear fresh as a daisy for the show. In spite of all this I am happy to report that Maestro Hyde recovered completely.

I greatly admired a lithe, long-limbed, blond beauty (for the nonce I skipped brunettes) appearing in a Brooklyn stage show. She was an amazing, exotic creature, born in China and spoke several languages including French and Chinese. We shared many enchanting evenings of rather torrid climate. I was proud to introduce her to many Broadway personalities to whom I described her as a real find. I especially stressed her delightful sense of comedy. It was Lou Holtz who brought her to real stardom in his show, *You Said It.* And so to Hollywood and a very promising career and—a man. Man happened to be married and couldn't get free, and Lyda Roberti committed suicide. I guess it's an old story, triangular and all that; probably happens more often than we realize. Still so many of us miss her deeply, a marvelous talent just beginning to bud.

There was still another time I felt that *something* happen in the presence of unusual beauty—and here I got considerably more involved than if I had been a mere manager. At the time I was in the anguishing throes of a hopeless love affair with a girl who will have to be (I beg your indulgence) nameless. The two of us sat watching a newsreel and suddenly on the screen appeared three girls modeling the latest WAC uniforms. The shot was from the back and then, one by one, the girls turned their heads toward the camera. The last was a luscious brunette with eyes of a certain Chinese quality and a beautiful, white-toothed smile. I was mesmerized but didn't dwell on the happenstance. That same week *Life* magazine ran stills featuring the same girls. I had to find out about the one I admired. Through friends in Washington I was informed that she was Jane Greer and made myself the recipient of her address and telephone number.

I called her and found that she and her mother had been radio fans of mine for a long time. When I explained that my interest was personal as well as managerial, she expressed a willingness to come to Hollywood where I would undertake to direct her career.

However, at that moment, fate decided to warm up my "hopeless" love affair (see above) and, in the interim, Howard Hughes stepped in to sign Jane and bring her to Hollywood himself for a career in pictures. Hughes forbade her to go out in public but she remembered my phone call and was soon singing at some of my Coast Guard band appearances. A more charming, talented, and gracious person I shall never know.

Ah yes, I was destined to be much more than a mere manager. Our wedding was military and as we walked out under the crossed-sword arcade created by my comrades-in-arms I had every hope that I had come to the end of my search for the perfect mate. But it just didn't happen. It was entirely my fault that it didn't. Fortunately, time (I hope) has brought happiness to Jane—successes in pictures, a devoted husband and children. It was my belief then, and always will be, that had she really desired to reach the heights, she could have been the Katherine Cornell (whom she resembles) of her generation.

I wish I could take the bow that so many people would like me to take for the appearance of the illustrious personalities that we were presenting throughout these years on our Fleischmann broadcasts. I did save Joe (You Wanna Buy a Duck?) Penner from a nerve-racking first Coast-to-Coast broadcast. I had worked with him at the Brooklyn Paramount and knew his act thoroughly. When I found him nervously trying to memorize a song that had been especially written for him on this show, I was aghast. It was a silly song—something about "Flies." It seemed that my co-director of the show (who represented the advertising agency) didn't feel that Joe's little song, "When the Pussywillow Whispers to the Catnip" had any merit. I knew better than my associate that Joe Penner was what we call in show business a "worrier" and that even if he were doing the same act which he had done a thousand times, this first broadcast would be a nightmare to him. But to ask him to memorize a new song which he might fluff would cause him to panic. Therefore, I insisted we permit him to do the "Pussywillow" song. It not only was one of the hits of the broadcast but became the theme song of his own radio series for my sponsors over a period of several years.

I cannot honestly take a bow for even the selection of Burns and Allen, Bob Hope, Milton Berle, Red Skelton, Carmen Miranda, Ezra Stone, Lou Holtz, and the hundreds of personalities who were first presented on our broadcast. I did suggest Kate Smith, but for the most part I was too busy with my theater appearances and one-nighters and other things that often took me out of town between broadcasts. I must pay high praise to the boys of the Thompson Agency who worked with me, for the countless hours they spent in weeding out talent and finding dramatic performers and the scripts for them. That's what made this series of broadcasts so memorable to so many millions of people.

Perhaps the only thing for which I can take credit is that I was enabled, through my own projection of the qualities of casual relaxation, to convey some of this tranquilizing effect to some of my nervous performers who appeared on this series. Sherman Billingsley has always said that he was frightened enough to faint but somehow my arm around his shoulders kept him standing there during our interview.

It is to the credit of Ed Gardner (whom most of us know as "Duffy" of Duffy's Tavern) that John Barrymore, in his last days, was to give such delight to those who tuned in on our Sealtest broadcasts from California. I seconded Ed's suggestion that we use Barrymore, although I reminded him that there would be days when we might wonder whether John would be there or whether something untoward might happen on the broadcast itself. But I'll never lose the thrill of working with that magnificent personality whom I had admired from afar as I watched him play Hamlet in London in 1925 before a packed house of swooning females. I never dreamed then that one day I would clown with him in a series of radio broadcasts that will never be equaled for the fabulous qualities of bombast and shading that he gave our simple but well-written scripts—scripts that were written by writers who today have combined salaries of fifteen or twenty thousand dollars a week and whom we then bought for several hundreds of dollars.

That John never missed a broadcast nor at any time ever gave any offense, but rather lifted our program to the highest rating it ever achieved, is tribute to this enigmatical but true genius of the spoken word. The recordings I have of these broadcasts are treasures that I prize more highly than I can say!

In 1941 while John was on our show, I was to discover two personalities whose great success today cannot help but fill me with a great sense of pride and satisfaction. One was a girl, who actually was discovered by my associate in our little agency of "Rudy Vallee Presents." Here was a gal with a voice so powerful and yet of such great clarity and bell-like quality that I still feel she has no rival in the singing of popular music and musical comedy. Although her broadcasting appearances were few, I had forgotten (until she reminded me of it) that I did arrange for her to sing at our Pirate's Den, a club which I had conceived in co-operation with Don Dickerman in Hollywood. In the pressure of my work I had forgotten about her and, although I had read somewhere that a Dolores Gray had appeared in several New York musical comedies and had received some help in her career from Mary Martin, I was not sure that this was my same protégée whom I had managed for a short time.

Then I read in a *Variety* spread-page advertisement the description of the final night of *Annie Get Your Gun*, which had run in London for over two years. The entire audience had stood up to cheer the petite star of the show, a blond girl named Dolores Gray. They had sung "Auld Lang Syne" to her on this her final night of triumph. I was sure that this could not be "our" Dolores Gray as the girl I had presented in Hollywood was a rather hefty brunette, a girl of Greek extraction. Later on, as Mrs. Vallee and I noted the opening of a new show in New York, a show called *Two on the Aisle,* starring Dolores Gray and Bert Lahr, I purchased two seats for the opening-night performance. I was delighted on opening the theater program to read (in the summary of her career) that Dolores Gray gave credit to me for having first put her on the air and, in a sense, having discovered her. The fact that she saw fit to single me out from the many who must have helped her along the way was most gratifying. But after the show, as we went backstage to her dressing room to congratulate her, to see her push everyone aside and scream that here was the man who had first discovered her filled my cup to overflowing. Frankly, I did little or nothing really to help Dolores Gray, but, in a sense, her exaggeration of my part in her career made up for the failure of some of those I *did* help ever to mention it publicly.

During my Sealtest broadcasts, I was getting close to my enlistment in the United States Coast Guard. War with Germany was steadily approaching. The head of the Warner Brothers radio station in Hollywood, Harry Maizlish, telephoned to tell me that he had a truly great comedian whom he wanted me to watch work. I suggested that he bring him to the Pirate's Den where I would put him on and let him perform.

This comedian with black curly hair and very dynamic magnetic eyes sought at first to interest me in his scrapbook. But before he could stop me, I had introduced him to the audience and before he had done two numbers I was falling off my chair in uncontrollable laughter. Although he insisted that I present him on my radio program, I told him there was only one broadcast that was tailor-made for him and that was the Bing Crosby show. On my show, between Barrymore and me, there was barely time enough for each of us to acquit ourselves satisfactorily and there would be no room for a third on our broadcast. I did ask him to do the warm-up before our broadcast the following night at which I would have the producers of the Crosby show to watch him work. Suffice to say that he left no laughter in our audience by which to test out *our* script that night! He literally wrung them dry. The next day I had the satisfaction of receiving calls from my own sponsors and the Crosby show. Both wanted him. I took this man, Victor Borge, to Grace Hayes, out at her lodge, where she immediately offered more money for Borge than I knew she would ever pay for any act. Later, I arranged for a screen test of Borge at 20th-Century-Fox. Unknown to me, he had been working in a gas station as a filling attendant, but I sensed somehow that his finances were at a low ebb. Although I had arranged for him to make three appearances on the Crosby show, these were still two weeks away. But I had no hesitancy in advancing him funds as I knew that this artist had a gift for the creation of comedy monologues and bits of business (with simple things such as a handkerchief, a chair, sheets of music) unequaled by any comedian of the past, present, or future. I made the prediction to him that he would be with Crosby for one year. So what! He made me a liar by two weeks. He was with Bing for fifty-four weeks. Eventually we had to release him to one of the most successful talent agencies, the Music Corporation of America, who along with the William Morris Agency and all the networks had failed to see this boy's great genius when he had been brought to them by Harry Maizlish weeks before.

Borge had skipped out of Denmark just before the Nazis marched in and had come to the attention of Ed Sullivan who, in the fall of 1940, wanted to use him in a stage show. However, there was a conflict of ideas about what Borge should do and, on opening night, Borge refused to go on. For some unaccountable reason he found his way down to Palm Beach, Florida, where he worked at the Everglades Club. There he came to the attention of one of the Warner Brothers, Albert Warner, who sent him to Hollywood to Maizlish. The latter peddled him all over the cinema capital—with no takers!

I am more proud of Borge's success, perhaps, than that of any of the personalities I have known or helped. It is still absolutely impossible for me to understand how anyone could have failed to recognize instantly that he was destined to become one of the most refreshing and different comedians of our day and age. The fact that he has, as a one-man show, broken records everywhere and has earned over a million dollars in the last few years speaks for itself. The fact that Borge never mentions my recognition of his talent and my careful guiding of his career at a time when he needed it so badly is not important. He is a great artist, and an artist is only supposed to remember his lines.

CHAPTER XIII

Home Is Where You Hang Your Hat

"A Wandering Minstrel, I"

THE LIFE OF THE ENTERTAINER TODAY
has considerable kinship with that of the peripatetic troubadour of
ancient times. I wouldn't be surprised to learn that paleolithic man had
his extroverts who wandered from cave to cave giving impromptu reci-
tals as they rhythmically banged away on the jawbone of a mammoth.
To make it then and to make it now you've got to have a touch of the
wanderlust, a dash of gypsy blood in your veins—or you'll go out of your
bloody mind. You've got to be a trifle crazy and ulcer-resistant to put
up with plane schedules, sleeper-jumps or the do-it-yourself bit when you
drive your car all night to make the next day's engagement hundreds of
miles away.

I've hung my hat in thousands of places through the years: from tiny
cubicles in the YMCA to de luxe hotels in Europe, the Pacific and the
Caribbean; from dingy, walk-up rooming houses to New York's finest
hostelries. Some of the accommodations I remember with pleasure; others
I would just as soon forget.

One of my most memorable pads happened to be in the sovereign state
of Maine. (My use of the modern idiom is perhaps imprecise—"pad" is
hardly the word, I suppose, for a three-hundred-acre estate with seven
buildings.) It was situated on Lake Kezar, one of the three most beautiful lakes in the world for ideal size, surrounding vegetation and mountains. I have this on no less authority than the *National Geographic
Magazine*.

Don Dickerman, of all people, was instrumental in getting me involved
in this property. I often recall how he made a nickel phone call to me
in New York and inveigled me into the Daffydill Club in which I dropped
about ninety grand. This time his siren song was on a penny postcard
by which instrument he apprised me of the sylvan grandeur of his camp
on Lake Kezar.

I thought no more about it until I happened to be in Westbrook during
a summer tour in 1930. There was a three-day celebration in progress

147

during which the square in front of my father's drugstore was to be renamed "Rudy Vallee Square." I chanced to meet a pilot from the Curtiss Wright company in Portland and he prevailed upon me to make my first flight. Since his craft was a hydroplane, it occurred to me we might land on Lake Kezar and pay Dickerman a visit.

I placed a call to him at his camp through the tenuous wire that led through the woods and culminated in his party-line "crank" phone. "Hello, Don—it's Rudy!" I shouted.

"Boy! That phone ringing sure shook me. I haven't had a call on it for three years," he said. "I thought the goddam thing was out of order!"

"I'm going to drop in on you this afternoon—in a hydroplane. How do you get there?"

He gave me the directions in detail. "There are five million lakes in Maine—look for a bright blue float."

We made it without any undue problems and discovered Don waving frantically at the water's edge. He showed me around and I fell in love with the locale. "I've got to get a place up here. Anything available?" I asked.

"Only thing I know of adjoins my camp here. It's a large tract, though. The owner will only sell the whole three hundred acres."

"Hell, I only want some water frontage. I don't want to own the whole state of Maine."

"Buy it, Rudy. Let me design you a dream castle. If you let me do that you can use my road through the woods."

"The old designer rides again," I thought. "Not again, Rudy—not again."

When he later found out that my plans did not include a "dream castle" Dickerman-style, he suddenly decided I'd have to build my own road, that the noise of our automobiles might disturb him or his guests!

So I had to have my own road built, with some fifty French-Canadian lads from Westbrook as my construction gang. They divided into two groups and worked their way toward each other like sandhogs building a tunnel.

It was a considerable bit of construction but it was a beautiful road, and one that I knew was my own. A Westbrook carpenter constructed a simple Cape Cod bungalow with warm gray shingles, three bedrooms and two baths, a long living room of simple-beam construction and pegged flooring, with a huge rock fireplace at one end. By the time the first building was constructed, I was appearing in *George White's Scandals* and the Pennsylvania Grill. One Sunday morning I flew twenty of my close friends in two planes for our first baptismal banquet in the new Lodge, flying back to New York on Monday morning.

During the summer of 1932 I purchased a fifteen-foot speedboat, several canoes and outboard motors, and decided that this would be an ideal spot to entertain my band and company of entertainers with their wives each year. Therefore, construction was hastily begun on two other buildings named Lodges B and C, with the Cape Cod designated as Lodge A. We also decided to build a huge boathouse with a float in front of it and in the upstairs of the boathouse a separate bar and pool-room. Work proceeded rapidly and in September, after a long summer of one-nighters and theater engagements, we began the first of a series of nine pilgrimages which followed the same patterns every year.

During the course of the Thursday evening preceding our trip to Maine, we would play a fantasy on the University of Maine "Stein Song" as it might have been written by various composers This would occur somewhere in the middle of the program. Then, as the program neared the closing two minutes, we reprised the "Stein Song" while Graham McNamee announced our departure for the Lodge. The last thirty seconds of the program, we proceeded to render the "Stein Song" in several keys simultaneously as our radio audience pictured the throwing of music into the air and general pandemonium. At the show's close we rushed from the studio to a waiting cab to Grand Central Station where the State of Maine Express was held three or four minutes past its departing time to enable us to board her. Some of the boys in the band and their wives would be on the train with me. Others in their own cars, the rest in a large chartered bus, would drive through the night for Old Orchard Beach, Maine, where they would swim if the weather was propitious and enjoy themselves on its long sandy shore.

Those of us on the train would arrive in Portland about seven-thirty in the morning. Meanwhile, a crew of ten women from the neighboring farmhouses would await us at the Lodge, preparing the beds and laying in the food we would consume. Friday night at Old Orchard Beach became a ritual, with the Governor of Maine always on the stage next to my Dad and Mother. The band began playing for dancing at eight o'clock and at nine-thirty on the dot I would make a long triumphant walk down the pier itself, a walk of about an eighth of a mile, saluting fans and friends of many years' acquaintance. I then put on an hour show with the various personalities whom I had been presenting in theaters all summer. Fortuitously, a Hollywood personality, Roscoe Ates, happened to be with us the first summer and thereafter I made it a point to have a film notable as our guest each year. At the conclusion of the dance at one o'clock in the morning, I would give autographs to those who requested them while we packed our instruments and prepared for the seventy-mile trip to Lovell, Maine and Lake Kezar.

On arrival at the Lodge at about three o'clock Friday morning, all lights were on, fires roaring in the fireplaces, with cold cuts, hot chicken à la King, sandwiches of every type, hot coffee, milk, champagne, and whatever else you might wish at our two bars. The staff of ten women would wait up to see that everyone had everything he or she might want. We generally stayed up all that night, retiring early in the morning; but at noon everyone was up for breakfast, and then fun out on the float, in the canoes, and in the water. The order of procedure at the Lodge was very simple. Everyone arose when he or she felt like getting up, and breakfast was served no matter what time of morning or afternoon it might be. Lunch was at one o'clock and dinner usually about seven-thirty or eight in the evening. We began a ritual in food, with leg of lamb on Saturday evening, charcoal-broiled steaks on Sunday evening with Cherries Jubilee, roast beef on Monday, and chicken on Tuesday. Wednesday noon a hot lunch was served as we departed for Worcester, Massachusetts, where we played a dance-pavilion date on the Worcester Turnpike. From Worcester we drove through the night, arriving back in New York ready for our Thursday afternoon Fleischmann rehearsal.

If the weather was sunny and fair, we returned to New York tanned, happy, and rested. But if it rained during our visit, with a group of forty to fifty persons staying indoors, playing cards, pool, imbibing perhaps a little too freely, tempers naturally became frayed and we returned perhaps the worse for our trip. But we were fortunate that in our nine yearly visits we were only rained out twice!

The profits from the Old Orchard and Worcester engagements were distributed among the band and the entertainers so that in a sense it was a vacation with pay. The Lodges continued to grow and improve like Topsy. I picked up ideas as I traveled throughout the country and incorporated them into the lodge itself.

I realized that women don't like to rough it and we secured the finest beds and mattresses and the softest sheets and pillowcases obtainable. A tile man was brought from Boston and all the bathrooms were tiled in beautiful colors, with fixtures to match or contrast. A wonderful Capehart phonograph (*the* de luxe record player at the time) played throughout the entire estate over a complex sound system. It was geared to play certain records on our arrival and certain records on our departure. It also provided soft music during the day from well-chosen albums which made the summer or fall afternoons and evenings romantic and more delightful.

I discovered musical cigarette boxes, made in Switzerland, that would play popular tunes of my choosing. As each room was named after a song that I or some friend had written and popularized or introduced, the cigarette box was painted to match the decor and play the tune of that particular chamber. My room, of course, was "Vagabond Lover" and my bathroom of black fixtures with cherry-red plaster and tile was

16. The Yankees augmented to ten men for *The Fleischmann Hour,* 1932.

18. Fay Webb emerging from plane chartered for flight to Maine Lodge, 1931.

17. With Alice Faye in the film, *George White's Scandals,* 1934.

19. Rudy's birthday party at the Astor Roof, 1936, with famous orchestra leaders as his guests. He is shaking hands with Horace Heidt; Ben Bernie and cigar is between them; others include Hal Kemp, Fred Waring, Shep Field, Buddy Clark, Russ Morgan, Jerry Cooper, and Jack Smith.

THE COMPANY WILL APPRECIATE SUGGESTIONS FROM ITS PATRONS CONCERNING ITS SERVICE

1201-S

CLASS OF SERVICE

This is a full-rate Telegram or Cablegram unless its deferred character is indicated by a suitable sign above or preceding the address.

WESTERN UNION (40)

R. B. WHITE
PRESIDENT

NEWCOMB CARLTON
CHAIRMAN OF THE BOARD

J. C. WILLEVER
FIRST VICE-PRESIDENT

SIGNS

DL = Day Letter
NM = Night Message
NL = Night Letter
LC = Deferred Cable
NLT = Cable Night Letter
Ship Radiogram

The filing time as shown in the date line on full-rate telegrams and day letters, and the time of receipt at destination as shown on all messages, is STANDARD TIME.

Received at 708 14th St., N. W. Washington, D. C.   1934 APR 14 AM 5 40

NA37 38 DL=NEWYORK NY 14 531A

ARTHUR GODFREY=

        STATION WJBS EARLE BLDG WASHDC=

MINUTES IN TRANSIT
FULL-RATE   DAY LETTER

ENJOYED YOUR BROADCAST FROM THREE TO FIVE FIFTEEN WHILE

DRIVING FROM PHILADELPHIA TO NEWYORK STOP BELIEVE YOU HAVE

ONE OF THE MOST FASCINATING STYLES AND VOICES ON THE AIR

A BLEND OF GRANNY AND BERNIE THOROUGHLY ENJOYABLE

MICROPHONICALLY=

        RUDY VALLEE.

20. Documentation of Rudy's early recognition of Arthur Godfrey's talents at 5:40 in the morning.

21. Living it up at Chasen's Restaurant in Beverly Hills, 1939. (l. to r: Wendy Barrie, Frank Morgan, Dad Vallée, Rudy and W. C. Fields.)

22. The fully-augmented Yankees as they remained from 1935 until *The Fleisch-mann Hour* went off the air. In this New York NBC Studio shot we see Benny Krueger, one of Rudy's sax idols, who helped with conducting chores.

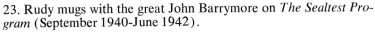

23. Rudy mugs with the great John Barrymore on *The Sealtest Program* (September 1940-June 1942).

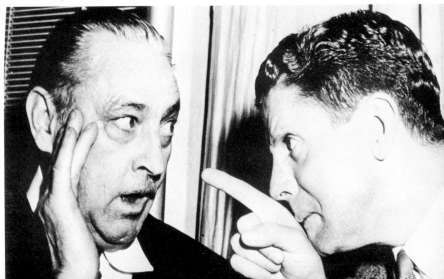

24. The Rudy Vallée-Jane Greer nuptials, 1943.

25. An 'all-out' Warner Bros. publicity shot, 1938.

26. Vallée's Coast Guard band, Eleventh Naval Dist., 1944

called "Lula Belle" from the Lenore Ulric play. The room that Alice Faye occupied in the summer of '34 was called "Nasty Man." There were other rooms such as "Stein Song" and "Saxophobia" in honor of my idol Wiedoeft. Then came "Deep Night," "Sylvia," and one bathroom in beautiful light and dark green tile and fixtures where the theme tune from *East is West* was played. Another room in red, white, and blue had "The Star-Spangled Banner." It was, however, unnecessary to stand at attention during each rendition.

As the years went on we added to the Lodge equipment bicycle boats, all sorts of rubber floats, archery, and other fun and games. Fishing was practically nonexistent since the lake was not well-stocked but there *was* a nine-hole golf course nearby. Since most of our guests liked to play tennis, I installed a tennis court and a beautiful clubhouse with vari-colored slate roof and a bar, so that after the cold chill of an October evening set in, hot buttered rum, hot toddies, and other drinks were the order of the evening. During the day, when a large group might be at the Lodge, the pineapple frozen daiquiri was my specialty. I sometimes made as many as two and three hundred of these masterpieces, using my Waring mixers which Fred Waring himself had personally installed during his visit to the lodge.

Guests often wished to present me with something in appreciation of a Lodge visit, and I asked that an engraved brass plate be put on each gift. Thus it was that the red Minnipiano was the gift of Edgar Bergen and Charlie McCarthy, Class of 1936, the year that Bergen first broadcast with us. And Frances Langford and Dorothy Lamour gave me the pool table and a large bar, each with a brass plate denoting the year they had left my management or employ.

On Sunday evenings I dictated that the Stokowski album of *Scheherazade* become the background to our animated conversations and arguments during the course of dinner by the roaring fireplaces. In the fall of 1935, Lodge A was enlarged to twice its size with a new "Vagabond Lover" bedroom, my old one becoming "Betty Co-ed." The big wood-beamed living room was now twice as large and a most delightful spot, and the room with the bar and pool table adjoining it was also made more spacious.

It was in the fall of 1935 that Eddie Cantor became ill and asked me to come down from the Lodge and pinch-hit for him on his cigarette program in New York. In appreciation of my willingness to do this for him, he gifted me with a magnificent Chris-Craft Cruiser, thirty-one feet long, which (believe it or not) could accommodate thirty persons. Our lunch thereafter became a nautical ritual with a phonograph aboard playing the records of previous broadcasts. There was also current for the Waring mixer to make our daiquiris on board and while our Filipino chef prepared the hot lunch, we cruised to the north end of the lake

and sat in the cool of the trees listening to the broadcast records of last
night's show and eating his delicious cooking. The smaller Chris-Craft
(our "tender") would race out with the ice cream which was hoisted
on board to make our Cherries Jubilee. On lovely moonlit nights we
could cruise up and down the lake wrapped in blankets with the phonograph playing Glenn Miller's "Moonlight Serenade" and other equally
relaxing music. Tough life!

Our departure for lunch on the boat was always accompanied by a
record from a 20th-Century-Fox picture, a sound track of the music of
forty of Alfred Newman's finest musicians. As we idled upstream, at a
certain juncture where the music with a chorus of feminine voices soared
upward, I gunned the boat and it leapt forward from the dock. Our return was always musically cued by the playing of "Jalousie" as recorded
by the Boston Pops Orchestra. The large Chris-Craft was called "Banjo-
Eyes" and bore a gold-leaf caricature of Eddie's head as it appears in
the Brown Derby in Hollywood.

Our basic provisions were plentiful. My sponsors furnished the coffee
and Royal desserts and the president of the Philip Morris Company saw
to it that his cigarettes were in abundance during our stay. The president
of the Planters Peanut Company plied us with nuts of every type, and
other friends and manufacturers saw to it that we were well supplied
with many of the things that made our visits more enjoyable. I myself
would pick up as many as three or four hundred large Persian limes for
our daiquiris on the Friday morning we arrived in Portland. A famous
chef who excelled at making blackberry and black raspberry pies would
make up twenty or thirty of his best delicacies, which we would take
along with us. I excavated a wine cellar underneath Lodge A in which
I stored in racks some of the finest of wines, particularly my favorite
pink champagne, which my friends not only on weekends, but throughout the year, were free to enjoy to their hearts' content.

Only one who has seen the countryside in October can appreciate
the beauty of an Indian summer in Maine. The leaves from the birch
and maple trees create a riot of beautiful colors so breath-taking that
when I show some of my motion-picture shots, it is almost impossible
to believe that these are actually pictures from nature. I have one shot
of a red canoe with a red sail, which truly epitomizes the song "Red
Sails In The Sunset." On arrival, I always arranged for a recital of Rudolf
Friml records, beginning with "L'Amour, Toujours L'Amour" while
the guests were assigned to their rooms and their things put away. On
the sad days of departure, from the sound track of a Crosby picture,
there was Bing singing "It's Easy to Remember, But So Hard to Forget."
This bittersweet number kept repeating while we loaded the luggage
and said a reluctant good-bye to the Lodge.

In 1933 I put in a pipe organ and one weekend I had the inimitable team of Lee Simms and Ila Mae Bailey as guests. One of the loveliest scenes in my memory is Lee Simms at the organ and the lovely voice of Ila Mae Bailey singing as she was dressing upstairs preparing to come down for dinner just when twilight was falling over the lake. The pipe organ, which I gave to the Catholic church in Westbrook, gave way to a Hammond Organ and later on a Hammond Novachord. It was my delight and the delight of many of my friends to pick up odd gadgets and pieces of equipment as we traveled throughout the country and each year the Lodge became more and more a thing of beauty and practicality.

During the winter a lone caretaker stuck out the long dreary months and plowed the road in the event I decided to come up for a winter weekend of complete rest, study, and preparation for new shows. But it was the summer and fall months that made the Lodge our dream place. Those I felt might enjoy a visit there were invited by a brochure that depicted on the cover the entrance with its two large field-rock gateposts. It carried the simple statement, "You are invited to the Lodge," and told the story of how it had evolved and what it had to offer. I was rarely in evidence as I generally had much work to do with study and preparation and research of songs. But when a bartender was needed, I was happy to perform my chores.

I discovered that some persons are by nature careless, untidy, and thoughtless, not only of their own welfare and comfort but of others'. For the enlightenment of my guests, I evolved my set of rules which were bound in birch-bark covers decorated with gaily-colored circles. This little treatise was entitled "Lodge Logic and Your Eccentric Host," with illustrations by my brother William. I stated simply:

> Your host is eccentric and admits it! . . . He is just **ODD** enough to hope that his guests here will read this list of requests and then not carelessly leave rooms and things in a disarranged and untidy fashion. . . . It is a great deal to expect an individual when through taking a shower, to put the used towel in the hamper and **THEN TO REACH INTO THE CLOSET FOR A CLEAN ONE AND TO PUT IT ON THE TOWEL RACK FOR THE *NEXT* GUEST** . . . But your host is just **MAD** enough to expect you to do just that! **WONDER OF WONDERS!** . . . He hopes that he is fortunate enough to have guests who take a pride and joy in being neat. Guests who are really concerned as to how they can save others from picking up after them. . . . Of course, this is contrary to **HUMAN NATURE** and most people apparently are not brought up any longer to be thoughtful and neat . . . (at least, not when there are other persons to do it for them) . . . In this modern age of extreme laziness it is difficult just what final caution to

leave . . . It used to be "Do as you would at HOME" . . . But
after seeing how untidy some people are in their own homes
that is a bad injunction!—PLEASE READ ON . . . (and so
forth covering a seven-page "rule book")

Most of the above may seem rather captious and perhaps a little super-
critical on my part. But having watched so many people suffer with a
bad sunburn, observing that one thoughtless person could ruin everyone's
sleep by playing the organ too early in the morning, or because someone
dropped bulky paper in the toilet bowl we had to go personally and
call the plumber who had to come from a distance of twenty-odd miles,
and having observed that the lake was deep and things could happen
that might result in tragedy, I felt these suggestions necessary. Suffice to
say that during the ten years I owned the Lodge, there fortunately were
no tragedies beyond a few family squabbles, a few bruises, and maybe
a few cuts on hands or feet. All in all I like to think that those who enjoyed my hospitality have, as I do, unforgettable memories of a few
days of relaxation and enjoyment on the shores of the "third most beautiful lake in the world."

In 1945, realizing that California was definitely my permanent home
and that the unoccupied Lodge was rapidly deteriorating due to the
difficulty of finding a caretaker (as well as being a drain on my income),
I sold the establishment for one tenth its value and have never permitted
myself to cast a backward look.

The remarkable place I happened upon and bought in Hollywood I
wouldn't trade today for the Taj Mahal. It is *my place* and will be till
I die.

Please bear with me through the next few pages while I show you
around "Silvertip." If I seem a trifle baronial, I beseech you to forgive
me—this dwelling is my pride and joy.

In the summer of 1941 I found myself becoming more and more dissatisfied with the California home which I had purchased back of Ciro's
on Harold Way. Up to this time I had laughed at those natives who
insisted that a pool was a necessity. It was the first time I had ever really
spent an entire summer in southern California and although the nights
are cool and delightful the days, while not irritatingly warm, lend themselves perfectly to the pleasures of the pool. I therefore assigned my
tennis-playing real-estate friend, C. Ralph Sentney, to do the impossible.

First, I asked him to look for a house near the radio studios of Hollywood as well as the motion-picture studios. Next it must be high, with
a sweeping view of the lights of either Hollywood or San Fernando
Valley. It did not seem possible to me that I would be able to secure
both. In addition it should have at least an acre or an acre and a half of
property, large enough for dogs to roam and exercise. I desired four

bedrooms, four baths, and a wood-burning rock fireplace. A room in which motion pictures might be projected would be equally desirable and if some portion of the house had a built-in bar, I wouldn't mind in the least. But above all, it must have a pool and, if possible, a tennis court. And my final admonition to Sentney was "find somebody in trouble." How finicky can a prospective buyer get?

After inspecting twenty-three homes, I came to the conclusion that it was as difficult to find *the* house as it was to find the ideal and perfect employee. If your employee did not drink to extreme, then he was girl-crazy. If he was able to handle his drinking and not interested in women to the extent that it interfered with his work, he was dishonest. If he was all right in the aforesaid three, then he had no skill either with his hands or brain. Or he couldn't drive a car. Or he had an irritating personality!

As we examined house after house after house, there were always one or two things that were missing. If it didn't have a pool, it had a court. If it had a pool, the court was lacking. There were either too many bedrooms, or not enough. And most of the houses were either in Beverly Hills or near Santa Monica, which made it a thirty- or forty-minute trip to the broadcasting studios. This could make it a near thing getting to a show on time of a Sunday when traffic was heavy.

I was being conducted on these tours of inspection by a tall, young, wavy-haired Greek god who worked for Sentney, a boy who had probably made a try at pictures and wound up selling real estate while he bided his time for the right part and the opportunity. When he finally called me the morning after an evening of pink champagne at the Pirate's Den and assured me that he had found just what I wanted, I climbed into my car and followed him up Laurel Canyon and headed east on Mulholland Drive. About this time the hangover hammers in my head were becoming unbearable. As we rounded curve after curve, I decided to toot my horn, bring him to a stop and tell him to forget about it. We would look at it on another day. But perhaps I had a subconscious divination of what awaited around the next bend. Whatever kind fate watching over my shoulder guided me at that moment deserves my deepest gratitude. At least I continued driving and forty seconds later I saw it—perched high on the peak of a mountain. It was a place that I've always stated would have been the first thing Hitler would have taken as his own American Berchtesgaden if he had conquered the United States!

It was built in 1930 by Ann Harding and her husband Harry Bannister, on the site of what was once a reservoir. Whereas I find it possible to describe my Lodge in Maine, "Silvertip," the name which I have given to the Harding estate, defies all descriptive and verbal powers. However, I can tell you that it has a view of each point on the compass. On the north the San Fernando Valley stretches for miles to the base of the Sierra Nevada Mountains. Therein lie the Warner Bros., Universal, and Republic Studios a long stone's throw from us as well as the Lockheed Airport and aircraft plants. From the patio on the south side is a stunning view of Hollywood with its myriad twinkling lights, frustrations, broken hearts and pulsating successes. With little effort on a normal day devoid of haze or smog you can see the oil wells of Long Beach and, as corny as it sounds, even when the day is not too clear, Catalina Island stands out like a cameo.

There is an imposing set of iron gates that swing from two huge brownstone posts and a gatehouse that leads into the estate. The flora is rampant, with fruit trees bearing avocados, peaches, limes, lemons, grapefruit, and oranges. And there's a lovely high summerhouse with flowers to delight the eyes. Then you discover the house itself.

Paul Whiteman, on visiting me for dinner one evening, noted the thickness of the walls and the massive beams in the living room. He confidently predicted to me that no earthquake, nay, *nothing* would ever do any damage to the house. It would last forever. (This surmise happened to be pre-Hiroshima.) There is a massive sunken living room and a rock fireplace fourteen feet wide and ten feet high. This room gives on a beautiful rotunda with red tile steps leading down a circular staircase to a beautiful entrance hall. There is a dining room with exquisite Italian furniture (table and chairs which came with the house), a small fireplace and a large picture window that looks down on Warner's and the valley. A secret staircase to a sun porch upstairs lurks off the rotunda. Once there you find beds which pull out of the wall for sun-bathing, etc. Westward (ho!) from the rotunda is a long, beautiful hallway carpeted in red. A children's playroom that I converted into a library, an attractive bedroom on the right, and a tremendously large master bedroom with large tiled bath complete the floor. At the end of this hallway are long glass doors set in intricate wrought-iron metal by master craftsmen. I am told they would be impossible to duplicate today.

The floor below houses a huge safe for valuables, another bedroom and bath, the hallway which previous owners used as a gymnasium, and a beautiful open porch that overlooked the swimming pool but which I have enclosed and now use as an office. Flagstone steps descend to two small bathhouses overlooking the pool and farther steps take one down from the three-car garage to another building affixed to the side of a great gradual slope, a building that is four stories in height. The roof of this building is, believe it or not, a championship tennis court.

Directly underneath the court one enters a long corridor which is the full length of the court, almost a hundred feet. It is marked at the entryway by a blue-and-white-enameled street sign which I picked up in Paris—RUE DE VALLEE. In France "Vallée" is a fairly common name as are "La Vallée" and "de la Vallée." In this long corridor are eighteen wall panels of semicircular design, each illuminated by a light bracket which hangs overhead. It was here, evidently, that Ann Harding had hung glossy 8 x 10 pictures of various scenes from her motion pictures. Fortunately she left the hooks and the lights and thus provided a perfect resting place for the several hundred framed copies of songs, personalities, announcements, cards, and clippings which for years had hung on the walls of our New York office.

A widely syndicated woman feature-story writer, Aileen Mosby, who took the forty-cent tour through the house, either had not too good a memory or deliberately sought to give the impression that most of the pictures portrayed my likeness. Actually, one-third of the pictures are of neutral subjects or personalities other than myself. Also here are the "Stein Song" piano copies as they appeared in France, Germany, Australia, China, England, and the United States; there are the gastronomic panels, the photographs of recipes from my good friend George Mardikian of the Omar Khayyam restaurant in San Francisco, the redoubtable Trader Vic and a rum formula that was an exclusive gift to me from Don the Beachcomber, whose rum creations are without parallel anywhere in the world. There are the Yale panels, the military panels, the panels containing photographs of those whom it has been my privilege to guide in their climb to fame and fortune. Scattered here and there are other songs, pictures of various parts of the lake regions of Maine, pictures of my pet canines, and announcements such as the card that described our opening bill at the Palace in 1929. All in all a fascinating gallery—fascinating, at least, if you are interested in show business and have some liking for one Rudy Vallee. As Frank Sinatra rather snidely put it as we left this particular corridor, "You would never guess who lived here!"

Miss Mosby, who tried to describe as honestly and as favorably as she could this castle in the hills, somehow imagined that she saw a framed photograph of Truman among the two-hundred-odd framed subjects. Frankly, I don't recall any one of them that even resembled the Missouri President, but she reported that it was there—even though I definitely know that he is among the missing.

Underneath the roof next to the corridor just described is a soundproofed theater with a stage at one end and a projection room at the other. The theater is capable of holding one hundred and twenty-five persons very comfortably and the quality of sound projection leaves nothing to be desired.

Miss Harding probably presented plays of some nature, as there are dressing rooms backstage, one of which we have converted into a ladies' powder room with poodle wallpaper design and another houses a refrigerator, electric range and sink, with a tremendous array of southern California pottery in various pastel colors, featuring fourteen-inch dinner plates on which the entire meal can be served for gastronomic enjoyment.

Backstage in a special panel are the thirty-odd color shots pressed into wood panels, showing my Lodge in Maine in all its pristine and colorful glory. These photos, and memories, are all I have left of it. Back of the backstage is a large knotty-pine playroom in which ninety people can move about without the least constriction. In this room is a rock fireplace equally as large as the one in the main house and a bar at which fifteen or twenty people can sit most comfortably. The room is in knotty pine with a carpet that will never wear out and large luxurious davenports on which a seven-foot man could stretch out and sleep comfortably. However, I don't recall ever entertaining any basketball players. The farewell Fleischmann program gift, the Capehart phonograph in Swedish blond oak, reposes in one corner of this room.

The playroom leads to what was a long open porch now glass-enclosed; I call it the "Christmas Room." On the walls are large redwood panels with gold frames in which I have placed Christmas cards received from friends in show business over a period of thirty years or so. If greeting cards were rated the same as rare and unusual postage stamps, this collection would be worth a fortune.

Underneath the theater-playroom are two more floors that house all the recordings I have made over the last three decades or so and shelves and shelves of orchestrations of music, valued at six hundred thousand dollars. Against the opposite wall are stored cases of liquors, spirits of every description and, from racks of Philippine wood, hangs a collection of wines containing over two thousand bottles. Every California vintner is represented by two bottles of his most choice vintage plus every other type of red and white wine that the palate might conceive. Stored here are electrical equipment, musical instruments, the saxophones of Rudy Wiedoeft and Benny Krueger, a collection of luggage for travel which alone would fill one-half of the average luggage store and a collection of furniture, particularly beds, which will eventually find their way into the newly built homes of some of our friends. Beneath this floor is a tremendous storage place in which we keep things not likely to be used or needed except at rare intervals throughout the years.

Outside, beside the tennis court is a pool. Slightly smaller than the conventional standard size, it is more than adequate for our summer enjoyment. At the west end of the pool is a flagstone barbecue fireplace with a speaker that pipes sound from the large phonograph in the living room, a sink and storage space for food, cans, and supplies for parties that we enjoy on warm evenings into the late fall.

A few feet down from the barbecue at the west end of the long theater and playroom building is a little playhouse with a miniature fireplace, kitchen, and everything that would delight the heart of a small child. There are so many evidences that much thought was put into this fabulous estate with respect to the comfort and safety of the child that Ann Harding and Harry Bannister hoped to rear in this setting. Some of the windows have tremendous iron grills which were to prevent any intruder or kidnaper from entering the house.

The sloping lawns, the trees, foliage, and shrubbery might really require the services of two gardeners but our one man keeps everything in excellent appearance and tidy condition.

My greatest pride and joy is escorting our guests through the large-beamed living room with its large rock fireplace, through metal French doors to a patio built in natural rock; huge boulders, approximately ten or twelve feet high, support the sheltering beamed roof which projects from the house. The view through the boulders, particularly at night, is exactly what one might expect to find in the Burma Bowl of the Himalayas.

Had the Fuehrer absorbed the United States into his Third Reich, this indeed would probably be the spot that he would choose to pace up and down while looking out at the broad expanse of rolling hills and mountains and the miles beyond leading to the sea.

As I have said, it is almost impossible to describe "Silvertip." There are stunning days when it is bathed in sunlight and the view of the mountains in the distance is so impressive that I almost have to pinch myself to realize that a punk kid from Maine who played a fair saxophone and who sang in an untrained, slightly nasal voice should have achieved such a breath-taking castle. It is a spot that never fails to thrill even blasé Europeans and hard-boiled Easterners who never dreamed that anything quite so beautifully situated and artfully conceived and executed might exist in this part of the world—or any other part, for that matter!

This domicile, plus the cottage for weekends in Palm Springs, is where I hope to hang my hat for the rest of my days.

CHAPTER XIV

London Revisited

"A Foggy Day"

FRANKLIN DELANO ROOSEVELT SAVED money that year, 1937. There were no moving expenses for him as the American public chose to keep him in the White House for a second term. It was to become habitual.

That was the year that sit-down strikes and the Big Apple dance came to America. Other great achievements were the invention of nylon, the completion of the Golden Gate Bridge, and the opening of one tube of New York's Lincoln Tunnel under the Hudson River.

Aviation was the big news then that space travel is today. Aviator and aviatrix alike were trying to see how fast they could get from here to there. Howard Hughes, for instance, broke the existing transcontinental record by flying from Los Angeles to New York in some seven and one-half hours. Amelia Earhart took her last flight. Her plan was to girdle the globe but she was lost somewhere in the Pacific. The German airship *Hindenburg* exploded and burned as it arrived in New Jersey, with a strange effect on one of our London broadcasts of which more later.

On the Broadway stage Orson Welles was at large: his modern-dress production of *Julius Caesar* often resembled a gathering of Mussolini's rat-pack *Fascisti*. The big musical was Rodgers and Hart's *Babes in Arms* but this genre also included two unique paeans for the working class: *Pins and Needles* and *The Cradle Will Rock*.

And radio? It was becoming an immense business. "The March of Time," "Myrt and Marge," "The Voice of Experience," "Kate Smith's Bandwagon," (which was later to give me very rough competition for an audience) and that strangely voiced reader of poetry—remember "Tony Won's Scrapbook"?

Some great movies appeared, all of which I am sure you have seen for free on television by now: *The Good Earth, Captains Courageous, Lost Horizon, A Star is Born* (the first version, with Janet Gaynor and Fredric March) and the famous Paul Muni tour de force, *The Life of Emile Zola*.

I guess I must have felt just a trifle "dated" that year as I read in the paper about Benny Goodman and his "swing" causing a ten-mounted-policeman riot at the New York Paramount. As I looked at the news pictures of the thousands of screaming and gyrating teen-agers, *my* first riot at Keith's 81st Street seemed a part of the distant past.

I think that for years I had the feeling that some day I would return to London. You know, the prodigal son and all that. The opportunity came about sooner and much more pleasantly than I could have ever anticipated. The advertising agency had convinced our sponsor that it would be a timely and brilliant idea for me to do two Fleischmann broadcasts from overseas during the Coronation in the summer of 1937, using all European talent and English musicians.

As I have said, I was associated with understanding and generous businessmen who had a warm regard for me and I had the same feeling for them. This decision had been telephoned to me while I was playing in Miami Beach in the spring of 1937 and on my return we discussed all phases of the plan. It was decided that I would miss one Thursday show by sailing on the *Ile de France* on a Monday. This would bring us into the docks at Southampton on the day after this missed Thursday broadcast, which unfortunately we would not be able to hear at sea. It was further agreed that Edgar Bergen would take over the show and fill in for us as master of ceremonies and top comedian. We were to have approximately six days in England to put our show together. The London J. Walter Thompson office had already interviewed and pretty well set most of the personalities, who included the Lord Mayor of London. An old American friend of mine who had become a British citizen, Sid Phillips, a brilliant arranger and director, was engaged with twenty-five of London's best musicians to handle those chores for me, although I was to direct the band as I had always done.

Thus, on a beautiful Monday afternoon, we backed out of the French Line pier on the luxurious *Ile de France* and turned the nose of our ship toward Europe. While the *Ile de France* had been dwarfed in size by the *Normandie*, it was still a fabulous vessel with cuisine to tempt the appetite of Brillat-Savarin himself. There were the choicest of fine wines and all you wished of them gratis at dinner or luncheon. Except for the fact that before sailing I had picked up some sort of an infection which gave me a high fever, the trip was a wonderful experience.

I felt better the third day out and, walking about the deck for some fresh air, discovered that among our passengers was George M. Cohan. He kept pretty much to himself and when I sent word down to him in his stateroom to ask him if he would become a part of the ship's concert which I had been asked to emcee the last Friday night on board, he declined even to take a bow.

I had become aware of the fact that George M. Cohan toward the end of his days, for all his great talent and fine artistry as a performer, had become an embittered man. His wrath was particularly directed at the new electronics: of sound on film, the microphone, and radio. Cohan had been born, so to speak, in a theatrical trunk and had come to his glowing success the hard way. He played all the "tank" towns in his vaudeville days and had known much privation, suffering, and hard work.

I recalled a night years before when I was playing the New York Paramount. My weekly salary was then at its highest. I received a wire from George M. Cohan asking me to appear at the annual Friars Frolic at the New Amsterdam Theater. Between shows on that Sunday afternoon I walked two blocks to the New Amsterdam to inform Mr. Cohan that I would accept with pleasure. After my last show at the Paramount I would come over and do a couple of songs with my own pianist from the Paramount, thereby not requiring any rehearsal with the orchestra that afternoon.

At approximately ten-forty-five that evening, I presented myself backstage at the Friars Frolic and introduced myself to the great producer Sam Harris (formerly Cohan's partner) who checked me on his list. I then peeked out from the wings to watch Chevalier and Primo Carnera *both* do an "imitation" of Chevalier! The entertainment proceeded with the other acts that comprised the last half of the evening show. Suddenly I noticed that the curtains were being lowered. The band was playing "The Star-Spangled Banner," signifying that the evening was over. To my amazement I found I was the only person left alone backstage.

My vanity was not affected deeply by this slight. If it was intentional, then I knew that Cohan felt that I was an adversary worthy to be challenged. If it was because he thought me unimportant—too unimportant to be introduced even though he had asked me to perform—it would leave me puzzled and hurt as to why he had asked me to perform in the first place.

Some of the Friars were mortified beyond words and descended upon me at the Pennsylvania Grill the following night, exhorting me to take a high post as their Dean, a position second only to Cohan himself. They wanted to give me a testimonial banquet at the Astor Hotel and the man who had sponsored me suggested I resign. I laughed it off and told them lightly that it was not terribly important to me, that it was forgotten and that I could accept none of these things they felt would be the propert recompense for this slight.

The sight of Cohan hunched up at the stern of the boat watching the wake of the *Ile de France* reminded me again of the night that he was toastmaster at the Friars' testimonial dinner to Maurice Chevalier at the Astor grand ballroom. In attendance was a most impressive array of religious and show-business personalities. Chevalier was about to leave America to return to France and this was his farewell appearance in this country. Four motion-picture cameras covered the event from the balcony and the ballroom was a sea of diamonds, mink, and ermine.

There occurred that evening the most spontaneous and explosive laugh-provoking incident I have ever witnessed at an affair of this nature.

Jesse Lasky, the pioneer picture producer who had originally brought Chevalier to the United States, was reminiscing about it. Being evidently a little tired, he lost his train of thought and absent-mindedly said, speaking into a microphone, "Where am I?" Like a jack-in-the-box, George Jessel popped up and close on Lasky's words said, "You're Jesse Lasky, this is the Hotel Astor, and the banquet is for Maurice Chevalier." The way Jessel said it, with his perfect timing, and Lasky's reaction to it with a true double-take, sent this audience off into a paroxysm of laughter that must have lasted at least two long minutes. It was a wall-to-wall boffola.

I was on the dais where I could observe Cohan very closely, about three chairs away. It seemed to me that he had had a cocktail or two, as he was exceedingly flushed when it came time for him to introduce the guest of honor. In essence, this type of affair is basically an effort to raise money for the Friars. Some "sacrificial figure" is asked to accept the honor and, while the speeches may ring with some sincerity, this bacchanal fills the depleted coffers of the club. I think even Chevalier knew that and was probably somewhat embarrassed by the encomiums that had been heaped upon him by various speakers. When it came time for Chevalier himself to speak, it was quite evident to me, at least, that Cohan felt a distinct hostility toward this personality, who quickly and dramatically had captured the United States in three pictures in the short space of one year. I can remember Cohan's words well as he fondled the gavel in a manner that distinctly indicated that he felt an inner urge to rap Chevalier over the head with it. Out of the corner of the famous Cohan mouth came this introduction which I recall so vividly: "We *admire* you, Mr. Chevalier. We *like* you, Mr. Chevalier. We *love* you, Mr. Chevalier. It now gives me extreme pleasure to introduce that star of stage, screen and that . . . er . . . what do you call it . . . radio!" In his introduction, Cohan revealed his contempt for my beloved medium of radio.

Not only did George M. Cohan not attend our ship's concert, but I did not see him at all during the rest of the voyage. Nor did I ever see him again.

The ship's concert afforded me an opportunity to get to know the incomparable Hildegarde better, and she really wowed 'em. There was also on board a small, dwarf-like, deformed German named Joseph Schmidt, who in my opinion was close to being the reincarnation of Caruso in a German body. I had heard a record from a German motion picture, *My Song Goes 'Round the World*, in which he sang with such beauty and power that I purchased a dozen of them and set about making the English translation of the German lyric of "Frag Nicht." I did this song, which was an exquisitely lovely one in melody and lyric, in both German and English on my broadcast. Schmidt was on board, returning to Germany, and unknowingly to his death. On his return, because he was a Jew, he was sent to a concentration camp where he died. He was a shy, pleasant individual, who at first refused to do anything during the concert, although he did attend. I finally cornered him when the orchestra was playing dance music later on for the assembled crowd. After I sang the "Whiffenpoof" with the band while the crowd waltzed to it, I insisted that my good friend Joseph Schmidt do several numbers informally standing at the piano. This he obviously was happy to do after the proper encouragement.

A very beautiful black-haired English girl who had won the title of "Miss England" or "Miss British Isles" was also on board. She was as devastating a black-haired beauty as I've ever seen but, during the two days' illness which confined me to my cabin after we left New York, my pianist moved in and stole her from under my nose. Toward the end of the trip, the night of the ship's concert particularly, she was back courting favor with me, but I would have none of her. She had played me false, and I said reluctantly, "Begone, fair lady!"

My good friend Jimmy Campbell, the music publisher, arranged for us to be speeded through the British customs. With all of my cameras, electrical equipment, and gadgets that I carry with me for comfort, pleasure, and utility this was a great help. Within two hours from the time we docked, I was ensconced in a handsome suite at the Savoy Hotel where, twelve years before, I had labored as a lowly saxophonist.

Our first night on the town my pianist and I, after a delightful roast-beef dinner at Simpson's on the Strand, found ourselves at Ciro's, a now-defunct night spot, which then was the playground for British royalty and the elite of London. Ciro's orchestra leader was Ambrose, a favorite of mine and one of the most prolific and imaginative of British orchestral recording artists. It was not until we had arrived that I discovered that our own American artist, Helen Morgan, was appearing there nightly. There was no line of chorus girls or assisting artists: she was the show. Shortly before midnight, Ambrose announced this personality whose immortal rendition of "My Bill" and "Can't Help Loving That Man" from *Showboat* will be long remembered. But when this sensitive singer whom I had watched completely captivate her audience at Tommy Guinan's Playground in New York in the fall of 1927 and in the Ziegfeld production of *Showboat* in 1931 appeared, I realized with sinking heart that she was in no condition to perform this evening. I wished devoutly that I was not present to witness this tragedy on the floor of an English night club. It was a heart-rending thing to see, embarrassing for everyone present, particularly those of us who admired her and wanted her to be at her best. Her performance was cut short and Ambrose assisted her to her dressing room.

I felt that there was only one thing to do and I asked Ambrose if he would let me step into the breach to see if I could do something to save the situation. He explained to me patiently that Ciro's never presented anyone from the audience. However, I insisted and reluctantly he introduced me. I then proceeded to try to erase the unfortunate impression that had just been created by a fellow American.

It could have been that the audience appreciated that I was trying to smooth things over. Perhaps they really did enjoy the numbers that I offered. At any rate, they kept me there for forty-five minutes and I closed with a ten-minute slice of musical Americana, a Rodgers and Hart composition that is one of my favorite offerings, "All Points West." It is a dramatic monologue with songs about a train announcer who has never been on a train himself and who envies the people who board the trains whose departure he announces. Near the end of the composition, the poor train announcer is shot by a criminal who is being taken to Sing-Sing. Although the railroad stations I announced were unfamiliar to this British audience, the theme of the train announcer and trains was naturally a universal one. When I finished, the audience was standing and roaring its approval. After I returned to my seat, Ambrose asked me if I would perform at Ciro's for a week. I had already agreed to play two vaudeville theaters during the course of my stay, sandwiching in the appearances between our broadcasts. Although I realized that I was taking on more than I should really attempt, nevertheless I agreed to play Ciro's the last seven days of our allotted stay in London.

In preparation for the Coronation the heart of London was sealed off with barricades that made it necessary for us to drive several miles on the outskirts of London in order to reach the Savoy Hotel. With the event only ten days away, the entire population of London, every phase of the city's industry and activity, was in dedicated preparation for these festivities so dear to British hearts.

Had I realized the tempo of conditions that prevailed during the Coronation, I would not have accepted the cabled offer which we received when we were three days out from London, to play the Finsbury Park Theater and the Holburn Empire Theater. I also accepted the invitation of Jack Hylton, the famous band leader, to be his guest at a soccer game the coming Saturday and that evening to witness his triumphant production of *Red, White and Blue* at the Palladium Theater. I wish I hadn't, as you shall see. In the first place, the population of London was much too busy rehearsing for the Coronation itself to go to a vaudeville theater during these hectic days; and my appearance at the Palladium was to be a devastating experience.

Saturday morning Hylton's chauffeur arrived at the Savoy to take me to Jack's apartment. After a light lunch we left for the soccer game which was played before an audience of over one hundred and twenty thousand people. I left the game early to return to the hotel for a nap and at eight-thirty was seated in a box to watch one of the finest musical productions I have ever witnessed in a theater. At intermission Jack invited me to come to his dressing room and asked me if I would take a bow. Naturally I told him that I was prepared to contribute something to the evening's entertainment and he asked me what I was going to do. Recalling the great success of "All Points West" at Ciro's, I told him that I would like to do that number.

At that moment, Jack was being dressed for his next appearance on the stage. With no explanation he quietly suggested that I do something else. Remembering my triumph at Ciro's, I reiterated my intention of doing the Rodgers and Hart composition. Hylton said nothing more, and I wonder to this day why he didn't tell me his reasons for asking me not to do it. He could have simply explained to me that two-thirds of his audience, particularly the balcony and the back portion of the floor, consisted of visiting firemen from the Lancashire district of the British Isles (a segment of the British populace somewhat comparable to our Ozark or Tennessee hillbillies) who had come down primarily to see the soccer game. With considerable boredom they had endured Jack's production of *Red, White and Blue* and were impatiently waiting for their idol, a lean, saturnine individual named George Formby. Unknown to me, this worthy was to be presented after Jack had introduced me. So sure was I that I would prove Hylton's distrust of my choice of number groundless that I rushed in where angels fear to tread. I had my pianist, Elliot Daniel, with me and I informed him that we would do "All Points West" when the time came for my introduction. I wish I hadn't!

I pride myself on having a sense of showmanship, a sense of timing, and a feeling for the appropriate thing to do. But had I had any intelligence at all, I would have appreciated that when Jack finally did introduce me, the hour was late—it was approximately ten minutes after eleven. I should have realized that the audience, even if made up of normal Londoners, had been seated, except for the intermission, since eight-thirty. Most certainly I should have made a quick salutation to Jack and exited gracefully. As I stood in the wings awaiting Hylton's introduction, I observed a lanky character with a small ukulele in his hand and vaguely wondered who the hell *he* might be. Once out in the spotlight, I acknowledged the audience's perfunctory applause and paid a tribute to Hylton for his splendid recordings and the fine show he had brought to America several years before. Usually such a tribute would have brought down the house. The tepid quality of the reaction of my compliment to Jack Hylton should have told me something was wrong! But there is no fool like an unseeing and obstinate one.

"Now," I said to myself, "this is my opportunity to prove to Jack Hylton that I know better than he what this audience would like." Then I proceeded to describe the composition I was about to do. Before I knew it, I was doing "All Points West."

The composition is approximately ten minutes long including the introduction that sets the scene. I was about four and one-half minutes into it when, to my horror, there began in the back of the theater the sound most dreaded by all performers, the sound of an organized, *systematic clapping!* That portion of the audience in the front half of the theater, for the most part in formal attire, turned and tried as best they could to stop it. Knowing that I had approximately five more minutes of the composition to do, I debated whether I should turn tail and leave the stage, or continue. What I really wished was that the floor would open and swallow me.

By some miracle the clapping ceased. I finished the composition, and received a nominal amount of applause, though nothing comparable to the reaction I had received at Ciro's the night before. It was an unnerving experience I will never, never forget. I still wonder why Hylton had not bothered to explain to me the simple fact that the large Lancashire portion of his audience was waiting impatiently for their idol, George Formby, and would tolerate no one else at that hour of the evening. Obviously, had he told me, I would never have attempted anything beyond a one-minute chorus of a song, if even that.

I have a feeling that the memory of this fiasco remains in British theatrical circles today. It is probably the reason why I have never received an invitation to play the Palladium, a stage that has seen the appearance of most of our top-line American performers during the last eight or nine years. I am not the only American who has known rough going on the stage of the Palladium but at least I am the only one who got the works without being paid for his misery!

Our first broadcast boasted a wonderful cast of European names, with the Lord Mayor of London as the featured guest and performers Will Fife, Richard Tauber, the German tenor, and several other outstanding Continental favorites. We had so much talent that time was left for only three musical compositions in which I worked with Sid Phillips and the orchestra. It was rather a fantastic thing to contemplate that our broadcast which commenced at one o'clock on a foggy Friday morning was reaching New York by short-wave radio at eight o'clock on the day before; quite as strange, it was reaching the California coast at four o'clock on a sunny afternoon.

The evening of the broadcast, I was already on the fourth day of doubling between the Finsbury Park Theater and the Holburn Empire. The matinees at both theaters (I was doing two shows a day at each house) were sparsely attended, since most of the British people had their minds on the crowning of a King and Queen. The evenings found the audiences larger and quite cordial to the little routine I had whipped up for this appearance. I played the saxophone and related how I had played at the Savoy Hotel with the all-English "Havana" band some twelve years before. Frankly, I was much relieved when the vaudeville appearances were over and I looked forward to my opening night at Ciro's. I felt it would be as happy an engagement as the evening I had stepped into the breach for Helen Morgan.

But my hopes of a triumph at Ciro's were to be short-lived. As I sat downstairs in the cellar awaiting my introduction, I observed that after the band had finished its last dance set, someone had announced the show was about to go on; but something was wrong with the public-address system! A feeling of fear clutched my heart. Was I going to be jinxed the rest of my stay in London? I heard the speaker's voice on for a second, then off for several seconds.

My introduction was delayed some ten or twelve minutes while evidently futile attempts were made to repair the amplifying system. Even though some glib individual tried to reassure me that the system had indeed been fixed, intuition told me that I was going to be in trouble.

Ciro's is a long room, with a capacity of about four hundred people, and was packed with an expectant and receptive audience. My voice and vocal chords are not powerful and I depend completely upon a public-address system to give me much-needed resonance. Without the proper amplifying system, I might just as well have stayed in bed. My first number was received well enough; the second item began to really bring them into camp, and then it happened. In the middle of my third number, the system went dead, came on for a few seconds, and then went completely and finally dead. Again I wished that the floor would open and that I might disappear through it, but I realized I was obligated to go on as best I could. I fear I would have been wiser to have simply walked off than to try to fill the spacious room when I knew that more than two-thirds of the impact of what I was doing was completely lost.

It could have been such a glorious triumph, as it was a friendly audience and one that I knew wished me well; but the fact that this establishment failed to have a technician capable of maintaining the vital bond between the performer and an audience completely ruined what might have been a happy, exciting moment in my career. If I had been a girl, I would probably have gone home and cried myself to sleep. As it was, it was one of life's darkest moments, and despite the fact that the succeeding evenings were happily successful, I could not erase the bitter taste of those agonizing moments.

But the supreme catastrophe had to come on our second and last broadcast from the British Isles, and this misfortune was in no way attributable to any fault of mine. We had assembled an even more brilliant cast for this program to the British Isles and the United States. There were J. B. Priestley, the London Scottish Pipers, the Weston Brothers, two extremely talented boys from Cambridge, Florence Desmond, the gifted British mimic, the Royal Horse Guards Band, the French actor, Fernand Gravet, and another appearance of Will Fife; all these plus an American musical-comedy star, June Knight. We felt we had a diversified and outstanding broadcast to beam back home.

The program itself went off without a hitch and we all retired to June Knight's apartment in a swanky hotel. Just as we were about to toast and congratulate ourselves upon a fine program, we were informed *that three minutes before our program went on the air,* the dirigible *Hindenburg* had crashed and burned at Lakehurst, New Jersey! I knew, of course, that for at least an hour following this tragic disaster, no American radio audience would be paying any attention to our program, good, bad, or indifferent. In our smug, placid ignorance, we might just as well have been broadcasting to the North Pole. But I also had the common sense to appreciate the fact that life is like that. We at least had done our best and what was done was done!

After a reunion with some of the musicians with whom I had played at the Savoy and a final evening in my honor at the hotel itself, in the very room where I had played the sax so many dreary hours, we sailed from Southampton on the German liner *Bremen.* It was necessary that we take this Nazi luxury liner in order to be back in time to do our Thursday broadcast. As we backed out of Southampton with all the fleet of the world lined up for the Coronation, I took pictures of the Nazi officers of the ship as they crowded to the starboard side intently studying the ships of the various nations moored in the harbor. Many of these very ships they and their comrades were to destroy a few years hence. The Nazi officers didn't like it as I trained my camera upon them but I secured highly prized shots of men who were quite possibly conspiring at that moment on plans of destruction.

My Jewish attorney, who hated the Nazis with a just, implacable hatred, had confided in me that as much as we disliked sailing on a German boat, we would find (he had to admit) that the cuisine of these boats was without parallel in all the ships of the world. I can only say that he was more than justified in his gastronomic estimation of the North German Lloyd's *Europa* and sister ship the *Bremen.* If we had found the *Ile de France* a delight, the *Bremen* was even more calculated to please those who traveled upon it. There was hardly an item or variety of food that was not to be had in varying styles and presentation. The crepes in particular that were a regular part of each evening's meal were as varied and delicious as anything I have ever known.

No matter how fine the fare, its taste was dulled considerably by a morbid ritual which took place each evening *after* the dining room was vacated by the passengers. All the members of the ship's crew that could be spared from their duties congregated in the spacious salon above the dining room. There, in abject worship before a bronze bust of Der Fuehrer, they sang Nazi songs of war.

For all the luxury the *Bremen* afforded, we were happy to disembark on the morning of the Thursday of our broadcast, happy to be back from a trip that from my standpoint at least, had been a series of unhappy memories. The only bright spot was the excitement of the Coronation itself and even that had taken place in a downpour of rain.

CHAPTER XV

From One Sponsor to Another— More Movies

"We Could Make Such Beautiful Music"

FOR ME PERSONALLY, THE BIG TRANSI-tional event of 1939 was the ending of my ten-year association with Fleischmann. For the Europeans it was to be a year of terror as the fanatical Fuehrer began to move like a rapacious cobra on the loose. Czechoslovakia was "peacefully" annihilated and pacts with Italy and Russia freed Hitler to turn on Poland. Europe was off to the races. We were too but we didn't know it. After all, this rumbling in the cockpit of another continent was many thousands of miles away.

We had other things to concern us, like the New York World's Fair and the visit of King George VI and Queen Elizabeth. The Daughters of the American Revolution occupied themselves with keeping Marian Anderson from performing in their auditorium, Constitution Hall, in the nation's capital. We were busy reading *The Grapes of Wrath* and Thomas Wolfe's *The Web and the Rock,* and, when we could get tickets (it took nearly eight years for everybody to see it!) we went to see *Life With Father.* Moviegoers occupied themselves with *Goodbye, Mr. Chips, Wuthering Heights* and *The Wizard of Oz.*

All in all it was a pleasant, peaceful time and you just didn't read the papers too carefully or ever, or rarely ever, look out over the Atlantic toward the anguished peoples of Europe.

Our last program for Standard Brands originated in New York in October, '39. It was a solemn and yet exciting occasion. We had had several birthdays through the years with special music being written and guest stars such as Winchell and others to celebrate these landmarks. Nevertheless, our final program, full of portent as we realized that this was our last show after ten years of happy comradeship in the attempt to bring to millions of listeners the best in radio entertainment, was a momentous and spine-tingling occasion. I had had my programs recorded since the year 1933 and have them all safely stored at "Silvertip." A short while back I listened to my farewell speech on the last program and ɪ think I was just as deeply affected as I listened to it as I was the evening I uttered it. Following a party at the St. Regis Hotel, where my sponsors gave me a beautiful Capehart radio-phonograph combination, I said good-bye to New York and returned to my home in the Hollywood hills. God! how I was looking forward to an indefinite vacation. No longer was I to be confronted with the ulcerogenic thought that on Thursday evening I must be ready, willing, and able, whether I felt like it or no. I contemplated a nice, long vacation with a great deal of relish.

But things didn't work out that way. My vacation was to be a short-lived one. The great combine, National Dairies, had made a survey among housewives to find out whether there was an interest in a new program with Rudy Vallee. The answer seemed to be that if something new and different was presented, these listening consumers would welcome me back on the airways. I met with executives of the company in Miami Beach, Florida, and presented my idea for a relaxed show called "The Rehearsal." This would, in effect, take the listener backstage and show him what went on in the preparation of a half-hour program.

This, of course, was not to be done in a technical, cut-and-dried fashion. It was to utilize, for instance, comedians as studio cops, secretaries, and librarians; this casting would be augmented by the band itself with outstanding personalities and composers. Everything was to be done in much the same manner that Jack Benny often utilized—with the impression given that his entire show takes place at his home instead of a radio studio. I had "mutual approval" on this show; that is, everything had to be mutually acceptable both to me and the advertising agency. However, I chose a director who, in cahoots with a large talent agency, weaned away the executive of our advertising agency. One night at the Brown Derby they were met by a brilliant young writer who sold them upon a series of historical sequences with me as Christopher Columbus, Captain John Smith, and other well-known figures. It was to use historical events as background material, all done in comedy style. Slapsie Maxie Rosenbloom was to be my man of all work and retainer. The bits would unfold when he accidentally knocked me out as we sparred in fun or when I fell from a ladder. Then the show would find me, in my unconsciousness, dreaming of an occurrence in the history book which I had been reading just a few minutes before.

On paper this looked like a solid, sure-fire thing. The writer assured us that these were historical sequences and personalities that even every schoolboy would know and understand. There was to be original music, done in the Gilbert & Sullivan style, with a chorus when needed. On my first show Mary Boland was to be Queen Isabella and Martha Raye was Pocahontas in the second sequence. Like many things that look good in script form, this had engendered enthusiasm in the minds of everyone. Everyone but me and a few others.

I knew that a good AFRA actor could portray my part as well as I, if not better. Moreover, I was afraid that the qualities that had been interesting to those who listened to me perform as myself on the Fleischmann show would not be at all evident in the role of a swashbuckling figure of American history. But rather than fight the agency, I agreed to give it a try, even though I knew it might be my own funeral.

The worst happened. We began with a seventeen rating in March of 1940 and tumbled to a summer rating of four. While we expected the rating to drop during the hot months, we didn't expect it to damned near disappear. We were selling dairy products and particularly ice cream, and needed as large a summer audience as possible.

Ratings at that time were compiled by the Hooper organization and were known as "Hooperatings." If your show had a bad "Hooperating" the sponsors and networks began sharpening the ax. The method used by Hooper was to find out how many of a few hundred listeners were tuned in to a given show. On this basis they were able to "rate" the shows by interpolating population statistics, numbers of radios in the homes, average numbers of listeners in an average domicile and, after a dispassionate discussion with the witches in *Macbeth*, they published the order of popularity of the shows on the air. Today there are other rating systems: Nielsen, Arbitron, Trendex and what have you—but, Trendex-schmendex, it is still the thumbs-up, thumbs-down of the Roman gladiatorial arena that determines whether a show lives or dies no matter what its intrinsic quality.

In the summer of 1940 when we moved to New York in deference to my request to be able to enjoy the Lodge in Maine on weekends, I suddenly found that the agency had fired my director and released Slapsie Maxie Rosenbloom. They then approached me with a list of directors from which I was to make my choice. I looked over the list. One name stood out—a man I knew could be difficult, obstinate, and as unpredictable as the winds. In spite of all this, this man had the great gift of finding outstanding writers and guiding them with almost sheer genius in the art of creating unusual situations and clever dialogue. At that time Ed "Archie" Gardner had not yet launched his "Duffy's Tavern"—in fact he was delighted to be working again as the director of a show. I turned the production over to him completely, with only one stipulation—that I would dictate the songs that I was to sing.

My faith in Gardner was more than justified as he took charge of our show. Our feeble rating immediately shot upward with his choice of brilliant writers including Norman Panama and Melvin Frank, who later made pictures with Danny Kaye after a brilliant career at MGM studios; Jess Oppenheimer who was the production brains behind the "I Love

Lucy" series; Frank Gaylen whose "Millie" show was a radio delight; Charles Isaacs who created and wrote for Jimmy Durante's television appearances; and the retention of Paul Henning, the genius who had conceived the ill-fated historical sequence. Henning later wrote material for Robert Cummings, after a long stint with Burns & Allen. To head these writers under him, to carry out his orders as executive officer, so to speak, Gardner selected a balding, bespectacled individual who looked like a disgruntled astro-physics professor. His name was Abe Burrows, and his great talent for story-line situations and funny dialogue is perhaps unequaled. After a stint on our show he received acclaim as writer of popsong parodies such as "The Girl With the Three Blue Eyes," was a nightclub performer, and had a lot to do with the success of the deathless musical, *Guys and Dolls.* (Of course, he achieved apotheosis recently as writer-director of *How to Succeed in Business Without Really Trying.*) And what a bargain we got! The combined salaries of all of these gentlemen (most of whom wrote for our show for two hundred and fifty dollars a week or less) plus Gardner and Burrows would cost any impresario today eighteen to twenty-five thousand dollars a week.

We utilized Dinah Shore who, with Walter O'Keefe and me, recreated a comedy of the feuding Hatfields and McCoys. It was one of her first Coast-to-Coast radio programs and was to bring her to the attention of Eddie Cantor who really launched her career as one of America's best-loved singers. As we prepared to move back to the Coast, it was Gardner who suggested, as I've said before, that we use (in his last days) the great Shakespearean, motion-picture, and stage personality, one of the very greatest, John Barrymore.

By the time we reached California in September, our rating was already climbing fast. With the addition of Barrymore we hit the twenties and never left them. Now everyone was happy. When I reflect the ease with which our show was put together and presented, in contrast to the travail and long rehearsal for the simplest TV show today, I find myself sighing with deep regret and longing for those days that I'm afraid will never return.

When I got back to Hollywood in the fall of '40 who in hell do I stumble over but Don Dickerman. Maybe it was coincidence but honestly it sometimes seemed that man was following me. After the Heigh-Ho and Daffydill fiascos you know what I did? No, I didn't tell him to get lost. I let him talk me into another club! Well, after all he did get me into the lodge in the Maine woods. That was something.

"This one can't miss, Rudy," he said in the same old way and I gullibled it up. "Errol Flynn is making *Captain Blood* out at Warner's, see? Okay, we get him to come in on the deal. Hollywood is just dying for a really different-type night club. We'll call it the Pirate's Den."

"How much will it cost me?" I said resignedly.

"Believe me, we can open for thirty-five hundred."

I went him three times better. *I* became a salesman and produced a line of backers which included Bing Crosby, Bob Hope, Fred Mac-Murray, Ken Murray, Jimmy Fidler, Tony Martin, Vic Irwin, Errol Flynn, and myself. I figured that if even *one* of the boys on this list would show up for dinner each night, word would get around in the hinterlands that the Pirate's Den was the place to see the stars. We couldn't miss.

All of us put up about a thousand each, but—the same old story: before opening night we needed a total of nineteen thousand. But, what the hell, it was kicks. Dickerman didn't skimp on a single thing. After all it wasn't *his* money. There was a Captain's bridge, several small jails or brigs, parrots hanging in cages, fishing nets, sharks' teeth, swords, cut-lasses, pistols, pirate weapons, all of them from Dickerman's remarkable collection of pirate paraphernalia. All employees from the *maitre d'* to the cigarette girl were clad in pirate regalia. Of course, one was wel-comed aboard to the clanging of a bell and on opening night it was an eight-gun salute from the wooden cannons that poked out from the roof of the building. Ah, atmosphere!

We got off to a great start. Opening night we had perfect coverage by the press, particularly *Time* and *Life* magazines. I have a forty-minute "newsreel" of the proceedings. There was Dorothy Lamour being thrown in the brig and pleading for her liberty; Fred MacMurray and I engaged in a flamboyant mock duel; Ken Murray and I planned to render a par-ody duet of "Sailing, Sailing, Over the Bounding Main," but by the time we were to go on, champagne had rendered us numb—I broke up as Ken pretended to be upset at my lack of artistry and the real trouper's spirit in a club that had been built with *his* money. We had two lovely "pirate" girls circulating with a hangman's noose to drop around the neck of some customer—the film shows the trouble they had getting it down over the bulbous nose of W. C. Fields. What a ball—we figured we all got our money's worth opening night!

But the best-laid plans of mice and men and Dickerman often goof. Business waned and we all sold out to Fred MacMurray at a fraction of our investment. He carried on alone for a year or so.

The Pirate's Den will always be memorable for the many pleasant evenings I had there. It was also the place I met a girl who was to change my taste in the type of woman I admired and, in a sense, to change the entire course of my life.

At that time the war in Europe was growing closer. Its nearness was felt particularly in Hollywood with its colony of British actors. Gene Lockhart was presenting a benefit one night for British War Relief which I attended accompanied by the usual dark-haired female. I was still in quest of the grail on the *College Humor* cover. After the function, we went to the Pirate's Den for an evening of dancing and something to eat. There I saw *this girl*. Until I saw her warm, broad mouth and stunning smile as she wandered out of the bar drinking from a glass of milk, I was a confirmed brunette-fancier. At this dazzling sight, my resolve to pursue always the darkly lovely ones melted quite away.

All my life, possibly because I am blue-eyed and light in physical appearance, I sought and admired my very opposite in the fair sex. Leonie Cauchois and Fay Webb, who epitomized the Rolf Armstrong creation on the cover of *College Humor* and, really, nearly every girl whom I had truly admired was always a brunette with pale complexion and vivid red lips. A fleeting glimpse of this combination of beauty would send my heart pounding. And yet Avory Monroe, the girl who had made the University of Maine an unhappy memory of a shattered romance, was anything but this particular ideal type.

Avory, my fair co-ed in the fall of '21, was certainly not a Pola Negri or a desiccated, white-faced Camille. Rather she had the healthy, warm complexion of an American farm girl which indeed she was. She used little or no make-up and her golden tresses were long, her face round and full with the glow of health. I can never account for this departure from the norm. Up to the time I saw this unforgettable vision at the Pirate's Den in the spring of 1941, with that one exception, I had been steadfast in my search for the perfect brunette sweetheart. There had been Gloria Youngblood of the Goldwyn *Follies* picture, a girl with Cherokee blood in her veins. She took hours to complete her make-up but, when she was ready, she presented a devastating picture in sheer perfection of brunette features. By the use of braided hair in various configurations she achieved a startling beauty that I know knocked most observers for a loop when they first saw her.

Then there was Hedy Lamarr who, in the opinion of many experts and critics, has one of the most beautiful faces in the world. It was a bit trying to escort Hedy and Gloria, as I liked each for her own particular charm and appeal, yet they were in many ways similar types. On one occasion while Hedy waited at the Cocoanut Grove, I fulfilled a dinner engagement with Gloria. A Canadian friend who entertained Hedy until I arrived for my show at the Grove reported to me Hedy's bewilderment. She asked him in her Viennese accent if it were the custom of most American men to keep one girl waiting while they ate dinner with another!

But I was a doomed man the night I saw this vision with her white fur draped over her lovely shoulders, her exquisite hands with beautiful long nails—the type of nails that had always been exciting to my eyes. She was taller than most girls I've known and whereas, at the time I met her, a girl with feet larger than size five would be unthinkable, she changed my tolerance in that direction completely.

It was a simple matter to have this girl and her attractive blond girl companion thrown into the brig. They were released by the pirate waiters on the condition that they give their names, addresses and phone numbers so that the Pirate's Den might "send them announcements about future activities from time to time." Oh, we were insidious all right.

Armed with this phone number I was talking to this girl at two A.M. She assented to meet me that same evening. If I had realized what would happen to me, I would never have called and asked for a date.

So we started out very casually. You know, a few laughs, dining, dancing, catching my broadcasts, the whole thing. Then on the day of the bombing of Pearl Harbor it all came home to me—the way a million things came home to millions of Americans!—there was a loneliness and a longing of love for this girl. She had gone to New York for the summer and I was on the West Coast, which we presumed would be overrun by the Japanese at the drop of a *sukiyaki*. I figured I would be in uniform very soon and I needed her desperately—*where was she?*

Oh, I was ripe and ready! For the first time in my life I was truly eager for marriage. Before, I had taken the vows with some slight, sub-conscious reservations. Don't get me wrong. This girl went along with me in style—she wore everything to please me: the right clothes, make-up, nail polish, and even perfectly applied false eyelashes. However, for reasons which shall be her own, she never seemed to enjoy my perform-ances on the air or in person. This was unfortunate but, when it happens, it can *kill* a performer. If a guy is a good mechanic at a garage, loves his work, and yet has a wife or girl friend who hates it—well, it takes some-thing out of a man. If I may be a trifle florid, I tasted bitter ashes in knowing that the appeal that I had hoped I had for her was merely an illusion.

And so I gradually began to bring our association to an end (who knows, in retrospect, was *she* working toward the same end—in a burned-out love affair I suppose each wants to believe he or she ended it!) and I told myself that it was all over. But, as Somerset Maugham so brilliantly put it in *Of Human Bondage*, a human being has a desperate time in free-ing himself from a deeply felt love affair. It is quite probable that some scars always remain and the memory of some persons in our lives never quite leaves us.

Of one thing I am certain! No brunette would ever capture my heart again. I had kicked the *College Humor*-cover fixation. Even while I was in the throes of my first unhappiness with this girl of the Pirate's Den, I was to meet at the annual Earl Carroll birthday party one of his former chorus girls. Believe it or not, this fabulous creature was seated com-pletely alone in an isolated section of the vast Carroll estate near a small pool where she had withdrawn from the crowd. She said her name was Yvonne DeCarlo. It happened she was as bored with the party as I was and we drove off into the night to escape. This deliverance was followed by successive evenings of pleasure together.

As I looked at her loveliness, I felt that there should be a definite spot in motion pictures for her. (I was admiring her for other reasons, as well, I must admit.) My partner Ted Lesser and I knocked on the door of every studio in an attempt to convince some producer that this girl had a great future in pictures. She could sing. She danced exquisitely. In fact, dancing was practically her whole life, and her intelligence was matched by a warm and captivating charm and personality. Always the reply was the same: she was too exotic, too oriental in her features. Still we continued to try to create an interest in her in some particular part. Two years later, ironically, I convinced Walter Wanger, who had been searching for the ideal girl for the female lead in *Salome*, that he should give my wife Bettejane Greer a test for the part. After doing so, Wanger insisted that Bettejane secure a release from her contract with RKO Studios as he had every reason to believe that this role would make the girl who played it a star overnight and he did not want any other studio taking a bow for something that he had wrought.

I was forced to tell Walter that it was impossible for me to get Bettejane away from RKO where I had placed her under contract. My disappointment, however, was short-lived, because I was delighted to note in the trade papers that Wanger had chosen for the role in *Salome* no one else but the girl for whom I had always predicted such a glowing future— Yvonne DeCarlo! That both Wanger and I were right in our enthusiasm for this talented beauty is more than evidenced in her great popularity with motion-picture audiences all over the world.

All the time I was changing sponsors, switching from brunettes to blondes, and acting as night-club impresario, I was not in the least neglecting that unique art form, the Cinema. I had appeared in *Second Fiddle* with Tyrone Power, Sonja Henie, and Mary Healy and had just finished a very weak musical for Columbia Pictures—in it I played a Harvard man who turned talent agent. To put it quite succinctly, it was a turkey called *Time Out for Rhythm* but, bad as it was, bad as *I* was, it brought about one of my luckiest breaks! You know you're never sure it pays to even get up of a given morning—but this one paid off in spades. The long-term pay-off was in the co-starring role in *How to Succeed in Business Without Really Trying* more than twenty years later— but there were other pay-offs in between.

Here's how it happened. It is a kind of droll lesson in "how to succeed without really trying." Preston Sturges, the great comedy director, decided to go to the Pantages Theater to see a Ronald Colman picture. It was part of a double feature and Sturges miscalculated his timing. He was therefore subjected to a portion of the other picture which starred that great thespian Rudy Vallee. Preston was astounded by the fact that each time I was required to be serious, the audience roared with laughter. "My God," he said to himself, "this guy is funny and doesn't know it!"

Now, if Sturges had been just idly catching a movie for divertissement I am sure nothing would have come of his rather penetrating observation. However, as luck would have it, he was at that moment planning a picture called *The Palm Beach Story* and needed someone to portray "the richest man in the world, John D. Hackensacker III." But luck is one thing and, in all honesty, I must volunteer the further intelligence that a member of Sturges' staff was related to my agent. That didn't do any harm either.

At any rate, I got the part. At the time it was about as off-beat an idea in casting as the industry had ever seen. It was as if you were to redo a Chaplin picture with Marlon Brando in baggy pants and derby. The front-office executives in both Hollywood and New York assumed that Sturges had finally gone completely mad.

When Claudette Colbert, who was to co-star along with Joel McCrea, was informed of the choice she was stunned. "Oh, *nooo!*" she gasped. Then she thought for a moment. "But, of *course*. Who else could do it?"

In case you missed *The Palm Beach Story* (chances are you have not since it played all over the country to healthy grosses and is now on TV) the plot in a nutshell is sketched below. I append this in some detail because in my role you can see the progenitor of J. B. Biggley, the part I play in *How to Succeed in Business Without Really Trying*.

After a quarrel over money to live on, Colbert runs away from her husband, McCrea, and boards a train from New York to Miami without a dime to her name. She blunders into chartered cars occupied by the "Quail and Ale" club made up of millionaire sportsmen bent on a hunting trip somewhere in the South. The members become drunk and obstreperous in the wee hours of the morning and begin to shoot skeet; that is, they have the porter set up glassware which they blow to bits with their shotguns. The frightened Colbert (she is their mascot by now) runs into another car, pursued by the hunters and their dogs, and climbs into an upper berth above mine. Hearing the noise, I poke my head out just in time to have her break my pince-nez by stepping on the bridge of my nose in effort to climb into the upper. In a moment three or four of the hunters' hounds climb into my berth and pandemonium reigns in the Preston Sturges manner.

The following noon I invite her to lunch with me. She is in pajamas with a Pullman blanket wrapped around her posterior presenting a rather grotesque yet attractive figure. (The cars of the offending hunt club have been left on a siding along with her clothes.) Of course, she doesn't know I am the richest man in the world and, as we carefully weigh the price of each item on the menu, she wonders if I can really pay for her lunch as well as my own.

We get off in Jacksonville where I practically buy out a department store for her as I have become sorely smitten. In the jewelry department I buy her a $25,000 bracelet and the store detectives start closing in. I show them my card and they are all apologies. We proceed to my huge Palm Beach home via yacht. There I give her a "surprise" by hiring a huge orchestra and singing "Good Night, Sweetheart" to her from the garden as she retires. McCrea arrives from New York and amid many complications wins her back, to my great sorrow. All is not lost, however—Sturges saves the day by providing a twin sister of Colbert (played, of course, by Colbert) whom I marry with Colbert and McCrea as matron of honor and best man. In short, pince-nez and all, Hackensacker is perforce a not-too-distant relative of Biggley. Aside to all actors and actresses: don't fret if you make a lousy picture—it may be the best thing you ever did!

Before three days' rushes on the picture had been shown, I had received five other offers, which is exactly what happened to Sinatra when he began making *From Here to Eternity*.

But by the time I had finished the next picture they wanted me to do, we were at war with Germany. It was a Technicolor opus called *Happy-Go-Lucky* with Betty Hutton, Mary Martin, Eddie Bracken, and Dick Powell. I heard of the position of Bandmaster in the Coast Guard base at Wilmington, California, said farewell to my movie career, and joined up. It was a twenty-piece band which was later augmented to forty-seven. It became one of the finest service bands in all the armed forces.

CHAPTER XVI

The Coast Guard Days
in World War II

"Oh, Say can you see ..."

IN 1942 JUST ABOUT EVERYONE WENT TO
war in one way or another—even tin-pan alley. Remember "I Left My
Heart at the Stage-Door Canteen," "Praise the Lord and Pass the Am-
munition," and "This Is the Army, Mr. Jones," for example? And the
Broadway plays—*The Eve of St. Mark, The Doughgirls, Priorities of
1942,* and, of course, *This is the Army.* The movies also had a whiff of
grapeshot about them—*In Which We Serve, Mrs. Miniver,* and *Wake
Island.* One of the best-selling books was, not surprisingly, *See Here,
Private Hargrove,* as hundreds of thousands of civilians were drafted
into the forces.

When I took over as Bandmaster in the Coast Guard, I was permitted
to continue my broadcasts since they did not interfere with my duties.
My radio salary was turned over to the Coast Guard Welfare Fund. They
felt the appearance of Chief Petty Officer Vallee on the Sealtest Show
would stimulate recruiting in that branch of the service.

There were the usual upsets, petty jealousies and skirmishes before
our band settled down to a rigorous routine of entertaining men in every
branch of the service. Since there was not enough band activity to keep
us busy at the Wilmington Base, I asked for and received permission for
us to play at Air Force bases, Army bases, "E" awards and dances for
servicemen. We wanted to play any affair that would in any way stimulate the war effort, recruiting and, above all, bring pleasure to lonely
and dispirited men in the Service.

I recalled the bleak existence that I had known in Newport, Rhode
Island, in 1917. There was no USO. The joys of radio and the multi-
tudinous other things that were now offered our servicemen in World
War II were unknown to us at the Newport Naval Training Station.
There it was so desolate and lacking in recreation that a suicide on a
Sunday was not uncommon.

I remembered those days when as an apprentice seaman in 1917 I discovered how inhospitable human beings can be to a man who is in training to risk his life to save these self-same jerks. We were not accorded "shore leave" in Newport very often because war had been declared and our training speeded up to a high pitch. This didn't permit much opportunity to get to Newport itself from the island on which the training station was located. But the few times I did get to Newport, I noticed only casually (for some reason their full significance was then lost on me) the number of signs on the lawns of even the small dwelling houses that read: "Sailors and dogs keep off the grass"!

An article appeared in a magazine during World War II listing the towns and cities in the United States that treated servicemen as though they were lepers or had a communicable disease. This same article also listed as shiny beacons the communities that treated servicemen with the realization that these were our sons, many of whom had been peremptorily ordered to go into training which would lead to combat, inviting possible death or disability. These friendly towns offered to these men of all types, races, creeds, and background some opportunity for relaxation, recreation, and pleasure away from their arduous hours of study and preparation for war.

Then someone conceived the idea of the USO. I'm sure I don't have to tell you what USO meant to these boys. Each USO offered its own variation. Of course the launching of USO in Hollywood had to be done in the usual grand manner of Hollywood openings. It was decided that the "première" would be held in the Hollywood Bowl. Needless to say, the elite of the upper strata of the film colony (of course, Hollywood does have its castes: the three-, four-, and five-thousand-dollar-a-week personalities) bent backward to lend themselves to this innovation; in fact, they vied with each other to present themselves prominently in the spotlight on this occasion.

For once it was not a question of finding personalities for the event; it was the simple matter of narrowing down the list to a favored few. As I recall it, Edward Arnold was to be one of the narrators or masters of ceremony and the list of those who were to appear was a veritable Who's Who. From the performers' standpoint, it was a star-studded show in every sense of that much-abused word. Next to their pilgrimages to service bases all over the world, this was an opportunity for the top strata of the high-bracketed luminaries of the silver screen and radio (who were able to stay at home and enjoy the somewhat curtailed delights of civilian life while hauling down their fat weekly pay checks) to make a contribution that might help save many a service man from going wacky in the regimentation and drabness of military life.

It was a show that ran for more than two hours, and even lured Judy Garland out of hiding to sing a song arranged by her ex-husband David Rose, one of the most ethereal arrangements I have ever heard. Each act was cut to the bone in an effort to cram in as many personalities as possible.

I was selected to direct the massed bands of the Army, Navy, Marine Corps, and Coast Guard, some one hundred and twenty men in all, and was ordered to report to Paramount Studios for a conference with the high muck-a-mucks, the geniuses who were to execute this glamorous occasion. The meeting was held in the office of the then-head of Paramount, Henry Ginsberg, a suave, sartorially elegant, and cultured gentleman.

I had enlisted in the Coast Guard to take charge of the band as a chief petty officer, which as anyone should know, is an enlisted man. John Philip Sousa, in World War I, a man of perhaps no greater repute than I, was commissioned a lieutenant commander when he assumed charge of his naval band. The Armed Services generally commissioned a man according to his reputation and earning capacity prior to entering the service. Thus, an ear, eye, nose, and throat specialist earning seventy-five thousand dollars a year might well enter as a major or colonel in the armed services. Still it has always been a sore point that music which can neither be seen nor felt, but only sensed emotionally, is usually an unrewarding profession for those who follow it. For years the services have not seen fit to give entertainers of international reputation (who in civil life were earning three and four hundred thousand dollars a year) more than a sergeant's rating. Rarely and begrudgingly, they made someone a first lieutenant or warrant officer.

I am not saying this with any pique as I could very easily have entered with the rank of at least a First or Second Lieutenant. However, a few weeks before I enlisted, a popular personality in show business was accused of bribing a commissioned officer to secure a commission and as a result of the headlines in the newspapers about the affair, every high-ranking official (when asked to approve a commission for a deserving personality in the world of entertainment) promptly drew in his horns and refused to have anything to do with the matter. These top brass hats feared the inevitable kidding by some fellow officer who might ask, "And what did you get for okaying that commission, pal?"

After the bribing incident, it was the kiss of death for the man seeking a commission if he listed as his occupation "Entertainer." My own pianist, a Harvard man with a brilliant mind, more than qualified for the position of an officer in the Navy and had thought himself set for a lieutenant's commission. Suddenly he found himself high and dry and was more than happy to accept the enlisted man's rank of "Musician First" in my outfit. In fact, we kept the medics of the Coast Guard in Long Beach in their offices long after regular hours to complete his enlistment on the night before he would have found himself in the Army.

In Mr. Ginsberg's Paramount office I found myself submerged in a sea of gold braid, silver stars, and scrambled eggs on hat visors. Naturally

27. Vallée takes a turn as a comic with Marie Wilson in *Ken Murray's Blackouts,* 1946.

28. With Sid Grauman as he autographs the famous concrete for posterity at Grauman's Chinese Theatre.

30. A publicity still for the film *I Remember Mama* made at RKO Radio.

29. Hamming it up with Monte Wooley on *The Drene Show,* 1946.

31. Photographed with his wife, Eleanor, aboard the U.S.S. America, 1955.

32. As an Irish priest in Jean Kerr's play, *Jenny Kissed Me,* (with Sally Fraser), Pasadena Playhouse, 1956.

33. Christmas (1960) celebrated at Silvertip, Rudy's Hollywood home, with Eleanor and beloved poodles.

34. A scene from the smash musical, *How to Succeed In Business Without Really Trying* with his stage inamorata Virginia Martin.

35. Vallée and Robert Morse, co-stars of *HTSIBWRT*, pose at the RCA Victor New York studios, where the original cast recording was made.

I, a lowly CPO, remained comparatively in hiding. Although it was really my function to pace the program through my direction of the orchestra from start to finish, I offered no opinion and remained unobtrusively in the background. Then my ears detected the mention of P-38s which were to be a part of the program during the early portion of the evening.

I have never made any pretense of being an aeronautical expert, but ever since my first airplane ride in 1930 I have been involved in considerable flying in all types of aircraft. This experience with planes, large and small, had taught me one thing—airplanes rarely take off at the precise moment they are scheduled.

At our contemplated affair in the Bowl, some knucklehead had the brilliant idea of having three or four P-38s zoom down over the audience to prove what I will never know. Nevertheless, they were supposed to play a very definite part in the evening's festivities. The P-38, as you may remember, was in its day a very fast plane, and one that gave considerable difficulty because of its construction which made it difficult for a man to bail out. While it was very effective in some respects it became a sort of "Peck's Bad Boy" in the field of aerodynamics.

Feeling like a small boy who raises his hand when he wishes to leave the room, I piped up with the observation that the planes might not arrive at the precise moment they were supposed to arrive and might thereby louse things up a bit. There was a deathly silence in the room, as though I had uttered a dirty four-letter word. A few stares were turned my way as if to inquire, "Who the hell is this?" Most of the high brass ignored me completely. Mr. Ginsberg, however, fixed me with a cold, fish-like stare and, in the same patient tone that one uses to a misbehaving child, proceeded to inform me that he had it on good assurance that the planes would take off on schedule and would be over the Bowl at the precise moment they were expected.

Properly squelched, I retired into my shell and proceeded to listen to the men on Mt. Olympus discuss the pros and cons of the show, men who for the most part had never faced an audience and who knew nothing of pacing, timing, or the ingredients that go into two hours of entertainment. It's always thus when amateurs get a chance to run anything in show business!

The night of the affair found the weather cool and pleasant, as it usually is in California. Our rehearsal during the afternoon had proceeded without any great problems or difficulties. That evening our initial overture, which I conducted, bringing forth from my one hundred and twenty musicians the best of their musical efforts, led to the introduction of the first personality. About thirty-five minutes later, according to my schedule of the program, although unknown to the audience, came the moment for the P-38s to zoom down over the heads of a surprised and delighted audience.

However, what with wind drift, the idiosyncrasies of airplane motors,

and many other factors that go into aviation, our P-38s did not materialize, as I had felt they would not. It was not until fifteen or twenty
minutes later, when the blond bombshell Betty Hutton was in her second
number, that out of the dusk (it was still fairly light, as we were on
daylight-saving time) there came the ear-splitting whine of an airplane,
followed by a second and a third as they buzzed down as close as they
dared to serenade our Hollywood Bowl audience. Miss Hutton made a
valiant but vain attempt to compete with several-hundred-horsepowered
propellor blades and then rushed off into the wings, crying hysterically.
For all I know, she may have thought the Japs were coming!

No amount of coaxing could persuade Miss Hutton to return after the
planes had left. She was followed by Burns & Allen, who began one of
their best comedy routines only to find when they were halfway through
that they too were competing with these noisy birds of the Air Force.
However, Burns & Allen were more philosophical. Having had years of
experience with every type of annoyance and interruption, they merely
leaned against the piano and watched in apparent enjoyment the planes
zoom down, and then, when the last aircraft streaked off into the sky,
continued with their routines.

Years later, when back in civilian attire, I ventured to kid Henry
Ginsberg, who produced the picture, *Giant*, about the P-38s in the
Hollywood Bowl only to be greeted by a rather quizzical look from him
which seemed to say, "What the hell are you talking about?" I think
this is perhaps one phase of his career that he just didn't care to remember.

The commissioned officer who had conveyed word to me that he
would like me to lead the Coast Guard band was a former musician in
Glenn Miller's civilian band. He was a lawyer who had dealt in sailing
boats as a hobby and who had enlisted earlier in the Coast Guard. This
man was as convivial a spirit as you would want to know, an honest guy,
and a likable one. I was flattered that he wanted me to lead the band.
He had already picked the twenty-three men who were to be the nucleus
of our group when he called me. However, for some reason, he was to
become a contradictory personality, an enigma, a character.

While he had been very careful in his selection of most of the men in
the band, he had enlisted three or four who were adequate but not outstanding. At a time when the cream of musicians were all anxious for
a berth in a band that was not likely to find itself in the trenches, on the
firing line, or on board a ship there was no excuse for second-raters.
Musicians rarely make good fighters. Their very temperament and screwball nature, their age, the lives they have led all seem to make them
unsuitable for the rigor of training and combat. There are those who may
take issue with me on this, but the truly gifted musician, while not always
exactly a screwball, is intrinsically unsuited to the life of a regular cut-
and-dried turn in the Service. For one thing, the fact that a musician's

life is usually one of retiring in the wee hours of the morning and sleeping until noon or afternoon is a handicap. For another, if he is truly an inspired and gifted musician, he is quite often a brooding, introspective misfit. In my opinion this meant that although he *might* work out in some other capacity, his best contribution in wartime is that of bringing pleasure to the thousands of less-gifted men and women through the stardust of his music.

My superior, having assembled a small group of men, failed to tell me that we were not an authorized band! In simple language this means that we existed by the grace of the captain of the Eleventh Naval District of the Coast Guard Area in Long Beach, a man who liked poetry, who was an authority on Greek and Latin, who loved music and who was willing to stick his neck out and risk censure by permitting the organization of a band which (and I believe I am accurate in stating this) was never actually "legalized" by proper military procedure and red tape.

It may have been for this reason that my superior lacked the courage to demand an office for me or a hall in which to rehearse. We were always being chased out of the one large room that we wished to use for band practice. We had no arrangers and I think you'll agree that they were necessary for a band of this nature. Even if we had secured arrangers, there was no music paper issued for them to use. The bandsmen used their own instruments, a saving for the taxpayer. However, within the ramifications of the Armed Services' supply system there was no provision for such things as strings, reeds, drumsticks, etc.: since the Coast Guard had not supplied the instruments themselves, they therefore did not exist. The men had to purchase such supplies out of their own pockets! Oh, we had a jim-dandy operation there, all right.

But since there is always a gimmick with which to circumvent the tentacles of red tape, we worked out a deal. Since I was continuing my broadcasts and turning the salary over to the Coast Guard Welfare Fund, we arranged it so the fund would buy supplies for the band! One hand was washing a lot of others.

There were other things that griped me about which my superior seemed indifferent. The men were asked to play dances until one or two o'clock in the morning. Then they were routed out of their cots and hammocks the same morning after only four hours of sleep, the same time as the other enlisted men who may have retired as early as eight or nine o'clock the previous evening. On some of the dances that we played for servicemen at other posts, the boys might not arrive back at the base until three in the morning. As everyone knows, three hours' sleep doesn't do anyone any good.

On our Saturday morning inspection parades, we used the same small bass drum that we used for dances instead of the large oversized bass drum necessary for use in parade or open-air concerts. It always galled the devil out of me every time I saw the large, beautifully booming bass drum that other naval and military bands used when we worked near them on certain occasions.

I rebelliously accepted some of these deficiencies at first while my superior was busy with a million other things. He was generally up in Hollywood looking for writers for the publicity branch of the Coast Guard, into which he evidently hoped to fit himself.

The final straw came when, after being asked by a group of Hollywood ladies to be the only source of entertainment for an evening in the Long Beach auditorium, we suddenly had our program interrupted by the arrival of Bob Hope and his entire company. Of course, they put on a terrific show but they completely disrupted the program we had planned. This was particularly annoying because originally it was understood that Hope and Company would *not* be able to be present. Our efforts were wasted that evening. My only thought was that my boys could have been back in the barracks sleeping instead of waiting to play the Exit March after an hour and a half of Bob Hope and Company.

I risked the ire of my superior and went over his head. I took the bull by the horns and made the acquaintance of our top man, the Captain. He asked that I make a written request for everything we wanted, and our wishes were immediately granted. We had our rehearsal hall whenever we wished to use it, arrangers were recruited, and it was definitely agreed that when the boys played a dance until one or two in the morning they could get at least eight hours of sleep on returning to the barracks.

Our affairs continued to be handled in a haphazard manner by our patron superior, who actually was a good guy and fond of me, until it culminated in a series of incidents that made it absolutely impossible for me to go on as bandmaster and maintain my self-respect. I had asked for the privilege of entertaining men in every branch of the service. On a Friday evening we found ourselves entertaining the Army Air Corps boys at Minter Field in California. I insisted that my boys wear white uniforms with black scarves, even though it meant a lot of laundering to keep their suits white. I wore a white mess jacket, with the black and gold shoulder boards. At the time of this engagement, I had been promoted to Lieutenant, Senior Grade, having served as a Chief Petty Officer for a little over a year. We finished our opening naval medley, a twelve-minute potpourri of Navy songs with a comedy and choir work *à la* Fred Waring, winding up with the Beethoven Victory Theme in a final triumphant chord that brought the audience to its feet roaring in appreciation, and we launched into a two-hour show that (particularly at Minter Field) was an electrifying evening for the audience and us. My superior had driven up in a car I owned which he was going to try to sell for me in San Francisco. We met afterwards in the Air Force restaurant which was kept open that night while my boys continued to play for a dance following the show. My superior had, frankly, been imbibing freely. In answer to my question as to where we were to play the following night, he somewhat incoherently informed me that it was to be Camp San Luis Obispo. This was in itself a commentary on the way our band was run. Instead of receiving specific orders in duplicate or triplicate, the way all military bodies do in moving from one spot to another, ours was a case of verbal understanding, which of course was slightly ridiculous. I informed him that the boys in the band had told me that they thought we were going to play Camp Cook, a large Army base about one hundred miles from Camp San Luis Obispo.

"As a matter of fact, sir," I interposed, "I was under the same impression as the men. I thought it was Camp Cook also."

My superior just looked at me witheringly. "Surely, Lieutenant, you remember Colonel Burgess?"

"Burgess?"

"Sure. He liked the band and show so much the last time you were there. He's asked for you back again. So it's San Luis Obispo tomorrow. Okay?"

Frankly, I knew nothing concerning San Luis Obispo, but I was in no position to argue. After a night's sleep in the delightful air-conditioned officers' quarters, I took off in a two-seated plane with a major in the Air Corps for San Luis Obispo, while the boys moved on in Army Air Corps buses to join me at our rendezvous.

On arrival at my destination, an amazed but cordial Colonel Burgess informed me that he had no idea that we were coming and could not use us as he had a USO show that evening! He added that he would be delighted to put the boys up. I informed him that he would not only have to put them up for the night but that he would somehow have to get transportation to take them on to San Francisco. The following day we were to perform at a Naval Aid Auxiliary show in the San Francisco auditorium.

Burgess informed me that he had no transportation but would find some way of getting the boys there. There was little left for me to do but to fly on to San Francisco with the Air Corps Major. Once there, I dutifully reported to my superior that he had sent us to a place where they not only did not know we were coming, but could not use us! He was flabbergasted when I told him this bit of news.

By this time enough things had happened to kindle my feelings to the boiling point. There were several other incidents comparable to our San Luis Obispo blind alley, and I felt I couldn't take this slipshod and poor handling of our programs any longer. Just as I was about to do something about it, we were ordered East for a War Bond Drive. We flew East in two large Navy planes, performing in Indianapolis where we played on the steps of a large monument in the evening. It was nice but we did not accomplish our purpose of selling bonds! We played a few more towns in Indiana and Ohio, performing for noon crowds in the street at which no attempt was actually made to raise any money for the war effort. And, too, there was the eternal diet of chicken which seemed to be the only thing the Service clubs who fed us could provide. When we arrived in Cleveland and the press asked me how the tour was going, I told them very frankly my honest feeling was that it was a waste of time. My superior informed me that I was not supposed to sound off to the press; but they had asked me and I had given them an honest answer.

In Cleveland our talents were literally wasted on thin air. We performed out on the football field on a foggy night without adequate amplification. With the dampness affecting everything we played, we accomplished nothing except the spoiling of some of our drumheads, and strings, and almost ruined our harp. We *could* have been indoors in a large auditorium seating ten thousand people, with admission at least five dollars in war stamps, and in that way could have accomplished our mission.

In Philadelphia we were to play in the Navy Yard for the workers during their lunch hour. The commandant of the yard had been involved in the Pearl Harbor disaster and was leaning over backward to avoid further criticism. He insisted that we could play for forty minutes during the workers' lunch hour and not one minute longer! A Coast Guard ensign picked me up in a station wagon and we followed the Navy station wagon in which rode my superior and a young naval lieutenant who had arranged our Navy Yard show. We entered the Yard and proceeded through the maze of lumber and materials stacked everywhere. To my ears came the sound of my band tuning up. *It was now two minutes of one*, with the concert scheduled to begin at one o'clock sharp! Three minutes later we had still not arrived at the stage which had been erected for our concert. It suddenly dawned on me that the naval lieutenant who had arranged this affair and built the stage, *was lost in his own base!*

Unforgivable stupidity, such as I felt this was, is the one thing that causes me to see red. I knew that all these workers were hanging from cranes, standing beside their tools of work, waiting for every minute of entertainment we could bring them, and here we were, wandering like rats in a maze, unable to find the band platform. As we tried another lane and came to a dead end, I sounded off by saying, "This is true Navy thinking—this is the type of thing that caused Pearl Harbor!" The knuckleheaded lieutenant reddened slightly and I knew that my superior made a mental note of my criticism of the sacred untouchable Navy. Of course, we eventually found the band platform but the four-thousand-odd workers must have resented my failure to be on time.

From Philadelphia we went to New York, where I envisioned our doing midnight shows at the Radio City Music Hall, the Roxy Theater, the Capitol, and other theaters of that ilk, with one-hundred-dollar and one-thousand-dollar war bonds as the price of admission. If I seem to be a bit arrogantly boastful in making the above statement, it is only because we had a two-hour show that I felt was one that in peacetime would be worth four dollars and forty cents a seat. In the first place, the solos that Robert Maxwell played on the harp were the same that brought him several thousand dollars a week in his concerts. I had a brass section unequaled by any other Service band in the entire country. I used some of the most choice bits of my repertoire of twenty years, and there were several excellent comedians in the band; and we had some arrangements and medleys which even the Glenn Miller Army Air Corps band and the Santa Ana band would have to admit were unique and highly imaginative.

By now we had streamlined the operation of our unit by the addition of three magnificent "rislay" performers. This is the type of act where two boys at each end of a totter board, by jumping on and off, somersault the third man into the air to land on each other's shoulders. Seaman Lybarger and his trio, which up to the time of their enlistment were known as the Flying Duanes (an act which usually received one thousand dollars per week), had been stuck over at our Catalina Coast Guard Base. I had arranged to have them transferred to our band to load and unload all of the band equipment and drive our truck to and from the engagements, in addition to doing their act during the course of our two-hour routine. These three boys were grateful for the chance to perform and get away from lonely Catalina. They worked like Trojans, making the operation of our unit more efficient and pleasant. We had "our own" public-address system; it was really my own eight-thousand-dollar Western Electric system which we used to amplify every section of the band plus one microphone, of course, for the announcements and vocal work. Milton Berle's brother Phil was assigned to precede us on War Bond drives to have the pianos tuned for our two pianists, to set the stage, the lighting and, in general, to effect everything that could be arranged in advance for the better presentation of the shows that we gave all over the West Coast.

So here we were in New York. Instead of being programmed in Radio City Music Hall, the Roxy, or the Capitol for midnight shows for New Yorkers who would have turned out to help the war effort and to welcome me back, we played in a *tent* behind the Roxy Theater. There the rain and dust poured down through the holes in the canvas and the price of admission was a twenty-five-cent war savings stamp! By this time I had written to our captain back at Long Beach asking him to transfer me to some other outfit. I felt that I could not take the accumulation of bad management, poor handling, and wasted effort any longer.

In the band was an arranger who, on the day that he was about to be inducted into the Coast Guard, was arrested for drunken driving in Santa Monica. When one of our officers had shown me his picture and asked me if I felt he should still be taken into the Coast Guard, I went to bat for the guy. Not only was he inducted but he was attached to our band as an arranger. This character seemed loyal enough, but I discovered that when my back was turned, he was constantly trying to undermine me with the rest of the musicians in the band. Although he knew that I demanded the best in food, accommodations, and transportation for the boys, he continually made it seem otherwise. On the few occasions that I could not be present at a function, he sought to ingratiate himself with the bandsmen and alienate them from me.

A cute trick was pulled in New York once on an afternoon when I had gone upstate. A secret rehearsal was held for a three-hour radio show, putting me in a very difficult spot for directing it as I had not been present at the run-through. That did it! I informed the boys that it was my intention to be transferred elsewhere unless they gave me an overwhelming vote of confidence. I asked for secret balloting as to how many wished me to remain as their director. I was frankly amazed and delighted to find that forty of them were happy with me. Six (among whom were some of the poorest musicians of the band, and who knew that I knew it) were hostile. One didn't care whether I lived or died.

Our next stop was Washington and on a Monday morning when we entrained, the great Winchell had an item that really shook me! It stated very simply that I was likely to be court-martialed when we reached Washington. On the trip down, my assistant arranger and two or three of the men who had voted "no" to my staying on were openly hostile with sneering remarks and rude noises. Apparently the entire band had seen the Winchell article and, frankly, all of us were wondering what the hell was really going to happen!

At the Washington station we were greeted by Captain Reed-Hill, who was really the guiding mentor of all the bands in the Coast Guard. He was also the man who engineered the Coast Guard stage show, *Tars and Spars*, which starred Sid Caesar and Gower Champion and which toured the United States to stimulate recruiting. This captain met me at the station, all cordiality and warmth! He took me to the Press Club for lunch, introduced me proudly to many of the members present and then asked me if I would, along with Vic Mature, be guest of honor at a tea that our Admiral Waesche was giving that afternoon at his home. I found it a little hard to believe but I accepted. At the tea I met the Admiral who was a charming and most personable leader, a man who was to die of cancer of the throat a few years later. During the gathering, I persuaded the Admiral to delay his trip to Chicago to catch our second show at the Capitol Theater that evening. At our first show, which was held at the Earl Theater, it came time for me to bring on our arranger to direct one of his scores. He came in weaving slightly, having hoisted a few before the show. He grabbed the baton from me and, after conducting the number, instead of handing it back to me as he usually did, he threw it to the floor!

This in front of the first three rows filled with Coast Guard brass hats! Such an action by an enlisted man to an officer was slightly unthinkable! I said or did nothing about it and proceeded as though nothing had actually happened. The climax came when, at our midnight show at the Capitol Theater, with our own Admiral up in his right-hand box, this character failed to show entirely. This, of course, was a dereliction of duty for which I could have quite easily reported and reprimanded him. I knew he was thoroughly disappointed in not having the Winchell prophecy come true. It must have galled him to find that the court-martial had actually been a party in my honor. It turned out to be a strange "red-carpet" court-martial.

At any rate, upon our return to the Coast, my superior bowed out and I was given complete direction of the band and its destiny. We stepped up our activity. In addition to the Monday night show at the base which we put on for the boys (on a night which I know from experience is the most lonely and gloomy night in the week) I occasionally defied the Hollywood Victory Committee by phoning direct outstanding personalities and film names, asking them as a favor to me to come down and play a part in our two-hour show. We took on more hospitals, "E" awards, dedications, dances, and appearances at bases which were stuck away in remote corners of the West Coast, where we knew the men and officers were starved for music and entertainment.

We had defeated Germany and there was rejoicing. Still the armchair strategists maintained and the consensus had it that the Road to Tokyo was going to be a long and hard one. Except for a favored few, no one guessed or dreamed of the atomic bomb. The best prognostication indicated a long, hard, and bloody year or two before we would conquer Japan. This time it was the Army Air Force geniuses who were asked to carry out a brilliant thought denoted in the phrase, "Stay on the job and finish the job."

The idea was to corral some one hundred thousand persons who worked in the aircraft plants and shipyards in southern California into the Los Angeles Coliseum. There they were to be bombarded with enough inspiration to make them want to feel that when they left the Coliseum they would want to go back that night—that very night—to their lathes, their riveting machines, and the assembling of their ships to create the munitions that would polish off the Japanese. It was believed that by enough galvanic exhortation, interlarded with a good military show in the Coliseum, this would perhaps be accomplished.

An Air Force major who had a part in the assembling of this particular project happened to be a chap whom I had saved from drowning at my Lodge in Maine. I assumed I knew Cliff Henderson well enough to offer a suggestion anent this idea of "Stay on the job and finish the job." In civilian life he had promoted the Cleveland Air Races, had later come to California to build the Pan-Pacific Auditorium, and I knew that he had great imagination and was inherently a fine showman. Since again I was going to be asked to participate with my band in the evening's program and since I had a very definite idea of what they sought to accomplish by the spending of a considerable amount of the taxpayers' money in transporting all the men, machines, and equipment for this show, I felt that I should say what I thought about it.

Although I knew that one of the top admirals of the Navy, and one of the top men in the Air Force together with the Governor and Robert Montgomery were to speak, I still had the intuitive feeling that none of these would really fire this audience of toilers with the enthusiasm that was felt to be needed at this crucial time.

I did, however, know of a man who is one of the finest speakers in the world—a small man who rarely smiles but who can take an audience and hold it in the palm of his hand for sixty minutes or even two hours, to move them from laughter to tears, from happiness to anger or any emotion he chooses. I had first heard his voice over the air as I was driving down to my broadcast rehearsal and had been so entranced with what he said and the way he said it that I sat in my car and listened until he finished. I did this even though I knew some fifty people were waiting in a studio for me to arrive to begin a rehearsal, a delay that was costing me (personally out of pocket) several hundred dollars. After he finished his broadcast I immediately called the station to inquire whether his speech had been recorded and if I could secure a copy of it.

I obtained his name and home address in Wichita, Kansas, and after considerable correspondence secured the copy of one of his speeches as it was recorded in Denver. On his subsequent visits to California, I met him and we became very good friends. His name was Ralph Carney and at the time he was vice-president of the Coleman Lamp & Stove Company in Wichita. Nevertheless, he devoted most of his time to traveling over one hundred and fifty thousand miles a year throughout the world making speeches. As he said, "That's over five times around the world, a record equaled by no man and approached by only *one* of our women!"

I knew that he might receive a thousand dollars for a speech, or do it for nothing if he felt the occasion merited it. In my opinion, he was the one man—the *only* man—who should speak that evening. He was the only one who, after delivering his talk would find the Coliseum emptying, the workers anxious to get back that very night to their work.

Henderson listened as I played some recordings of Carney's speeches but he said he was powerless to rearrange the program which had already been set. So it went ahead, inflexibly following the orthodox, stupid pattern that the crackle-brains who arrange this type of affair always follow.

Not that the affair from any standpoint of showmanship of forces was not well-handled. It began with the entrance of marching men from every phase of military endeavor. There were the Navy Seabees with their shovels glistening in the moonlight as several hundred of them marched in. There were the light tanks that fired salvos over the heads of the audience in the Coliseum. As the gridiron portion of the Coliseum filled with all these marching men, it was my turn to clamber up a short series of steps to a platform at one end of the field and direct the mass bands in "The Star-Spangled Banner." God, how close I came that night to falling on my rear end as I came down the little stairway and creating a spectacle to haunt me until my dying day. Fortunately, I reached the ground safely, saluted the assembled gold braid at the east end of the Coliseum, and walked smartly off to the place where my band and I were to remain for the first portion of the evening.

The speeches began, with the Air Force general and the admiral (both of whom had been imbibing freely at a cocktail party at the Ambassador Hotel) not only mangling the English language but actually at times making little or no sense. It has been my contention, not only because I am a purist in speech and seemingly a lone crusader for better grammar in these United States, that the Naval Academy and West Point should have courses in the art of speaking in public. They should make these courses as tough and as important as the science of war for these prospective admirals and generals. No one can know which man later on in life will be called up to make a speech at a dedication of a hospital, an "E" award, or some public function. Instead of the inane, halting, and bumbling speech that so often comes out of the mouths of high-ranking officers, there could flow pertinent thoughts, well-phrased and eloquently spoken.

I personally recall the admiral who, at the dedication of the Long Beach Naval Hospital, at which my band and I functioned, asked the assembled crowd to stand and to remain *rising* while the band played the National *Emblem!* At the thirty or forty "E" awards at which my band and I officiated during World War II, I had plenty of opportunity to hear more Navy admirals stumble and falter through simple speeches that were not worthy of a ten-year-old grammar school student.

Both of these men at the Coliseum that evening were an embarrassment and an affront to the services they represented. Then followed more pageantry and show from the men of the armed services themselves. Every thirty minutes monstrous planes zoomed down as close as they dared to the Coliseum. All these planes but one were apparently not expected at any precise moment. This one plane's arrival was supposed to occur near the end of the evening when out on the gridiron was being staged a dramatic battle between the Japanese and some Americans beleaguered in a small fort or hut. The Americans were to be saved by a bomb dropped from this plane overhead. But the plane was apparently lost in transit, with the result that we had a monstrous and agonizing stage wait of some eight minutes, while all the performers out on the gridiron remained frozen in their respective spots, awaiting the flash of a putative high-explosive on the field and the triumphant exit of the Americans from their trap. This part of the performance was a "bomb" all right!

The climax of this comedy of errors, this "lead balloon," was furnished at the east end of the stadium underneath the scoreboard. My band and I had been instructed to move to this area for the last event of the evening, the playing of "God Bless America," which was to follow what I can only describe as "The War Widow Bit." Someone had conceived this tear-jerker as the real climax of the evening. It was to be a sort of tableau in which a woman who had lost her husband in battle was to be picked up by the spotlight as the crowning symbol, the final proof that the workers assembled must stay on the job and finish the job to avenge her loss. Of course, it was not necessary that we play "Hearts and Flowers" as she was presented, nor did she have to be an old crone, to dress in tatters, lean upon a cane, be supported by two nurses or appear in a wheel chair. But I was totally unprepared, as was probably most of the audience, for the appearance of a statuesque and most attractive woman, with beautifully styled hair, in a mink coat that must have cost at least eight thousand dollars and, to cap the climax, a sheath of orchids that looked about two feet long! As the spotlight picked out this glamorous creature—the exact antithesis of all that she was supposed to portray, I said to myself, "That's all, Brother!" I didn't know whether to laugh or to cry. I just stared quietly in amazement. What a production!

And yet I look back on this phase of my life as one of the happiest. I've always said that if the time ever came that I had to work for nothing, I would work just as hard as though I were receiving thousands of dollars for my efforts. There were those who pooh-poohed this statement, never believing that the time *would* come when I would practically have to do just that; but even during the first year as a Chief Petty Officer, with a salary of a few hundred dollars a month, I labored more energetically and tirelessly and with more excitement and pleasure in my work than when contracts and engagements paid me thousands of dollars a week! It was a glorious band. There was the thrill of giving a downbeat and hearing my powerhouse brass section with its astounding quality of trumpet tone and the response of the entire organization, with even the malcontents almost always giving me their best. It was a gratifying experience that I will always cherish.

CHAPTER XVII

The "Drene" Show
for Procter and Gamble

"Oh, What It Seemed to Be"

WORLD WAR II CLOSED IN 1945 AFTER A long run which played to millions. FDR died that April 12 on the very brink of the victory in Europe—a mere eighteen days later Herr Hitler blew his top for the last time in a Berlin bomb shelter and Germany fell apart. Things changed fast: it was from Roosevelt to Truman, Churchill to Attlee and, of course, from Stalin to Stalin, all three of them at Potsdam, starry-eyed and choked up with emotion as they contemplated a brave new world of peace.

Men were being released right and left from the services and I, like a few million other service men, asked myself, "Why not me?" Several fine radio offers had come my way for shows which were to begin that September but the prospective sponsors had to know whether I would still be "under contract" to Uncle Sam at that time. Therefore, I asked for my discharge from the Coast Guard—and got it. Jimmie Grier took over and carried on as leader for the few remaining months of the band's existence. And the whole crew made a trip to Manila which I envied.

It was not at all a happy severance. Wearing the uniform had been enjoyable and in spite of the occasional petty upsets and annoyances that occurred, I had taken genuine delight in directing musicians who were, for the most part, of the highest caliber. But above all I enjoyed the presentation of many thousands of hours of music, comedy, and entertainment to the military and civilians alike for whom the music was a tonic, an inspiration and, if you will, an anodyne.

The flood of radio offers was, of course, inspired by the fact that when I received my commission in the Coast Guard and bowed out of the Sealtest broadcast, our rating was an exceedingly high one. Now I realize that the Music Corporation of American and my sponsors, Procter and Gamble, as well as the advertising agency, probably thought that I would come up with another John Barrymore and Joan Davis with the inevitable high rating. They will probably never forgive me for only bringing Pinky Lee into radio popularity.

However, this was a most unique contract. For the first time in my radio career, I was to produce and direct my own show from top to bottom. I was not particularly anxious to do this—not that I have ever shirked responsibility or lacked the energy, the time, or the desire to handle completely the reins of a broadcast. But I knew that I did not have the great creative imagination we had found in Ed Gardner for guiding the various writing talents. And too, I was not very familiar with the available writers then in and around Hollywood. Although I knew the agency would help me find the best talent around, I was aware that it was not always easy for one to be at the same time performer, director, and producer.

But the agency now felt that my idea of the backstage rehearsal format should be given a try. It was similar to the one we had considered, then abandoned, for the Sealtest show. I outlined my ideas on it and we secured the services of a most capable associate producer who for several years had guided the destinies of the Maxwell House show.

I believe that both the agency and this gentleman who became my associate producer did believe in my rehearsal format to a limited degree. However, I realize now that the only way my unconventional format could be produced to perfection was to have everyone believe in it—everyone from those of us who conceived it, wrote it, directed it, down to the bit parts and the members of the orchestra. Also, we were doomed from the start, as the attempt to use four personalities in the course of the twenty-seven minutes or so allotted to the actual execution of the entertainment portion of the show, made my format impossible.

The show began with passengers presumably ascending in an elevator, the operator of which functioned as the usual "billboard" or person who announces the cast and scenes of the production. To be off-beat, we had this character do his bit in a very bored and unenthusiastic manner. This, of course, was the antithesis of all radio advertising and flew in the face of radio executives who always felt that these announcements must be in the bombastic style of a Don Wilson. As a matter of fact, on our first show our elevator operator deliberately pretended to confuse Ingrid Bergman with Greta Garbo and presumed to be not the least interested in either one, although we paid Bergman five thousand dollars for a five-minute dramatic sketch. Our audience was instructed to be quiet at all times. No applause! Instead, we "punctuated" and filled pauses (where audience reaction usually might occur) with great sounds of tympani and triumphant brass. We tried as much as possible to convey the impression to the listener that this was indeed a rehearsal, without the presence of a studio audience. In fact, our elevator operator warned the "passengers in his elevator car" that this was a rehearsal during which no applause was permitted.

We tried, *à la* Jack Benny, to simulate moments of trouble with executives of the broadcasting company who were quibbling over certain sound effects or lines in the script of our broadcast. We used Fritz Feld in the characterization of an impressionable and excitable French librarian for the orchestra's music and strove to recreate on the air some of the natural accidents and situations that do happen in the life of an orchestra and a group of personalities trying to work together at a rehearsal.

Well, it never quite came off—in fact great gloom descended upon the Music Corporation of America the night of the first show. It improved somewhat as we went along, although we never did get around to using our female Hollywood commentator, whose brilliant and caustic column in the *Hollywood Reporter* was, in my opinion, one of the best-written and most exciting columns on the doings in cinema land. We used Les Paul and his trio of string wizards, without anyone paying the least attention to his brilliant work. Long after he left the show, an accident befell Les, and during his convalescence a wonderful idea struck him which resulted in those brilliant recordings in his own garage that catapulted him and his wife, Mary Ford, to great popularity. But few ever remember that Les Paul was on our broadcast for over six months, week in and week out. And few will recall that we used a little vocal group led by a boy named Mel Tormé who subsequently clicked big as "The Velvet Fog." He was truly a very gifted artist, a master of several instruments, an inspired writer of music and a fine interpreter of song.

In spite of all our struggle for the evolution of this rather radical idea it just wouldn't work enough to give us the "fourteen" rating we felt we must have to justify our existence. The main thing wrong with the show was the agency's insistence on using four acts in a half-hour broadcast. There simply wasn't enough time to develop the relaxed believability of a Burns and Allen or a Godfrey.

However, I was renewed for the second forty-four weeks solid the second year. It was decided that in the fall of '46 we would use Xavier Cugat and his band for the music, as the agency offered him to me for a ridiculously small figure. Cugat later blamed me for this although I merely accepted an offer from his own representative. Later we were fortunately able to secure the services of Monty Woolley and to create a comedy situation centered in and about my Hollywood home in the hills.

This format, while offering possibilities, eventually merged into what I felt was the most believable story line for me. It was the idea that our show would take place in a night club owned by Billie Burke, where anything could and did happen. The cast of characters included gangsters, racketeers, a dumb but beautiful cigarette girl, a checkroom girl, a doorman with an accent of some ear-catching proportions and, above all, a bus boy named Pinky Lee.

I had met Pinky at the same Earl Carroll party where I met Yvonne

DeCarlo. Pinky, who perhaps is the most hard-pressing comedian I have ever known, was on my tail for a considerable portion of the Carroll party to use him in radio. Apparently his previous attempts to crash the medium had been unsuccessful and he was working at Earl Carroll's theater for much less than his actual worth. He offered to go on the broadcast for nothing. I told him that that was ridiculous. He would be paid and we would give it a try.

Pinky's first program was indeed a triumph, with MCA signing him under my nose the following morning. I protested to the Music Corporation of America's representative, whose decency resulted in one-half of Pinky's contract being assigned to me. Pinky also gave me privately a letter stating that I would have the first option on his services for future programs in the event this one terminated.

As Pinky grew in popularity, so did our program. As always, I bowed out of the spotlight and insisted that the writers, or writer whom Pinky had chosen for his own lines, throw most of the show Pinky's way. Our sponsor and advertising agency seemed fairly contented.

During the occasional visits of the very dignified and reserved executives from Cincinnati, I think they were rather frightened by my occasional outbursts directed at members of my own staff who all too often put the program in jeopardy, by their inattention or desire to clown around in the control room, instead of devoting every faculty and ounce of energy to its successful execution.

I have the patience of a saint but cannot tolerate repeated stupidity or inattention during costly rehearsal, when the success or failure of a very important contract is at stake. But the boys from Procter and Gamble, who rarely if ever would have raised their voices even if the walls had come tumbling down about them, were, I am afraid, somewhat flabbergasted at times by my fulminations.

This is a truly American phenomenon that makes it an horrendous crime for anyone, at any time, to raise his or her voice. All too often the individual who has just committed a stupid, grossly inexcusable blunder seeks refuge by twitting the individual who really suffers from the mistake by saying, "You're raising your voice, you're raising your voice!" And I bless the article in the April, 1954 *Reader's Digest*, which only *Reader's Digest* would have had the courage to offer to its millions of readers. It set down the simple thought, the heresy, that: "we have come to regard strong feelings as a sign that something is wrong with us. The truth is that it may be more dangerous to be *under*emotional than to be *over*emotional." The bird-brains, lightweights, and knuckleheads who surround us everywhere will perhaps not be transformed into intelligent, fast-thinking, or perceptive individuals by a bawling out or a harsh dressing down; but the person who has been seriously affected by the failure of others to carry out oft-times too-simple duties and obligations and who bottles up his righteous annoyance within himself is only subjecting his nervous system, his glandular system, and his blood pressure to an ordeal that can lead to downright ill health.

Let the supercivilized, the noble, dignified, and reserved, turn-the-other-cheek characters bottle up their anger and grandly overlook and forgive the bumbleheads who surround them. Personally, I'd rather risk losing the good will of a nitwit whom I should never have hired in the first place and keep my emotional good health. This could be the chief reason that I enjoy life without ulcers which plague my more gentlemanly, forgiving, but repressed associates.

Our program of broadcasts for the soap-makers emanated from Hollywood at seven-thirty, which meant that it reached the Middle West with its millions of listeners at nine-thirty and the Eastern seaboard, where the greatest segment of radio and television-set owners exist, at ten-thirty. As we were still just coming out of the war with its derangement of the household, with many thousands still overseas, engaged in war plants, or seeking diversion in theaters, night clubs, and places other than the home, it was axiomatic that our rating would suffer.

I doubt that, even if we *had* found a Barrymore, our rating could have achieved a very noble status. The Cugat-Pinky Lee-Billie Burke triumvirate, combined with my best efforts and the best of our writers did not suit our advertising agency or sponsor. We were only able to average eleven points in the computation of our rating nemesis.

In the spring of 1947 I was offered the third year for the Cincinnati soap-maker with the understanding that I permit someone else to produce and direct the show. Had they suggested an individual as capable as Gardner, Dick Mack, or some of our other creative and experienced operators, I would have been very happy to relinquish the reins. But the gentleman named was one about whom I knew very little, and that little was hardly likely to encourage me to entrust my career and show to him. Although the amount offered me was even more than I was netting from the previous two years' arrangement, I bowed out.

I had every confidence that if Pinky Lee and I were offered to a sponsor in the fall and given a better time and an earlier origination from California, with a rebroadcast by transcription to the East, we could together satisfy any sponsor who might come along. To my dismay, I noticed the obvious wooing of Pinky Lee by the advertising agency and the boys from Cincinnati. Although Pinky was obligated to take a gamble with me in the fall, it was apparent that he preferred the sure thing of a forty-four-week firm contract to taking a chance with me the following September. In the best downcast-eye-and-toe-digging-in-the-carpet manner, Pinky made clear to me his unhappiness at the thought of taking a gamble. I therefore released him from the contract with me, although I warned him that he might find that the sudden warm friendship of the advertising boys would be cordial only as long as he was important and useful to them.

Under the direction of the dilettante who supervised it, the third year of the soap broadcast starred Don Ameche who presented a feminine film star each week to do a portion of some favorite sketch or film which *he* had always wanted to do. It found Lee in the unusual situation of working with a male headliner who would not subordinate himself to Pinky. Pinky's spot or spots on the program became shorter and shorter until he found himself dumped from the program after the first thirteen weeks.

Although they were obligated to pay him for the remaining weeks of his contract, the ignominy of being dropped from the show cut Pinky very deeply. It was to have an even more disastrous effect upon *my* fall career. The Ameche program itself never rose above an average of eight points! Maybe I was more prophetic than I realized.

I had heard fantastic stories of an advertising-agency president, such as that he won a perfume account by dressing his office staff in dusters and having them busy themselves with office equipment and paraphernalia to impress a French perfumer. He was legendary in advertising circles for other stunts and methods used in achieving his prominence. I was told he was a hypochondriac, which meant little or nothing to me, inasmuch as I was not going to play nurse to him.

Having been asked to send some of our Drene broadcast records to him in the East, I was soon requested to appear before him in his West Coast office. I had been warned that he was a strange and difficult person and I should have risen from my chair and left his office without a word when he instantly put me on the defensive by saying that he had heard about the difficulties my Cincinnati soap sponsors had had with me. Beyond an occasional difference as to the choice of some of the personalities we used on our show or a difference with the talent agency about the writers we should use—honest differences of judgment and experience—our relationship had been pleasant enough. That I had been tentatively offered a third year at five thousand dollars a week if I would entrust the reins to someone else speaks for itself. The debacle of the third year of the shampoo program was also eloquent rebuttal. When the gray-haired executive made this crack concerning our supposed difficulties, I let it pass. He then proceeded to tell me that the president of a great cigarette company which had placed their advertising account with him was interested in a show similar to the one they had heard, in which we had the Villa Vallee as our format and Pinky Lee and I worked together.

Shortly thereafter, during the making of *The Bachelor and the Bobby Soxer* with Cary Grant and Myrna Loy, I received a call from New York from the president of the cigarette company who told me he was very interested in having me for the same type of show he had heard on the Drene records. He said he understood that Pinky Lee was not available but expressed the opinion that we could find someone who would work equally as well. I was pressed by my radio representatives to send a wire confirming my availability for thirty-nine weeks, and this wire was in effect a contractual agreement on my part to perform. Two weeks passed with no confirmation of the acceptance of my wire from the advertising agency executive. Suddenly I got word that he was coming to the West Coast and would see me at the Beverly Hills Hotel.

Again I made the mistake of not walking out on Mr. Hypochondriac. After listening to a record by a comedian we all felt might replace the unattainable Pinky Lee, this executive invited me into the garden back of his suite. There he quietly informed me that the National Broadcasting Company would not accept this program. This was the first time I was aware that a network may refuse to take an artist even if a sponsor wants him. The network may take this stand if it feels that the artist or his program is not satisfactory. It was as though I had uttered blasphemies or obscenities on the airways or had suddenly become a moral leper as far as radio was concerned. To say that I was flabbergasted is to put it mildly. We were nearing the Labor Day weekend, and this executive asked me if it would be possible, with no notice or preparation whatsoever, to do a reading for him in a radio studio with the comedian in question.

Not suspecting a trap and in order to make it possible for this gentleman to enjoy a yachting trip over the Labor Day weekend, I agreed to a simple reading of a hastily prepared script in a radio studio without orchestra or audience and a cast of personalities hastily assembled with no rehearsal.

I should have had my head examined for my courtesy and willingness, especially since I knew that this man was reputed to be a very dangerous one in our business. The rotund comedian and I did our best. We had a fairly good script, but lacking an orchestra and an audience, with all the stimulus these factors give, it was hardly a true sample of what he or I would offer in a finished program. This show was recorded and piped to New York to the top NBC hierarchy *as an example of the type of show I wished to present that fall!*

There then followed the most humiliating and trying experience I've ever known in my career. On his return from the yachting trip over the Labor Day weekend, the advertising executive disappeared and became impossible to reach. Utilizing the West Coast head of the network and the columnists, who were fed vicious and untrue reports, I was harassed and treated like a stumblebum. The West Coast network head informed me that the Villa Vallee format, regardless of the comedian we used (even though this format had been chosen by the president of the cigarette company) was not acceptable to him. When I then asked him what format we should use, I was given evasive answers and double talk.

Our program starting date was nine days away, and I still did not have a contract to begin the first program. I had been previously warned by the former West Coast network head that our hypochondriac advertising executive would "crucify" me. At the time of this warning I had not yet sent the wire of confirmation to the East, but later, secure in the belief that there was no way that this executive *could* "crucify" me, I had sent the wire, which left me completely at his mercy.

The thirty-nine weeks of this broadcast became a nightmare of continued torture, mortification, worry, and actual persecution. To be sure, two of the network representatives who played a part in the "crucifixion" were dropped from the network. There is little question in my mind that when they lay their heads on their pillows at night their consciences are not happy ones.

Our program ended in the spring of 1947 after two broadcasts from Las Vegas, which was just then beginning to expand into the strange wonderland it has since become. The termination of my association with this executive left me a sadder but wiser man. The fact that he was later involved in a headlined scandal that came perilously close to serious trouble for him, is beside the point. I'll never understand why he saw fit to single me out for such a punishment, but since I believe that there is a justice here on earth, I believe that time will take care of Mr. Hypochondriac.

(I wrote the foregoing account some years ago. It gives me some solace to recount that, since then, this gentleman's powerful agency has blown up in his face like a megaton bomb in an episode fraught with chicanery unusual even for Madison Avenue. And too, a number of the other bastards connected with this unhappy show have met their come-uppance. As I have mentioned, I only hold a grudge a decade or so.)

CHAPTER XVIII

Eleanor

"Some Enchanted Evening"

As I stepped out on the beach, out of nowhere appeared a man of medium height, and whether or not I observed it then, wavy hair, blue eyes, and facially the type that I had always admired. I would have said that he was thirty-five or possibly a few years less. Actually, Rudy at that time was forty-four. He wasted no time with social amenities, but immediately asked me if I would like to go that evening with him to the Cal-Neva Club . . . "No, thanks," I said very politely. He would not be put off so easily and began a systematic third degree. From me he secured not only my name but my father's name and where he lived. Then, apparently satisfied that I wasn't going to meet him and with obvious disappointment written all over his face, he turned to rejoin his friends in a little bungalow near the exit to the beach. . . .

(The preceding words are those of my wife, Eleanor Vallee. She wrote her own version of our meeting and subsequent "courting." From time to time in this chapter I may let her pick up the story—her prose will be italicized.)

Like most lovers' meetings, this confrontation on the beach was sheer happenstance. Just what in the hell was I *doing* on the edge of Lake Tahoe, on the California-Nevada line? What quirk of fate led me to be having cocktails with some Princeton friends on the porch of a lakeside bungalow at which time I was hungrily ogling a gorgeous sixteen-year-old redhead—so help me, she looked at least twenty-three or twenty-four, so help me! The redhead was Eleanor—and here's how I came to meet her. . . .

It was getting along toward July the Fourth, 1945, and I obtained a weekend leave from the Coast Guard. Along with Errol Flynn, Bruce Cabot, Jack Kramer (a fellow Coast Guardsman), and a group of tennis stars, I appeared in exhibition games in San Francisco for a bond rally. We drew a big crowd and sold several hundred thousand dollars' worth of war bonds.

With me on this trip was a Cleveland pianist named Charles Wick, for whom I had secured a position with the William Morris talent agency. He had booked a performer, Emil Boreo, into a Lake Tahoe club and nothing would do but that I come along to catch his opening there on July 2. I wasn't too enthusiastic about the two-hundred-mile trip, but Charlie talked me into it. When we arrived at the Cal-Neva, Boreo and the character who owned this fabulous spot (one-half of which was on the Nevada side, the other half in California) were waiting for us. Without any ado, the uncouth Boniface, who was later to be indicted for income-tax evasion, made it clear to Boreo that he was to call upon me to perform on his opening night performance.

Not only did Boreo call upon me for the early show but the late show as well, while the tab at our table was astronomical. I didn't mind getting up (with Wick assisting me at the piano) and knocking my brains out for thirty or forty minutes, but I thought that the lobster-faced character who owned the joint might at least have sent us a bottle of champagne or a cocktail. This sad sack had a contempt for musicians and performers, although he was willing enough to take advantage of them if he could get away with it. So much for opening night. The following night, July 3, I was again called upon for the early show and late show, with again no courteous acknowledgment on the part of our host for my contribution to the evening's proceedings. But the next day, the most Glorious Fourth, was to prove quite eventful for me as I was to discover on the beach my present bride.

It was apparent that she enjoyed the water as she and a little boy remained out in the deep for at least two hours. The whole beach was agog that a celebrity was among them. However, this tall gal, who was only sixteen but looked so mature that I debated as to whether she might be the mother of the boy, was oblivious to everything but her pleasure in swimming.

I warily watched her out of one eye and as she finally came past me I jumped off the porch and asked her if she would like to be my guest at Cal-Neva that evening. There was no mistaking her lack of interest in me as she flatly refused my invitation. I suggested she bring her mother and dad if she wished, in fact her whole party if that was what stood in the way. Unknown to me, she had a date with a young kid who worked at the soda fountain.

I didn't introduce myself to Eleanor Norris, as I assumed of course that she had recognized me. I could have been Cary Grant or Clark Gable, for all she knew, as she rarely went to movies. She dashed off into the woods, and I rejoined my group on the porch. A few minutes later she was back again. My fallen spirits were immediately revived as I consoled myself that she had seen the error of her ways. Again I stopped her and again I assumed she knew to whom she was talking. Again she flatly

said, "No." I then asked her her name and her father's name, where she
lived and if it was listed in the phone book. That was all I needed.

. . . and Rudy asked me, "Do you ever come down to Hollywood?"

"Oh, once in a while—"

*"Good," he said. "Very good. When you do please be sure and look
me up."*

This is one thing I made a mental note not to do . . . .

At the conclusion of the last show the night before I had told Boreo
not to introduce me on penalty of death at either show on my last night.
Wick and I had become a little annoyed at paying fifty dollars for each
visit. Our table had become the gathering place for all the moochers on
the spot, who ordered drinks and steaks with abandon. So you can imagine
Boreo's surprise when I breathlessly told him to be sure to introduce me
for the first show that evening as I naturally assumed that, since Cal-
Neva was about the only spot on that part of the lake to which everyone
came, she would have to be in the audience. I really knocked myself out
and, as I performed, I searched as well as I could under the spotlight to
see if she was somewhere in the audience.

The ironic fact is, as I learned later, that she was alone with the kid
with whom she had been swimming: she had canceled her date with the
soda jerk. She was standing on a chair at the entrance, peeking through
the curtains. She was unaware that the guy working in Coast Guard
uniform was the character who had asked her for a date that evening.
In fact, I guess in my bathing suit I looked like the ad which read "Send
this boy to camp." While her father and mother wandered around the
slot machines, my bride-to-be watched the show and admonished the
little boy to "look out for that Hollywood character—if you see him, tell
me so I can hide."

At the conclusion of the show, I wandered all over Cal-Neva itself,
inspecting the occupants of each table, the big bar, and all the gaming
rooms but could find her nowhere. I went to Cal-Vada, a smaller spot
next door, over to the bowling alley, and even down to the little theater
near King's Beach where, with the practiced eye of an old usher, I wandered up and down the aisles and in the little balcony upstairs to the
intense annoyance of all the couples in warm embrace. This last evening
at Lake Tahoe, under the full moon that was shining so brightly, was
indeed a night for romance, and I was determined that this gal with the
long red hair, well-scrubbed complexion, and the lithe frame was to be
my last romantic memory of this picturesque locale. After the second
show, in which I again poured out the best of my repertoire, I again
searched in vain for her and finally retired in disgust.

*. . . You may imagine that I am conceited about being sought so much,
being so desired by Rudy Vallee that first time. My satisfaction is tem-
pered by his frank revelations that I was not the first girl he had pursued*

with such thoroughness. In fact, Rudy's whole life has been one of a pursuit of romance for romance itself. . . .

My good friend George Mardikian of the Omar Khayyam restaurant, knowing my interest in wines, had arranged for me to visit some vintners: the Beaulieu Winery as the guest of Madame De La Tour, Beringer Bros. at St. Helena, and finally the establishment of Louis Martini, whose red wines had intrigued me at an Italian restaurant several weeks before. We should have met Mardikian at an appointed rendezvous at about two o'clock, which would have enabled us to visit all three wineries leisurely and with thorough enjoyment. But I insisted that we stay at King's Beach until one o'clock to see if my goddess would show.

It was a dismal afternoon with much wind and no sun and it was definite by one-thirty that neither she nor anyone else was going to brave the elements. So we dashed on with our friend Jack Bates, who owned the car, to the wineries in and around Napa County. We had called Mardikian to inform him of our delay and we missed the visit to Beaulieu altogether. Still we were able to manage a quick but wonderful tour through Beringer Bros. By the time we reached poor Louis Martini, he not only reeked of garlic from his dinner but had drowned his sorrow at our delay in his own wines. Although he conducted the tour with great pride and propriety, it was evident that he was having difficulty with his speech.

By this time we were loaded down with the best wines of both Beringer and Martini and we headed for San Francisco and a midnight meal at the Omar Khayyam.

. . . as far as I was concerned, the meeting with Rudy was forgotten . . . for Rudy, however, the chase had just begun. . . .

On my return to Los Angeles, I wrote a letter to Eleanor Norris at the address I found listed under her father's name, Harlie Norris, in the Berkeley phone book. In this missive I asked her if she had a picture of herself. When Eleanor came home from school, the household was in a dither. They had seen from the return address that it was from me, and everyone was waiting breathlessly for her to open it. On learning that I was the Hollywood character who had invited her and her family to Cal-Neva, she became the butt of much kidding for not having accepted an invitation which would have meant steaks and champagne and the thrill of being with a performer in the show.

Mother suddenly said to me, "Do you remember what he looks like?" and for the life of me I couldn't picture the Vagabond Lover. We all made a beeline for the rumpus room where we kept stacks of movie magazines and began feverishly fumbling through them, looking for a picture of Rudy. We found one that was taken when Rudy made The Palm Beach Story *at Paramount in which he portrays the wealthy "schnook" wearing the pince-nez which is cut to fit the droop of his eyes.*

It was a particularly atrocious pose as Rudy and the studio intended it to be, one in which Rudy pursed up his mouth and assumed the very prissy facial expression which has been glorified in some fifteen or sixteen pictures since. I dropped the magazine in disgust saying, "Good Lord, I don't want to go out with him."

I received a call from the Navy to direct the Seabees band at Camp Parks, just outside of Oakland, and phoned Eleanor to ask her if she and her parents would be my guests at the show as well as for dinner at the Omar Khayyam and dancing at the Mark Hopkins.

There followed a whirlwind two evenings: the first night with my good friend Mardikian outdoing himself at the Omar Khayyam, beginning with many Omar's Delights, one of the most delightful cocktails in the world, followed by every dish that George could concoct and an evening of dancing.

I've always made a fetish of the looks, the sheen, and the feel of satin on a fair lady. When I observed an attractive woman wearing this sensual fabric and stated very simply that I hoped someday to see Eleanor in a dress like that, she really felt that I was out of my mind. But she has since come to appreciate what a tight-fitting satin dress can do for a woman. In fact, she is more appreciative of what that material can do for a woman than I.

On the next evening, after the concert at Camp Parks was finished, I asked her father if he would mind if Eleanor rode with me in the Navy station wagon to Trader Vic's where we would all meet for Vic's rum creations and his unusual and exotic Tahitian gastronomic delights. Dad Norris had apparently liked me from the start. Even though Eleanor behind me was vigorously telegraphing a negative head-shake to him, Dad said that he would be delighted and that he and Mrs. Norris would follow in the other station wagon. The Navy chief who was driving my car was a smart cooky. He fixed his rear-view mirror so that it was obvious that he was not watching us and I prepared for my great moment as I drew Eleanor close to me for a kiss that had been all too long delayed. But I was doomed to disappointment, as she would have none of me. When we finished our drinks and food at Trader Vic's, Eleanor will never forget how I very courteously thanked all three of them for having been my guests then bowed out quickly, leaving her father and mother to take her home.

Our affair might have ended there as VJ Day came along and that evening was celebrated with another lovely lady of great charm and beauty. I had spent all afternoon opening thirty or forty cases of wine, putting them in specially constructed racks while the radio blared forth the excitement in the streets of Los Angeles and San Francisco. This attractive divorcée who shared the excitement of that memorable evening with me was a woman I had admired at Ciro's, a duplicate of my lost love of the Pirate's Den, but I knew even before that evening (it was our third or fourth date) that it was not to be. In the meantime I had also made the acquaintance of a very attractive and gifted young lady, a fashion designer, with whom I was to know countless hours of wonderful companionship and pleasure.

Eleanor by this time had gone on to the University of Nevada. We were pretty much out of touch with each other except for an occasional card and two surprise visits to Los Angeles, where I shunted her off to someone else. If anyone had told me that I was going to marry her, I would have said he was crazy.

Dore Schary, who was then the head of RKO Pictures, had a feeling that the part of the District Attorney in *The Bachelor and the Bobby Soxer* should be cast in an off-beat manner. I was called to appear one afternoon to try out for the role. Unknown to me, that same morning a very fine professional actor had already tested for it and everyone agreed that he was the man to do it. Frankly, he out-acted me a thousand per cent and was exactly what the average director, producer, and audience would expect in the role.

Like the dumb calf being led to slaughter, I showed up for the test with everybody laughing up his sleeve. I said to the young director, "I'm going up to Lake Tahoe for a couple of weeks, do you think I'll be back in time for the start of the picture?" He had difficulty in keeping a straight face as he wanted to say, "It could be that you can stay there for the entire summer, if you want." But when I stepped in the door and asked Myrna Loy to tell Shirley Temple that I had arrived (I learned this later) they all looked at each other and said, "Who are we kidding? This is the guy for the part. In a sense he's all wrong, but he gives something to it that is different."

My trip to Lake Tahoe was with a group of friends and this young lady who was my favorite at that time. We all stayed at a spot next to King's Beach, the same beach on which I had first seen Eleanor. And again, on the night of July 4, I agreed to emcee the impromptu party at Brockway Lodge, which strangely enough was the spot that Mrs. Norris herself had suggested as the ideal place to stay on the lake. Before the show began, I saw Dad and Mother Norris with Eleanor (a very obviously reluctant Eleanor) approach the entrance to the room in which I was going to work. She had not seen me, and was trying to hide between her father and mother so that I might not know she was there. And of course she died when I approached her with an expansive and cordial welcome. I think that was the beginning of wisdom for Eleanor, as when she saw the cultured, charming, and lovely creature who had honored me with her presence on this trip, the spark of jealousy really began to burn in my bride-to-be.

. . . this very attractive girl was extremely glamorous . . . a typical

Hollywood movie-star type ... at no time did I feel any pangs of jeal-ousy. ...

But again, if anyone had told me at that time that I was going to marry Miss Norris, I would have laughed. I had known great happiness with the girl who made the trip with me and seriously contemplated asking her if two could live as cheaply as one.

But Eleanor and I became smitten in the moonlight of Palm Springs, where we were almost accidentally thrown together when she and her mother were there for a short vacation. This meeting coincided with the conclusion of my third engagement at the Cocoanut Grove in April of 1949 and a slight quarrel with my beauteous dress designer, who had piqued Eleanor's envy and jealousy, left the track open for Eleanor and me to fall in love.

Unless you've known the incredible beauty, warmth, and "something" that Palm Springs has, particularly in April and May, you'll never know how really easy it is to fall in love. If the object of your affection seems to be difficult to win, take him or her to Palm Springs during those magic months. If conquest is not yours there—take it from me, it never will be.

... Palm Springs, Rudy and I feel, is the most relaxing garden spot in the world for anyone who is a sun-lover and a Garden of Eden by which all other places fade in comparison. ... The season was over and the Ten-nis Club was practically empty the night that Rudy and his friends drove down. Mother and I and Dad's secretary had had dinner at the club and wondered if Rudy was going to make it at all. No sooner had Rudy breezed in than he asked me to dance. While dancing he held me very close and began to tell me that he liked me very, very much. In fact, I think if I had let him, Rudy would have kissed me right on the floor, as it was evident that he was very passionately fond of me. ... Rudy has the quality of making a woman—and particularly me—feel as though she were a queen on a throne. Somehow when I was with him I felt that I was the only woman in the room. ...

About two nights before we left, Rudy took me to an ice-skating show at one of the small hotels in Palm Springs. In our party that evening was Walter Gross, the superb pianist who had worked with Rudy in the early days of '29 and '30 and who had accompanied Rudy at the Cocoanut Grove just prior to the trip. At that time he had just finished writing the unforgettable tune "Tenderly." After dinner and the ice show we all returned to Rudy's Palm Springs home but, as the hour neared one o'clock, we stopped in and asked Mother if I could stay out late. With-out realizing how late it already was, Mother assented.

Mother had gone back to sleep for a while; when she awakened sud-denly and looked at her watch she could hardly believe her eyes. It was 4 a.m. Mother awakened Marge, Dad's secretary, saying "Good heavens,

*what is that child doing out at this late hour with a man of the world
like Rudy Vallee!" Marge very laconically replied, "You'd better find
out." Mother needed no urging. Jumping into her pedal pushers, in a few
minutes she was in her convertible driving over to Rudy's place, only
to discover all the lights in the house were out; more important, Rudy's
car was gone. That of course meant only one thing—that Rudy and I
must be on our way back to the Town and Country, the "ranch villa"
hotel where we were staying.*

*Taking a back road short cut, Mother broke all speed records, hoping
to arrive there before Cinderella and her Prince should appear. All this
effort was in vain, however. Just as she drove up in front of the hotel,
Rudy and I were rounding the corner. Rudy very casually said, "What
on earth is your mother doing up this time of the morning?" Laughingly
I replied, "What do you think?" But frankly, deep down inside I was
just about as embarrassed as I knew Mother would be. Mother started
into the hotel but Rudy yelled to her. She came over to the car feigning
a nonchalance that I'm sure was quite transparent. Then the unpredictable
Rudy said with great aplomb, leaving Mother stunned, "Mother, dear,
don't worry—I'm returning your daughter just the way you gave her
to me."*

*Not long after this Rudy finally declared he couldn't stay away from
me any longer and made a special trip to San Francisco to ask Dad for
permission to marry me. . . .*

Eleanor had always desired a church wedding with bridesmaids, ushers,
and all the trimmings. I wasn't mad about the idea but I was so in love
with her that I finally gave in. It was the first time that I was to be married in a church and receive the sanction and blessing of a priest. In fact,
it had been decreed that my three previous marriages, not having been
performed in a church, were in the eyes of the Catholic hierarchy, at
least, not marriages at all. This may explain for those of the devout how
this seemingly incomprehensible act was accomplished.

At the reception, amid the popping of champagne corks, was Charlie
Wick who was responsible for the trip that led to the finding of my
bride and who was now married to a girl whom I had found for him.
Even the burning of Eleanor's veil as she leaned backward into some
candles, which might have resulted in a tragedy had I not acted with
precision and quickly smothered the flame, did not mar the happy
occasion.

Although neither of us realized it, this was the beginning of a long
honeymoon of night clubs and hotels, the "court of last appeals" for a
performer. It began with the SAE convention at the Biltmore Hotel only
two days later, followed by the taking of the wrong train to Vancouver,
British Columbia. I guess I was so much in love I couldn't read a schedule
properly. Then we took the right trains to Cleveland, Buffalo, Pittsburgh,

Maine, Boston, Florida, New York, Providence, Minneapolis, Chicago, Texas, New Orleans, Colorado, back to California, only to begin the same vicious cycle all over again. There is hardly a place in these United States where we have not been, including Puerto Rico, Panama, and Hawaii. They have been glorious years, with our forty-eight pieces of luggage, living on trains, out of bags in hotels, packing, unpacking, and repacking. It has been a great experience, albeit at times a very trying one. The night-club and hotel-room field is the most difficult of all. But I have been fortunate in having a very understanding, patient, sympathetic, and loyal companion, who has made this grueling grind more bearable. It has been an experience in which I have matured and polished my basic talents in the task of entertaining human beings.

All the same, it's pleasant to settle down in New York for a while in *How to Succeed*. It's really lovely to come home from the theater every night—to the same address for a change.

CHAPTER XIX

Into the Hecklers' Paradise—
Night Clubs—Play-Acting—TV

"Dear Hearts and Gentle People ..."

AND SO IT CAME TO PASS IN THE YEAR OF
our Lord, nineteen hundred and forty-nine, that I took my fourth wife.
I was crazy about her and the rest of the country was crazy about
canasta. A great number of the people were apprehensively looking under
their beds for Communist spies and sure enough they found a few.
Truman began his first full term after flabbergasting everybody (except
those who voted for him) by overwhelming Dewey 303 electoral votes
to 189.

America was steadily beating most of its swords into plowshares; it
retained some measure of preparedness, however, since the previous year
Congress had passed a peacetime Selective Service Bill. There was much
public criticism of this action by Congress in 1948. After all, we had
the atomic bomb, so what did we need with a lot of soldiers? No one
would dare attack us as long as we had the bomb. Things just had to be
peaceful from now on, right? Then in September, 1949, the month I was
married, an atomic explosion was reported to have taken place inside
the boundaries of the U.S.S.R. In the immortal words of Jackie Gleason:
"And awa-a-a-ay we go!"

On Broadway the best play to open also happened to be the most
commercially successful. It ran nearly two years, got a Pulitzer prize, and
was called *Death of a Salesman*. Rodgers and Hammerstein opened a gold
mine entitled *South Pacific* and *Gentlemen Prefer Blondes* also entered
hot-ticket heaven. Hollywood turned out some fine films that are finding
renascence on the TV grind circuit: *All the King's Men, Letter to Three
Wives*, and *Twelve O'clock High*, to name a few.

By this time radio was feeling the unpleasant competition of what the
British call "the telly," what *Fortune* Magazine called "motion pictures
in the home." Since broadcasting had become intolerable to me, I decided
to go out to the grass roots and play the clubs and hotel rooms—some

luxurious, well-staffed, and beautifully appointed, and a few flea-bitten cocktail lounges in which I never imagined I should be found dead. This "honeymoon" which was to continue off and on for a decade or so turned out to be one of the most fascinating and exciting yet exasperating phases of my life.

I have an unfortunate knack of embarking on certain phases of my career at exactly the wrong time. I guess I used up all my allotted luck when I hit radio right on the nose! When I began on the club circuit, it had been on the wane for a couple of years and is even now a moribund business mainly suffering from an overdose of TV competition. Nevertheless, I barged in fearlessly, mainly because I didn't know this part of show biz was a bit over the hill. Of course, I did the tried-and-true items like the "Stein Song," "Whiffenpoof," "Vagabond Lover," etc., but I played down nostalgia and built an act that would kid my age (I called myself the "Pat Boone of the Stone Age"), my marriages, and the image most of the audience remembered, that of the romantic crooner with the megaphone. I amassed a huge file of stolen jokes, one-liners, humorous stories, and songs in dialect. My God, I even did a fair ventriloquist act with three dummies called Ezry, Sally Ann, and Linoleum. I tried a little of everything as I realized I couldn't rely on the old radio pattern of singing, emceeing, and fronting a band. It was a revelation and, not so incidentally, a living—a chance to develop my memory and command of audiences to a degree I never dreamed possible. Between 1949 and 1961 I was to develop four one-hour night-club routines, each "socko" with 65 per cent humor and the best collection of minister, priest, and rabbi stories ever told.

The January before my marriage I had "returned" to New York, playing a date at Lou Walters' Latin Quarter. I was a little annoyed that most of the columnists and reviewers described this action as "staging a comeback." The newspaper space and excellent, warm reviews were gratifying, of course—but the writing was sicklied o'er with the implication that I had staggered out of a wheel chair and fought my way back to the Main Stem. It was as if I had decided to come out of retirement. Retirement! For Christ's sake, I was just a kid of forty-seven and as far as retirement was concerned, I had been making a goodly number of movie appearances. Maybe they weren't *Gone with the Wind* or *For Whom the Bell Tolls* but they were nothing to be ashamed of.

"Rudy, you ought to go into television. You know, do a kind of TV Fleischmann Variety Hour. You'd kill 'em! Just the way you did in radio."

I must have heard scores of variations on the above theme from well-meaning friends. At first blush it appeared to make sense, but you can't equate the early thirties with the late forties. Too much water had run under the bridge, too many electrons had been agitated in vacuum tubes.

In the early years with Fleischmann it was shooting fish in a barrel—
we had little or no network competition and had almost unchallenged
choice of a fabulous talent pool from Broadway to Hollywood. We
couldn't miss. We were to radio what Ed Sullivan was to the early days
of TV.

Speaking of Sullivan, I was offered his show early in 1949. I had made
a guest appearance one Sunday and had done the French-Canadian song,
"Alouette." I did a chorus, then invited the crowd to join in—a sort of
sing-along routine. (Maybe I should sue Mitch Miller for royalties?)
At any rate, the crowd *didn't* join in and I yelled at them. "Oh, boy—
do you *stink*!" They loved it.

On the show Ed predicted that I would be even bigger in television
than radio. He couldn't have been more wrong. In his column, John
Crosby gave me an excellent notice and also predicted a great career for
me in this budding medium. As you know, it didn't happen at all.

Still, the day after the show (it was called "Toast of the Town" in
those days) Stanley Abrams, the executive producer of the program for
the then sponsor, Emerson Radio, called me over to look at the kinescope.
It wasn't a very clear picture and I was something less than enchanted
with my visual impact. Nevertheless, Abrams offered me the program
for myself. Mind you, this was just one of four or five TV offers I got
after the guest-shot. American Tobacco wanted me to do a series for
them at $10,000 a week and the William Morris talent agency was after
me for several TV projects.

"I appreciate your offer, of course," I told Abrams, "but I can't accept
it."

"But why? This is a great opportunity!"

"I know that, Mr. Abrams. No question about it. But I don't want
to stay in New York for one thing. I like California living too well.
Also, if I take this thing away from Ed, he'll never forgive me. I realize
he is the very antithesis of a master of ceremonies and you need more
of a professional. But if I took the show, Ed would never forgive me.
And that goes for the other columnists, too."

I often wonder what would happen if Sullivan were to go to a network
casting office today as an unknown, looking for work. "What sort of an
act do you do?" the casting director will say. "Uh—uh—I'm an M.C.,"
replies Ed. "You're *kidding*!" answers the casting director.

It is my theory that part of the reason for Sullivan's success is the
very fact that he is not a typical M.C. His dead-pan delivery, his wooden
demeanor and "no-talent" talent are his strength! The viewers identify
with him—they feel that, by God, *they* could do just as good a job as he.
Ed has always had a good show—many many great shows, partly due to
the producer, partly due to Ed, partly due to his entire organization.

His ratings through the years prove that he's got to have *something*.

Later on, TV lightning almost struck me again. I am sure you all remember a little bagatelle called "The $64,000 Question." Walter Craig, one of the agents working on the show asked me to his office and outlined the format.

"Jesus, this thing can't miss!" I said excitedly. "Whoever emcees this one will be better known than the President of the United States!"

"I'm glad you're enthusiastic about it," the agent said, "because we think you are the right person to front the show."

"Are you sure?" I asked. "You know, if you're looking for a Bert Parks-Milton Berle type—big smiles, peppy, jumping all over the place— count me out."

"Not at all, not at all. This is going to be a very heavy quiz show. We need someone who is erudite, cultured, who speaks well and can pro- nounce difficult words, foreign words, technical questions, et cetera. You know, restrained, casual, underplaying. We want you. Now, we'll want a reading before the sponsors in a few days. Just routine—"

The day of the reading came and Joe Cates, one of the execs involved with the show, dropped by my suite at the Park Sheraton. In great detail he filled me in on the format of the show, the framework, gimmicks, the "plateaus," and all that. As he was leaving I made a remark that was to cost me the job!

"Joe, I wonder why in hell they want me for this thing. It sounds like a warm show with lots of empathy. For God's sake, I just don't like people." I didn't mean it in quite the way it sounded but, really, I'm not in the least gregarious. In this way I am not at all like my Dad— he would always have time to chat with strangers who would drop in the drugstore or even those waiting for a streetcar out in front. You know, where-are-you-from, what's-your-line-of-work, how's-the- family and all that crap. I have enough on my mind about my own prob- lems and those of persons dear to me without being interested in strangers.

Cates said nothing to me about my remark but lost no time in convey- ing the gist to the sponsors—Revlon, I believe. Came the reading and— there was no film in the camera! That's an old Hollywood expression for a screen test that nobody gives a damn about—they don't even bother to put any film in the camera! I had to open my big mouth—of course, they didn't use a camera but if they had you can bet there would have been no film. After they had heard about what I'd said to Cates, I was as dead as Kelsey's pendulous extremities.

The man they did select, Hal March, is rather my type in height, build, curly hair, and general facial characteristics. I was intrigued to find that he underplayed the role cagily in just about the way I would have done it. Coincidentally, March had been under my management in California years before. He had come down from San Francisco with his partner Bob Sweeny (Remember "Sweeny and March"?) with some recordings of their radio shows and I never heard such audience response and funny routines in my life. I immediately put them on my Drene show and got them in touch with producers of other programs. March has developed into an excellent actor, starring on Broadway in *Come Blow Your Horn*, a comedy that became the "sleeper of the year" in 1961.

I descended into the maelstrom of the hecklers' paradise, the night-club scene, knowing full well what awaited me there. As any entertainer knows, it can often become at best a source of irritation, given the presence of roistering drunks; at worst, it may develop into an arena of combat.

When I decided to make the transition to this new field of endeavor, it was inevitable that I should recall my past jousts with members of the audience during the one-nighters and club appearances of yesteryear.

While it was merely a figment of newspaper imagination, for some reason through the years I had gained a reputation as a stormy petrel, a man who was always ready with his fists, the Mickey Walker of show business. For instance, Bill Cunningham, a brilliant, fearless orator, commentator, columnist of the *Boston Post*, a man who flatters nobody, took great pride one night in describing one of my "bouts." I was appearing at Boston's Copley Plaza and Bill was re-enacting the incident for his daughter in vivid detail. "This heckler had been riding Rudy all night," he said. "He took all he could and finally just walked over to the pest and laid him out cold with a vicious right!"

One-punch Vallee! I wish I could justify Bill's enthusiastic estimate of my prowess in the art of fisticuffs. After all, it could often have come in handy in disposing of the loudmouths every entertainer is a prey to in personal appearances. The truth of the matter is I have only *once* in my career ever connected with anyone, heckler or otherwise. In that case I only grazed the man's cheek and, astoundingly enough, it turned out to be the wrong guy! One-punch Vallee, indeed!

Here's how it happened. It was in Canada and I was standing with my back to the audience directing a band in a soft waltz when I felt something strike my right ankle, turned and looked down and saw an empty liquor bottle—Scotch at that, which I don't drink. But the more infuriating thing was to turn around and stare into a sea of impassive faces, registering complete apathy for the most part, neither hostility nor friendship, nor any indication of a willingness to point out the villain who threw the botle. It is this unique complicity of the herd, this apparent willingness to stick together in perfidy and felony, that is so maddening! It would be a relief, at least, if you turned around and faced only one-half or one-third of them giving you the bird. But no, there is a bored detachment on every face, as though nothing whatsoever had occurred.

At least it was this way in Toronto on our second appearance at the Canadian National Exposition, one of the biggest events of the Dominion, which occurs every fall. I looked over at my public-address system man who was operating our eight-thousand-dollar amplifying system with his coffin-like box of controls out in the audience. He pointed to a giant of a man (he looked about six-feet-seven!) who stood about three feet away from the control box. With my lips and face, I mirrored the expression, "Are you sure?" Murray moved his head up and down and continued to point. There was no mistaking which man he meant. As I approached this monster, who looked slightly villainous with the mustache he was wearing, I looked again at Murray for confirmation. I guess I was praying he was mistaken but it was too late to back down. Again he indicated definitely that this was the one.

As I approached the Canadian man-mountain, I let fly a right which grazed his right cheek. Had he lifted one of his huge arms and fists, he probably would have pulverized me. Yet he made no move whatsoever. He merely looked at me sadly as he said, "I didn't do it." And the amazing thing is that I knew instantly that he had *not* done it. I felt conscience-stricken and extremely unhappy. I quickly apologized and made my way back to the band platform and continued to the end of the dance set. However, I was not entirely in error. This young giant was the scion of a charming, titled dowager with whom I had had lunch the day before at her fabulous farm, the operation of which was only a hobby with her. Her income from one of the most successful gold mines in the world was so stupendous that she could run one hundred farms like it; but hers was unique in that the cows slept on varnished floors while beautiful recorded music played throughout the day for all of the denizens of her entire rural estate, including the pigs. I had not met the young man during the luncheon but he was apparently the black sheep of the family. Perhaps he may have resented my visit to his mother's estate for some obscure reason and had brought a group of his aristocratic snobs with him to our show and dance. He was with and directly in *front* of the individual who actually threw the bottle and my boy Murray had seen him rising up after he had ducked while the other man behind him had thrown the bottle.

The affair wound up with our young aristocrat, becoming more annoyed as the moments went by, coming backstage for revenge only to face one Umba, an even bigger giant from New Zealand or Australia (I forget which) who tried to calm our boy. Umba was retained by the Exposition management as factotum, bouncer, and pacifier. Umba finally moved the aristocratic nose over to the ear, a feat accomplished by the simple expedient of taking the aristocratic head under his arm and proceeding to effect this plastic surgery with one blow.

That was the only time that I ever actually even slightly landed with my fists. Oh, I've studied boxing. In 1929 while I was at the Brooklyn Paramount, I was considered such a strong radio plug that Johnny Green, one of the bantamweight contenders of that day (whose brother Bud Green was a very successful song writer), spent several hours over in my dressing room at the Paramount attempting to teach me the manly art of self-defense. In other words, trading a pug for a plug of his brother's songs! Then in 1938, out in California, Bob Howard, who conditions producers and directors and gave Cole Porter a new lease on life after Porter's tragic polo accident, also proceeded not only to condition me but to introduce me to the punching bag. He even invited me to land a few on his chin.

Still my boxing instruction in no way justified my ever walking off the band platform as I did in Wilkes-Barre, Pennsylvania, in 1930, but it would have taken the patience of a saint to withstand the taunts and insults of a florid, shiny-faced coal miner who stood there pouring it on for a little over an hour. Finally the French-Irish in me decided that something had to be done about it. I walked off the stage toward him. Fortunately, the crowd swarmed in and our miner friend was somehow removed from the place. It was a blessing for me as he would probably have knocked me into oblivion and maybe terminated my career once and for all right then. It's practically impossible, I believe, to play a sax and sing with no teeth!

There was one glorious satisfaction about the Wilkes-Barre event, however; it showed me what my band thought of me. As I turned, I discovered that my entire band, with the exception of the drummer and pianist, were in various spots behind me just in case anyone else pitched in and the fight became unfair. Even though I bawled them out when they did dumb and stupid things, by their simple eloquent gathering behind me I knew from then on that my boys were with me.

The time I came closest to getting it was in Raleigh, North Carolina— the Carolinas where we had so much trouble with an insolently impatient crowd which booed Alice Faye and me as we came on to begin our show, where one of our promoters decamped with the money due us, and where the sleet and rain ruined two of our best dates. Garden Spot of America! There in Raleigh, on a Monday night, with a splitting headache, I found myself being constantly given the bird by a tall, professorial-looking character out on the floor who had the most diabolical, leering smile I've ever seen on a man's face. Between my headache and the unhappiness of our tour in that part of the country in general, this was too much. Again I was off the platform seeking my quarry. This character, however academic his features, clearly registered an intent to mayhem and murder as he stood there with his fist raised in the air waiting for me to get close enough to land a punch. Fortunately his actions had been observed by two police. What with the crowd surging between us and the ministrations of the two coppers, our friend got the bum's rush.

It was at North Adams on a summer's evening that another one of these babies decided to be rude and obnoxious for minutes on end. However, this character remained in hiding in the crowd, and I had no recourse but to announce over the amplifying system that if he would kindly come up on the stage, I would proceed to knock his unprintable teeth down into his unprintable stomach. To my great surprise, this brought a roar of approval and applause from the audience, who stopped dancing to watch for what they hoped would be a good melee. I very honestly hoped he would come up, regardless of his size or ability, but I was frankly relieved when he didn't. The dancing resumed, but it remained for my personal secretary and my agent Ed Fishman, who resembled Paul Whiteman, to come in looking for the character. They heard my announcement over the speakers as they sat out in the car cooling off. Locating the poor guy, Fishman pulled a plastic job in Umba style (or at least so he says) and gave our heckler something to remember us by.

While I speak of these encounters lightly (as I can afford to do now since they are past) I realize how stupid I was to let my temper get the best of me. One well-placed blow could have knocked my front teeth out, thereby sorely curtailing my ability to play the saxophone. And too, I might have been disfigured for life. Since I have little enough to offer the cameras anyway, this was hardly desirable. I have counseled many others in my profession who have asked me what to do in such circumstances. Although I didn't practice what I preached, I say it honestly and with the greatest conviction: no insult or heckler, or any amount of vilification, is worth the risk of physical disfigurement, possible permanent crippling, or even death if the fight waxes to such proportions that the blow sends one reeling to strike a pointed or hard object with the back of the head. The candle just isn't worth the burning.

As I continued to do night-club work, the most grueling of all entertainment work, in a smoke-filled atmosphere, with mean, vicious, cruel individuals whose natures, inflamed by alcohol, lead them to consider the entertainer out there on the floor who is trying to earn a living, fair game for their sadistic torture, I became able to curb my emotions and only lose my temper on a few occasions.

I have also memorized a flock of phrases that are calculated to make a bum out of the offender (who is generally too drunk to do anything about it). While this is not the perfect solution, it is an indication that I have reached at least a certain level of maturity. Actually, of course, it is the obligation of the management, if it is an alert, capable one in a fine hotel room or night spot, to remove such offenders quickly and quietly. However, sometimes the entertainer is crucified on the altar of greed and the patron who tips liberally may often be permitted to have his fun at the expense not only of the entertainer but the rest of the audience as well.

A perfect example of what "greasing the palm" will do occurred at the Cocoanut Grove in the fall of 1938, our second season at this popular institution. It was Ben Gage, then Esther Williams's husband, who introduced me to the short, rotund fellow whose owlish face in the midst of eight or nine others at the table looked harmless enough; but when I discovered that everyone in his party had deserted him, that should have told me what was going to happen.

Before we began our show we presented a roller-skating comedian who wanted to do a five- or ten-minute audition for the management. His monologue was so completely ruined by drunken taunts and blasphemy from the fat man that our skater rolled off in confusion and defeat.

My windup of the Cocoanut Grove show was a composition called "Where To" in which I portrayed the thoughts and feelings of a taxi driver as he encounters several types of personalities in the course of his day's cabbing, last of whom is a gangster, who proceeds to shoot and kill the cabbie as they flee from the police. This was a number which I particularly wanted to show off to some skeptical advertising men who doubted that the number was as effective as I told them it was at the Grove. The room was packed with a crowd which included Governor Lehman of New York and a few movie celebrities, among them Loretta Young. It was necessary for us to put a special table on the floor for my associates in J. Walter Thompson of New York, the agency which was producing our Fleischmann broadcast. Normally our show would have really "wowed" that audience. There was that good feeling in the air that bespoke a friendly and receptive group. Nevertheless, from the beginning of our show, Ben Gage's pal was really letting us have it. I instructed my two boys, Sam and Ralph, to stand behind him and if he became too abusive, particularly if he let out one crack during my "Where To," to lift him, chair and all, and with a hand over his mouth, give him the bum's rush.

For some strange reason, he didn't bother our ventriloquist, Bob Neller, too much and he left Al Bernie alone. He did, however, every now and then, release a string of oaths or obscenities which were not calculated to help our routines or to make my fellow performers feel very relaxed. But for me the big test was whether, when we got to "Where To," he would ruin the dramatic qualities of this five-minute monologue with music.

As I began my explanation and set the background for the number itself, he warmed to his task and really started to insult me. I looked at him to my right and should have remembered that one of the characters I portrayed in the number was a drunken senator from Washington, one of the cab driver's fares. I failed to anticipate this and, sure enough, by the time I came to the drunken-senator bit, our inebriated patron imagined that I was making fun of *his* intoxication. It was amazing that this somehow penetrated his alcoholic haze but it did and he really let me have it with both barrels. I could see my two boys standing behind him, and could only wonder *Why don't they take him out?* As we came to the end of the number where a green spotlight pinpoints my face as the cab driver, dying, says, "I say, copper, I'm asking you. Where to? Where to? Where to?" I prayed that he would be silent and let me have my dying moments in silent peace. Fortunately, by this time he was either worn-out or, possibly, the effect of what I was trying to do had somehow got through to him. At any rate he remained fairly quiet. The audience rose to its feet with a roar when the number was finished, chiefly I think for my courage in carrying it out with patience and fortitude.

I bowed low to the audience, turned and brought my band to its feet. We bowed together, the band and I, to the audience, and to each other. After one more bow to my audience, I strode briskly across the floor, put the palm of my hand under the chin of our drunken offender, gently pushed him over backward in his chair, taking great care that he would land on the soft, plush carpet. This brought forth an even greater roar of approval from the gathering. In a matter of seconds, two of the captains removed him, chair and all, from the room.

To reveal his name would be unfair as he has since apologized. As far as any animosity is concerned, the incident is closed and forgotten. Whether or not my agency friends were impressed with "Where To" I never found out. All the same, I never see Ben Gage but that I recall an hour at the Cocoanut Grove that seemed like an eternity.

But, as always, it is the female of the species who is more deadly than the male night-clubber. The male heckler, whether drunk or sober, usually is aware of the fact that he is giving someone a bad time. As annoying as this is in itself, the performer at least has the consolation that it is a direct challenge. But there are few things worse (and you can take it from one who knows) than the inane, light-brained chatter of a female ringsider. This cacophony can really tear the heart out of a performer. The timbre of the female voice cuts through the hubbub of a night-club atmosphere, the voice of the performer, and even the background of the orchestra, like a hot knife through butter. The amazing thing is that the female offender is usually the most surprised of all when she is finally, if ever, made aware of the fact that she has been disrupting a well-planned production.

Our final and fifth season at the Astor Roof was brought to an inglorious finish by such a harridan who rattled on aimlessly for fifteen or twenty minutes during some of the best things that my company and I could offer in rebuttal. I finally resorted to an artifice that I have used with loudmouthed women. Unfortunately it is too subtle to be appreciated by more than half the audience and least of all by the culprit herself. I usually call for a drum roll or a fanfare of trumpets and make a formal announcement.

"We have with us this evening, ladies and gentlemen, the winner of the hog-calling contest of the State of Iowa." (I *hope* they raise hogs there!) Then, pointing to the lady in question, I ask her to take a bow.

If (as she usually is) the miscreant happens to be three sheets to the wind, she finally brings her locomotive chatter to a halt, looks bewilderedly about, and even sometimes takes a bow! Of course, I'm afraid my sarcasm is lost upon most of the assemblage. They applaud vigorously, believing that this gal is really the female most adept at calling denizens of the pigpen in her native state.

At the Hollywood Restaurant in 1935, there appeared a very attractive dame (though getting on in years) who was obviously out on a clandestine spree with a young wavy-haired Lothario. The latter was slightly embarrassed at the raised voice of his illicit amour, who was attracting the attention of everyone. In spite of the fact that I was doing my best Chevalier, I finally stopped in the middle of my impression and let this gal have both barrels. When the boy started to remonstrate, I assured him that he would go out feet-first too if they kept it up. The press agent of the joint, who was a real rear-end-kissing sycophant of the columnists' press, rushed over to me in panic. Literally shaking from head to foot and white-faced, he informed me that I had bawled out the wife of one of the top executives of a New York tabloid. His anguish was somewhat mollified when I pointed out to him the top executive himself at another table, roaring blind drunk—so drunk, in fact, that he was totally unaware that his wife in an equally besotted condition was seeing the town publicly with someone else. Verily, yea, verily, it is the woman, particularly in a night club, who has the last word!

The thought just occurs to me that, although almost all performers are subjected to the strictures of the heckler, perhaps there is a reason for the frequency of my encounters with this alcoholic exhibitionist so endemic to night-club audiences. Some word about my podium deportment may not be amiss.

All right, so I don't jump up and down and don't bob all over the place every time an audience applauds. Yes, I know the typical American gesture is to bow as though you've just been presented with the Nobel Prize and smirk and smile. As the average American performer says nineteen times if he and his musical aggregation have done nineteen numbers, "Thank you, ladies and gentlemen."

To that trite pharase, I say, "Nuts!" And why do I take such a perverse attitude? Not only because I can't bring myself to do what everyone else does but because I have an abhorrence of things trite and trivial. I've watched Frankie Laine, for instance, performing—at the end of every number whether it was good, bad, or indifferent, whether the applause was heavy or light, he would say, "Thank you, ladies and gentlemen." I early resolved something that I have followed meticulously all my life: never to do or say the typical, effete things. If I couldn't be *different* in my speech and work, at least they'd remember one thing—that I was an entertainer who didn't use the ordinary tired expressions or do things in the accepted Broadway manner. I wouldn't use the words "swell" or "wonderful" over and over or, when bringing on an act, I'd rather choke than say, "Let's give him a nice big hand."

Somewhere, 'way back in my ancestry, in that stream of English (yes, there's also a dash of English), Irish, and French, there was a progenitor who has really flowered in me. He must have been a character who told some member of the English nobility, some Duke or Lord, to go to hell. Or on the Irish side of me, some ancestor must have existed who defied all the Irish leprechauns—on a night when there was no moon and all the Irish banshees were rampant, someone had cautioned him, "Don't cross that bog!" He had, of course, done so with complete abandon. Or from the French lineage of my father, this ancestor dared defy all the conventionalities of the kingdom of France, its royalty and its tradition. The first Vallee came over with Lafayette on his second trip to fight with the American colonists, later to settle in the Province of Quebec in the little town of St. Anne de Bellevue. And I, too, like independence.

I have always been self-analytical and honestly critical of what gifts or lack of them I had inherited from this stream of ancestry and thus at no time did I ever kid myself. On the other hand, I was fully aware that, willy-nilly and through no effort on my part, I had inherited a keen ear for musical pitch, a high sense of consonance and dissonance in music, and the gift of being able to create rhythmic patterns, manifested by my early love of the drum. Add to this a very high quotient in the art of tonal, verbal, and word memory and several other musical gifts, including a metronomic musical mind which enabled me to tell when my rhythm section picked up or slowed down the slightest fraction of the correct tempo. These musical gifts, which I later had measured and verified by the Carl Seashore musical talent test, all flowered in me to a very high percentage.

Knowing that I was the very unworthy carrier of these propensities (knowing that they were just as much inherited as the color of my skin, the wave in my hair and the impossibility of ever becoming bald, the color of my eyes, about all of which I can do little or nothing) has made

me conscious that the applause that greets some of my efforts to entertain should really be given to those ancestors who passed these gifts on
to me. That is why, as critics have often noted, I rarely bow very long
but rather hurry on to my next number or into the next phase of the
program.

For a while I was not cognizant of this fact but I was always embarrassed by demonstrations of applause in the theater. It was vividly
brought home to me one afternoon at the New York Paramount Theater
in 1929, when Jack Osterman, a brilliant but unhappy comedian-wit of
the Roaring Twenties stage-production days, did an impression of me
singing through the megaphone. He imitated the way I parted my hair,
the stance I took when I held the megaphone, the way I stopped and
looked at the violin section as it played, then at the woodwind section,
and then at the piano. But Osterman's greatest critical appreciation of my
refusal to "milk" the applause or take deep bows came at the conclusion
of his impression. He turned around and deliberately stuck his rear end
out at the audience! Well, my boys nearly fell off their chairs and the
audience, who may have sensed this tendency in me not only during this
show but in previous shows, roared with laughter and applause.

So—methinks I mayhap ask for it from hecklers. Maybe I play it too
cool but that is the way I feel about it. You may not agree with my
attitude but you must admit that it is one of substantial foundation. Oh,
you *don't* agree? Are you, gentle reader, that florid, shiny-faced miner
I faced that night in Wilkes-Barre?

In '54 I chanced to do a turn at summer stock. It wasn't my first
appearance in a straight play. In '39 I had appeared in *The Man in
Possession* and it was my misfortune to have Brooks Atkinson review it
as follows:

> ... he [Vallee] is reported as willing to spend considerable time
> to learn the profession. To judge by his acting last evening,
> this apprentice period is going to last long enough to try the
> patience of his friends. ...

No matter. A pox on Mr. Atkinson, say I. An agent friend of mine
had twelve weeks lined up for me in *Jenny Kissed Me*, written by Jean
Kerr, author of the comedy hit on Broadway, *Mary, Mary*. She and her
husband (Walter Kerr, drama critic of the *New York Herald Tribune*)
had known a priest after whom the main character was drawn—a crusty,
cranky old curmudgeon whose bark was worse than his bite. The minute
I had read a few lines of it I knew she had written it with Barry Fitzgerald in mind which, as a matter of fact, was just what she had done.
For its Broadway run, Fitzgerald was unavailable so Leo G. Carroll got
the role. Carroll is a very devout Catholic which I am not. When he
donned the priestly robes, he seemed to regard the role of Father Moyni-
han in a rather serious light. In addition, there was a lot of friction among

members of the company and this attitude was conveyed across the footlights—I believe the show folded after about eight weeks.

Alexander Cohen, the producer, caught our stock production one rainy night. "Rudy, if you'd been in the New York show," he said, "we'd still be running!" He went to CBS and tried to interest them in a series based on the play but at that time they felt that the religious aspect represented a difficult, nay, dangerous subject. Ironically, MGM is now preparing a series for TV based on the famous property, *Going My Way*, in which Bing Crosby and Ingrid Bergman starred when it was a motion picture. The series will star Gene Kelly with possibly Barry Fitzgerald's brother playing the role Barry created in the film. If I had been free, I would have been storming the gates at Metro to have a try for the role because I would have had a lot of fun doing it.

So we did the twelve weeks in various straw-hat playhouses in and around Maine with the new film star Lee Remick in the starring female part, to generally favorable reviews. In '56 we revived it for a successful run at the Pasadena Playhouse. The fine response there was heady brew— I decided to take it to San Francisco, where I lost my shirt. The tab came to $14,000 of my own money.

For some goddamned reason we opened on a Sunday night during Lent! The house was packed but the night was rainy. I think the rain outside did something to their innards because the crowd didn't react at all the way they had everywhere else. San Francisco doesn't go for sweet and charming plays, somehow. There isn't a risqué line in the play and when a newspaper critic mentioned this in his column we were dead. I mourned the debacle because I love the part so much. It's a kind of one-man tour de force and I romp through it smoking cigars the while. I hope one day to do it as a 90-minute TV spectacular. I believe the morning after the show a lot of people will be amazed at my ability to handle such an off-beat (for me) characterization.

And so it went, through the fifties. A skein of club dates and then back to Hollywood or Palm Springs for a lot of lovely loafing in the sun. For a while in '59 there was a modest sort of ground swell, a jerry-built bandwagon "clamoring" for me to run for Mayor of Los Angeles. I was intrigued but unfortunately the incumbent was Norris Poulson, an SAE brother of mine.

Every once in a while I would run into Poulson and tell him I was thinking of getting his job. He would just stare at me as if I were out of my mind. Now, as a fraternity brother, he could at least have acted polite! I never went through with this civic attempt for the simple reason that I refuse to rise before noon except in extreme circumstances. If I had been elected, they would have had to put the city administration on a late-shift basis.

CHAPTER XX

How to Succeed in Show Business
by Really Trying

"I Believe in You"

JANUARY HAD ROLLED AROUND IN THE second year of what someone had dubbed the Soaring Sixties. With the "East" and "West" brandishing bombs, the big ones, I hoped it would not become the Searing Sixties. I was beginning '61 in a way I have cherished for years—sopping up the sun on my hilltop in Hollywood and generally taking it easy between night-club and hotel dates.

My dozing was interrupted by a phone call from Bill Josephy of the West Coast office of General Artists Corporation, a man I had known years ago when he was in the dress business. This call was to begin a chain of events leading to my role in the Broadway musical, *How to Succeed in Business Without Really Trying*, a segment of my career running the gamut from supreme satisfaction to shattering discouragement.

"Cy Feuer is in town, Rudy," said Josephy, "and he's got a part for you in a musical. You know, Feuer and Martin."

At the time I knew only a little of this duo but I later learned that Feuer (correctly or traditionally pronounced *foyer* yet everyone calls him *fewer*—it's the *eu* that does it; after all you don't say *Frood* in speaking of the renowned Freud) had begun as a lowly Brooklyn trumpet player and had risen through the position of music department head at Republic Pictures to his present pre-eminence as a legit producer. Cy is a rather warm individual as opposed to his partner, Ernie Martin. The latter was known even to his best friends as a cold-blooded operator in his business dealings. He began his career as a page boy for a network and, before striking it rich on Broadway, he had become an agent and producer for radio shows.

"Oh, yes," I replied. "Can you tell me more about it?"

"Why don't you come on over to the hotel and let Cy fill you in. He's at the Beverly Hills."

There Feuer outlined the story briefly—the, by now, fairly well-known saga of the onward-and-upward progress of the guileful window-washer who becomes chairman of the board of World Wide Wickets. Like most show people pitching a production, Feuer laughed uproariously at frequent junctures which he felt would be the comedic highlights.

"You'll be J. B. Biggley, the president of the company," added Feuer.

I thought about it for a moment. "Can you give me your idea of what sort of a person this Biggley is to be? Visually——personality—"

"He's you, Rudy. We thought you'd be perfect."

"Yes, but—well, is the role sort of a Jim Backus, bluff and hearty? Or is it prissy, sort of Edward Everett Horton?"

"Frankly, I don't see him specifically, in detail, so to speak. That is, not yet."

"Very well. Let me think it over."

About a week or so later Josephy called me again with further information. The rehearsals were to begin in May, I believe, with the show opening in July. This meant I would have to forgo playing Bermuda, something I looked forward to each June. Taking part in the show would mean moving to New York for the run and I did not relish leaving "Silvertip" for any length of time; I knew I would have to sign for a minimum of a year. Furthermore, as I reconsidered the part the way Feuer had sketched it out, Biggley sounded like a one-dimensional, unrelieved SOB with little chance to ingratiate himself with the audience in any way.

"I'm sorry, Bill," I told Josephy. "I don't see the part as one for me at all."

A couple of weeks later Josephy called to see if I'd changed my mind but I was still adamant. It didn't seem worth the headaches and I assumed that this was the end of it.

In March I was playing Orlando, Florida, and received a wire and a call from the New York GAC office. It seemed they still were interested in me for *Succeed*.

"We'd like it very much if you could arrange to come to New York and sing some of the numbers for us on a theatre stage," said the GAC man. "Of course, we'll pay your fare here."

I did a slight burn. It was obvious that Frank Loesser wanted to hear me sing to be sure I'd be able to handle his music. Now this was understandable, really, but I figured it was pretty late in life for me to be running around auditioning for Loesser. "That's a long way to get back to California—via New York. It's really a pain in the neck and I'm not terribly enchanted about the part anyway. Tell you what," I countered. "Pay my fare to New York *and* on to California and I'll do it."

They refused so I went on back home figuring that I was definitely not going to "Succeed."

The week of April 24 I was booked into a small hotel and supper club in London, Ontario, where I had played about nine months before at a good fee and where the audience reaction was always excellent. We were rehearsing Monday afternoon when I got a call from Marty Baum, an agent at GAC whom I had never met. I knew he had been involved previously with Baum and Newborn, a firm now a part of GAC. They had previously acted as my theatrical representation and had asked me to do a Broadway legit show with Eartha Kitt called *Jolly's Progress*. I told them it was a bad show, that my part stank, and I believe it folded on Broadway after about a week. Evidently Baum had drawn the assignment to get me for the Loesser show.

"They're still interested in you for *Succeed*," he told me. "Can you swing down to New York after you finish in London and talk it over? They've postponed the May rehearsals. You can still play Bermuda."

"Oh, hell, Marty. It's impossible. I've got to get straight back to the Coast. They've scheduled a recording date for me." This was a black, barefaced lie. I wasn't playing hard to get, though; it was the only excuse I could think of to get out of coming to New York. I was homesick for my bride and home in the Hollywood hills.

When I'm working in a hotel, I always leave "No Disturb" instructions at the switchboard. No calls until two or three in the afternoon since I often don't get to bed until three or four in the morning. Nevertheless, the following Thursday the phone rang at eleven A.M.

"Is the godammed building on fire?" I grumbled into the mouthpiece.

"It's me—Abe Newborn," came the answer.

"Where in the hell are you calling from?" I'd never met him.

"Downstairs in the lobby. Cy Feuer is with me. Boy, what a trip—we flew commercial to Toronto and then had to rent a private plane to get here. Would you believe it—the pilot was sixteen years old. I swear to God! We've got Act I with us. Will you read it?"

"Of course I'll read it!" I exclaimed. I was impressed at their safari with the sixteen-year-old aviator.

I met them for a bit of breakfast, picked up Act I and went off alone to read it. Now I've got a pretty fair reputation for picking tunes which become hits, artists who become stars. Therefore, you've got to believe this is not Monday-morning quarterbacking—when I read Act I, I was bowled over. It was, I felt, a palpable hit. Never in my life had I put a dime in a show but I began reaching for my wallet then and there. The delightful story idea seemed to me to be permeated with the sweet smell of success.

I told Cy and Abe to count me in and, after the former excused himself, I talked to Newborn about such details as salary, dressing room, and "house seats" (tickets set aside for an actor at each performance which he may buy at box-office prices on his own option). The pair then returned to New York and I at the end of the week to California.

In May I worked my way East again playing clubs and rooms pointing to Bermuda in June and the beginning of rehearsals in August. Before taking off for Bermuda I signed the show contract for a year through GAC and met with Loesser, Feuer, Martin, and the choreographer Hugh Lambert backstage at the Lunt-Fontanne Theater. We decided upon the keys for the songs I would do in the production and Loesser gave me a recording he had made of his own versions of the tunes. I was to take it to Bermuda and bone up.

On August 4 we began the tedious grind of rehearsals in a studio designed for such things, as depressing a milieu as could be imagined, certainly not surroundings conducive to eliciting the best from a performer. For some goddam reason this is theatrical tradition—there is a strange rationale in the theater (and I don't suppose they will ever change) that a production must begin in some scruffy loft, some moth-eaten ballroom in a third-rate hotel, or a barren, colorless rehearsal hall in the Broadway area. I can only assume that this choice of arena has to do with budget considerations. At any rate there is always the joyous atmosphere of a cut-rate funeral home.

At the outset of our first gathering, Abe Burrows, the director and one of those responsible for the show's book, enlightened us on how gifted he was as a writer, director, and utility godhead. Further, he informed us in a warm and most encouraging way that some of us present would not be with the show in a few weeks. Then with jape and quip and quotes from George S. Kaufman he sketched out the various duties at hand pursuant to mounting the show. We waded through the first reading (just the lines, no songs) and then dispersed into different rooms by groups to work on various parts of the routining.

As I watched these segments being polished, it became obvious to me that here was a production which could well become a veritable gold mine. Before I had gone to Bermuda prior to the rehearsals, the publicity boys had told me they already had $500,000 in the till from advance ticket sales.

"All kidding aside, Rudy," they told me, "most of that advance is because you're in the show. People order tickets for the 'Vallee Show.' Maybe they can't remember the title, it's so goddam long."

I had made a few casual feelers toward investment in the show with Ernie Martin but had gotten only evasive answers. On August 14 I stopped beating around the bush.

"With or without me," I told Martin, "you've got a smash hit. It's a combination of *My Fair Lady*, *Guys and Dolls*, and *Of Thee I Sing*. Not a bad parlay at all! Ernie, I'd like to put some money in it."

Martin is always grinding away on a piece of gum. He just glared at me and gnawed the gum. "No," he said, "I don't want any of our personalities investing in the show." Three days later I was to realize why he was so evasive.

The next day the *New York Daily Mirror* columnist, Bill Slocum, came by to do a story on this epic now in rehearsal. It was a flattering column and stated in part: "Mr. Vallee thrilled me with an expert sense of timing, a gift I never suspected he had." (So I couldn't have been *all* bad.)

There are always annoyances in any theatrical undertaking. Some are sizable, some petty. One thing that galled me was the paltry rehearsal salary—five weeks at $87.50 a week; everyone in the cast got this from the lowliest "walk-on" to the stars. Now this is commendably democratic but since I was paying $150 per week for the apartment I had rented (most of the others in the cast were already living in New York) I was at a disadvantage. I had asked Newborn months before what the rehearsal fee would probably be. "Oh, I don't know exactly. It's just a token salary—probably a couple of hundred," he had said vaguely. This sounded reasonable since I had received one hundred a week with *George White's Scandals* thirty years before.

When I learned about the $87.50 I smoldered awhile and then on August 16 wrote Newborn to try to get $150 weekly at least to defray the cost of the apartment. It seemed only fair for the producers to cover some of my out-of-pocket expenses. If the show folded quickly, I would wind up way in the red on the venture.

Next day, August 17, during a rehearsal break, Abe Newborn suggested we duck out for some refreshments. I assumed he had gotten my letter about salary and wanted to discuss it.

We settled down at a table in the Hotel Edison Green Room and Newborn let me have it.

"They want you out of the show," he said evenly.

If he had suddenly hit me in the face with a wet towel or his fist I could not have been more surprised. Of course, I thought that I had misunderstood him.

"That's it, Rudy," he repeated. "They want you out."

"Well, if that isn't a crock," I thought to myself. "But why—I haven't made a pass at any of the producers' wives. I haven't tried to rape a chorus girl or set fire to the theater."

Newborn continued. "They don't think you're right for the part. You are not projecting."

"Well, I'll be a son of a bitch!" I exploded. "I have been begging Burrows and the producers to give me some indication as to how the part should be played. All they say is the character should be virile. Virile! Goddamit, a director is supposed to direct and Burrows has been wishy-washy in telling me exactly what he wants in J. B. Biggley. I don't think they know what in hell they want in Biggley."

"Don't feel too bad," Abe said. "Remember, Rudy, we have a pay or play contract. Now, technically, they will have to pay you full salary by contract for fifty-seven weeks. It comes to about eighty, ninety thousand. They told me they'd settle with you, free and clear, for forty thousand. If you demand the full payment you can't work at anything for fifty-seven weeks."

"Nuts! I want the full fifty-seven weeks! I'll take it and sit on my ass. The hell with them."

Most performers gladly take a settlement because it permits them to continue working at other things. And too, if the show folds in a few weeks or months they are still way ahead of the salary they would have gotten. *But I knew this one was going to be a hit* and I wanted to be in it.

"Tell you what you do, Abe," I suggested. "Go back to the boys and ask them if I can continue for two or three days. Maybe we can remedy whatever seems to be wrong."

Newborn returned shortly with the reply. "If they give you the extra days and you still don't suit them, there'll be no fifty-seven weeks' pay. That's the deal."

"If that's the way they feel, the hell with it. I'll leave but they're going to pay off in full. Why should I suffer the humiliation of getting fired and have them pay off at half-price."

"That's what Ernie Martin has in mind," Newborn said. "He says when he makes a bad bargain, he pays off. It's as if he were at the race track."

I wasn't going to give up that easily. My pride was cut to the quick. I don't take this type of thing lying down. I went back to see Burrows and Feuer at the rehearsal hall to find out exactly what their objections were.

"Frankly, Rudy, we're afraid you won't be heard," Burrows explained. "The 46th Street Theater seats about fifteen hundred people and we don't think your voice will carry."

"That's nonsense! For years I worked to an audience of five thousand at the Paramount!"

"But this is quite different from a stage show. It's a different type of production altogether."

There was no use arguing the point even though many of the things I had done at the Paramount were quite comparable to this script. Moreover, *both Feuer and Burrows knew of special microphones used by performers in Broadway productions when further amplification of the voice was necessary. And there'd be microphones in the footlights for everyone!*

"Do me one favor," I said. "Let's go over to the Lunt-Fontanne Theater and let me read a few lines with one of the cast. I want to prove something to you."

So Feuer, Burrows, and I took Virginia Martin, the girl who plays my red-haired inamorata in the show, and proceeded to the Lunt-Fontanne, which, incidentally, is owned by Messrs. Feuer and Martin. I read one of the scenes and Feuer came up from the auditorium and said that he thought I would be all right.

Not so Burrows. He kept reminding me of the pressures and difficulties of the out-of-town tryout in Philadelphia; he felt I might not be able to take the physical punishment. Whence came this sudden great compassion for my feebleness, decrepitude, and senility I can never fathom; nevertheless, he seemed certain I would never be able to make it. The matter of my continued employment was left up in the air and I was told to go home. They would give me their decision the following noon.

While we were reading the lines I did not notice a figure seated in the very last row of the theater. I learned about this much, much later. It was Abe Newborn giving my performance and vocal projection the acid test by listening from the farthest reach of the house. After I left, he bent the boys' ears until eight-thirty that evening, and finally convinced them that I should stay. But Feuer admits that the prospect of having to pay me eighty-seven thousand dollars was the clincher that finally kept me in!

The next day at noon the phone rang. It was Newborn. "They've decided to let you stay," he said. "Perhaps this happens for the best."

This last remark infuriated me somehow. How could an insult, a cut, a humiliation like this be for the best? Of course, from then on it was a wonder I could do the goddam part at all.

I reported for rehearsal as if nothing had happened, with one slight but important difference. As I have said, from the time Cy Feuer had first sketched the plot line for me that day in California, I had been begging for direction as to how the character of Biggley should be portrayed. On this particular rehearsal day I substituted a pince-nez for the regular "templed" glasses I had been wearing for the part. I "played" to the pince-nez, I guess . . . and it is quite possible that the substitution contributed a little something toward the characterization for those who couldn't visualize it otherwise.

Speaking of this pince-nez, I had planned a bit of business with it. In the "Heart of Gold" number in *Succeed*, the redhead hits a high note that rattles the woodwork. It is really overpowering and overpoweringly funny as well. I was going to rig a thread to the pince-nez and when she hit this note I would have the glasses pop right off my nose.

During one of the last rehearsals in Philly, Bob Fosse, who was staging the musical numbers, had an idea. "Rudy, when she hits that note can you fix it so your glasses fall off?"

"You son of a bitch," I laughed. "I was saving that as a surprise for opening night!"

At any rate, the bit is in the show now and never fails to bring down the house!

The night before we were to leave for the Philly tryout run late in August, we had our first complete run-through—no stopping, no coaching, no whistles (Fosse always blows a goddam whistle to stop a number for corrections), with just a piano in the pit, no make-up or scenery, *and no amplification of our voices at all* before a small, invited audience. I romped through my role just as I had done it all through the rehearsal grind.

In the first act I have several moments offstage and, as I sat there in the dark, several singers and dancers approached me saying, "You are wonderful—great!" It was the manna of vindication.

Once during a rehearsal, Larry Kasha, who is Feuer and Martin's casting director, had quietly remarked to me, rather cryptically, "I want you to be good. I have a great stake in this thing." I couldn't understand what the hell he meant! I later learned he had originally suggested me for the part of Biggley. He must have been rather apprehensive the last few strife-torn days to say the least. At intermission that night of the first run-through, he passed by me saying, "I love you!"

Some of those who had wanted to crucify me a few short days before were most effusive in their praise. Abe Burrows, with whom I had done about a hundred radio shows years before, approached me after the performance saying, most solicitously, "May I help you out to your cab—take care of yourself—drive carefully down to Philadelphia—"

I have since learned that firings like this are common. But usually the victim is a newcomer.

I had Frank Loesser problems from the outset. A few days before the New York rehearsals began he phoned me to drop by his office to go over the tunes. His half-humorous parting words were, "I am going to put you on the rack."

This annoyed me faintly and I immediately called Abe Burrows whom I felt I knew well enough to use as a confidant. "Now look here, Abe," I said. "If I am going to have a lot of headaches with Loesser about my singing I'd rather bow out right now. Who needs that crap? I'd much prefer to get the hell back to California."

"Now, now, Rudy," Abe replied. "Just calm down. Don't worry about it. It'll be all right."

That first day Loesser's office became a conservatory of music with him acting as voice professor.

"Rudy, you're singing incorrectly," he said. "You're closing on your consonants."

"Maybe you're right, Frank," I said. "Fortunately I've managed to squeak by with this handicap for about thirty-three years. I guess it's a little late in life to acquire a new technique." I had been wined and dined by composers as great or greater than Loesser to persuade me to introduce their tunes.

He gave me disks on which he had recorded the three songs I was to do in *Succeed*. I took them to Bermuda for study. Two of the songs, "Grand Old Ivy" and "Heart Of Gold," were what tin-pan alley would call corny—they verged on the old-fashioned Gay Nineties style in both melody and lyrics. As a college marching song "Old Ivy" never would have taken any prizes but because of my association with the Maine "Stein Song" the former opus acquires a certain nostalgic cachet when performed in the show. "Heart Of Gold" has an old-time quality reminiscent of "A Bird In A Gilded Cage" or "You Made Me What I Am Today, I Hope You're Satisfied," but the way Virginia Martin and I do it on the stage gives it, in my opinion, a plus not inherent in the number itself. In fact, most song pluggers I know would characterize both songs as dogs. The third number, "A Secretary Is Not A Toy," I thought was very bad—quite rangy and not very tuneful although the lyric was extremely witty.

Three days before the firing I was ordered into Loesser's small office off the rehearsal hall next to the Edison Hotel where the maestro again instructed me on the proper interpretation of the songs. The fact that I had chosen thousands of songs over a period of three decades and given them a style that was studied by Sinatra and others, meant nothing to Loesser.

As we discussed the rendition of the numbers I began to realize that Loesser regarded them as true works of art and, as befits masterpieces, proper performances could only come from considerable rehearsal on my part. If there is one thing that heats up my blood it is when someone tries to make a big thing out of nothing. And here is where the composer's feathers got ruffled.

"Frank, don't you realize that these are extremely simple songs?" I said politely and candidly. "I can do them about as well the first time as I can the thousandth."

"Understand one thing," he replied. "I've got a great deal of money in this show. I don't intend to have it ruined by your not performing the songs properly."

I should have realized that the dictates of a director-producer-song-writer in the legitimate and motion-picture fields are rarely questioned or contradicted. Loesser probably had never had anyone speak as frankly and critically about his songs as I had. So he was boiling about it.

He was not the only one building up a head of steam—I felt I was being sold short on the tunes given me as I listened to those given the other members of the cast. It seemed to me every other number in the show consisted of melodies a song writer dreams of having, they were so desirable, while the tunes I was assigned I would never have even programmed on one of my broadcasts.

At any rate, after I had gone through "Heart Of Gold" several times with Miss Martin, I felt I was singing it as well as I ever could and I said so. I suppose Loesser expected me to stay in the stuffy little rehearsal room doing the song over and over the way the boys and girls in the cast had to do with their material. It is quite possible that my frank and practical attitude rankled Loesser.

On the evening of August 16, the night before the firing, just before we were dismissed from rehearsal, Abe Burrows began to criticize me quite angrily, particularly about my love scenes with Miss Martin. No indication had been given me in the script and for the previous eight or nine days I had been reading the amorous lines quite straight with all the sincerity at my command. Burrows was not able to put into words exactly what he wanted but I gathered he was seeking more of a tongue-in-cheek flavor.

There were only Burrows, his secretary, and, I believe, Miss Martin in the room when Abe suddenly jumped on me about my theatrics. I thought I had known him long enough (since the 1940 Sealtest days) to voice an honest difference of opinion in something I had to do in the show. I realize now that he was quite possibly angered at my refusal to accept abjectly his direction. I had torn it with another of the bosses.

The following morning, August 17, bloomed clear and hot and I guess I should have sensed that something was in the air. Bob Fosse had just been brought into the show, being touted to us as a magician with his choreography and the staging of songs. When I was ordered into Room 2 to find the entire group of big brass seated there like Supreme Court judges to watch me go into a rendition of "Secretary," I knew that something was up.

This number was originally intended for Paul Reed who has a strong trained voice (the type of voice used in musical comedies to sing things like "Stout-Hearted Men"), a voice that indicates he has hair on his chest. Actually I had never felt that "Secretary" needed delivery by a trained voice as it was a sexy lyric and a trite melody best suited to a natural-voice singer such as I am. Furthermore, a believable tycoon would not sing in the trained-voice style. Fosse had devised some movements for me as I sang the number with all the male singers in back of me. We were ordered to go through it two or three times and I did it as well as I can do that type of number, giving it all the animation and voice I could muster. Perhaps I should have been aware that they were not pleased with my rendition but I frankly felt that I did a good job of it and was not looking for any on-the-table criticism of my method of delivery. Evidently it was the straw that broke the camel's back because a few minutes later the agent, Abe Newborn, walked in and asked me to go down to the Edison, where he gave me the bad news.

One of the cast later on explained to me that probably the reason I was asked to leave was that all of our brass were running scared. Remember if you will (something that I did not know at the time) that Feuer and Martin had had a four-hundred-thousand-dollar flop in a show which they had written together, Feuer had directed and I understand it was a miserable production called *Whoop-up*. I'd assumed that they'd had nothing but successive hits and I did not know that their last show had been a complete bust. Loesser had just had a very bad flop in a show called *Greenwillow* in which he'd attempted to have Anthony Perkins sing songs I understand were too much for him to handle. That was at least a two-hundred-thousand-dollar loss for Loesser. Abe Burrows had had an expensive disaster in *First Impressions* which he had written and directed. Another show, *The Golden Fleecing*, was a very so-so production. Fosse had been thrown out of a musical which had also collapsed to the tune of $500,000. The fact that they were all running scared still did not justify in my mind their making me the whipping boy. In rehearsal I was doing my lines in the same manner that I am doing them today—but men's egos bruise easily and it is my honest belief that my standing up to Loesser and Burrows was a signal for the lynching. Burrows, at least, was honest enough to say "All right. We were stupid. So let's forget about it."

It seemed a long, long time since Cy Feuer had first limned the story line of *Succeed* for me that January day at the Beverly Hills Hotel. He had started the whole thing and I found out he was the one who wanted to end it—he was the one who brought to a vote and to a head the suggestion that I leave the show. You see Ernie Martin, the cold-blooded business man, handled the finances on the shows and left the artistic details to Cy Feuer, the "rather warm" individual, who delighted in popping into rehearsals, *looking for trouble!*

Feuer has a rather peculiar theory to which he adheres tenaciously. As you probably know, there is a so-called "first reading" by the entire cast (seated) on the first day of rehearsal. This is a more or less routine run-through. Believe it or not, Cy Feuer believes that the members of the cast *who read well* at this juncture, who seemingly have caught the nuances of the script this *first* time, invariably proceed to go downhill and lose that something they had at the first reading. He actually believes this always happens!

He liked my reading the first day although I had a bad throat and didn't do as well as I would have liked. Apparently from then on (based, I suppose, on Feuer's Law) he became disenchanted with my delivery as the hours ground away in the sordid rehearsal rooms.

In addition I am sure he received word from Loesser that I was not giving my all to the two simple songs allotted me. Burrows may have told him I was not projecting (whatever the hell that means)! Abe didn't buy Feuer's Law at all. He had some trenchant opposing comments.

"Actors who tell me not to expect them to give out during rehearsal," he said very sadly, "rarely make good on their promise to 'come alive' when the chips are down."

I had still another view: an actor doesn't have to do or die every run-through; if he's running in high gear all the time he'll go stale and dull the final presentation. To me, rehearsals are mainly for line-learning and movement.

Another reason which may have prompted Feuer et al. to harpoon me was a matter of contrasting styles of delivery among the cast. I have always been noted for underplaying because that is my nature (*vide* my role as the schnook in *The Palm Beach Story*). I saw the J. B. Biggley part as a sort of Anglo-Saxon, Protestant, college-bred character calling for restraint in speaking the lines. Alongside the effusive, pressing portrayals of Robert Morse and Charles Nelson Reilly (who plays the part of my nephew in the show) I most certainly seemed subdued and lacking in *projection*. Nonetheless, I never doubted for a moment that I would be believable before an audience *doing the part exactly as I was doing at rehearsal!* Subsequent events proved my contention.

At any rate, we left New York for the tryout in the City of Brotherly Love. I survived the hours and hours of rehearsal where they wasted even more time than they had in that lousy New York rehearsal hall, with endless changes and changes of changes. No matter. On opening night with microphones in the footlights for everyone, the applause for all of us rocked the theater and my strong suspicions that a hit was brewing were thunderously confirmed.

The rest is theatrical history—we came to Broadway and became the "hardest-ticket" attraction since *My Fair Lady*. The critics unanimously saluted the production and I must blushingly admit that my own notices were flattering. The New York reviewers apparently didn't agree with the boys running the show. I sometimes imagine a little tableau that goes as follows:

A well-wisher approaches one of the *Succeed* brass and burbles, "What a stroke of brilliant off-beat casting—how on earth did you *ever* think of Rudy Vallee for the part?"

The brass assumes an all-knowing look of genius, thoughtfully taps the tips of his fingers together, and modestly says, "Well, you know, an awful lot of thought and care go into a major production—"

End of tableau.

After we opened in New York I was still smarting about the near-firing. I was telling an old friend, Sam Narefsky, about it one evening and he, being a loyal buddy, grew quite incensed. Sam had worked for me for several years in the late thirties—setting up public-address systems, driving, and a thousand other jobs we would encounter on tour, a kind of major-domo. He now is a manufacturer of metal products as owner of Tempo Design on Long Island. A few days after I told him the story, he appeared with a metal plaque on which was engraved (in oriental lettering) the legend, "Teahouse of the August 17 Moon." It hangs in my dressing room as a memento—as if I needed reminding! After all, I have already gone on record about my grudges.

The most unhappy aspect of this whole undertaking is the fact that I was denied the opportunity to invest in *Succeed*. It would have been the first time in my life to make some easy money. I have made a lot of money in my time but it was always very soggy with blood, sweat, and tears. The fact that Ernie Martin refused my offer of money to back the show (probably because he was thinking of firing me—why do *Vallee* any favors?) has cost me the privilege of capitalizing on my inherent sense of what will be successful!

It is ironic to note that the much-contested tidbit, "A Secretary Is Not A Toy," was no longer my number when the show came to Broadway. After all the furor it had caused! When I would do it in rehearsal, I would take slight liberties with the beat in certain places and this distressed Loesser immensely. He wanted it done in strict three-quarter time, hitting every note over the head. As the pressures mounted concerning my performance, I said to my wife, "If he'd only let me do it lightly and brightly, I think the bad melody would be less noticeable. It will seem more cute and clever. That's the way I think it should be done for best effect."

After several attempts to have other members of the cast have a go at it, "Secretary" was eliminated altogether.

Suddenly it reappeared in the show one day in Philadelphia, this time as a song-and-dance number with the boys and girls popping in and out of doors, moving swiftly about the stage, into and out of the wings—lightly and brightly so the melody is hardly noticeable. In such a guise the number always gets a fair hand. Once in a while Old Man Vallee does call a shot.

I am supposed to be a very tight man with the dollar! Actually, alongside some Broadway producers and our own Messrs. Feuer and Martin, I'm a free-wheeling spendthrift! These fine gentlemen think no more of a dollar than you do of your right eye.

My lovely bride, Eleanor, starry-eyed and optimistic as always, was looking forward to the Christmas gift that Mr. Feuer and Mr. Martin would surely bestow upon us at Christmas. Let's face it: my name must have helped get them great billing advance they needed—and received; but whatever value to the show the handle Rudy Vallee may actually have, the show notwithstanding, is a smash hit. So Eleanor felt we were due something that Christmas, not only in return for what I gave every night to the part, nor even in atonement for the humiliation they caused me to suffer when they fired me on August 17, but chiefly because they had flatly refused me the chance to invest in the show when I asked them for this opportunity during rehearsal.

It would have meant all of one half a per cent of the weekly gross (about $335.00) or maybe even one per cent! Hell! A Rex Harrison gets four or five per cent of MY FAIR LADY and a Mary Martin maybe as much as *twelve* per cent of THE SOUND OF MUSIC! Well, why not one little old per cent for an internationally known name who is (according to the critics) doing a reasonably fine job in the show?

Or perhaps Eleanor had her heart set on a bonus—five or maybe even ten thousand dollars to assuage the hurt of that day back in August that right now they'd all like her and Rudy to forget! Hell! If the like had ever happened to Burrows, a Niagara of Jergen's Lotion could never have soothed the hurt to *his* vanity.

Well, it came!

A box was delivered to the dressing room bearing the card of Messrs. Feuer and Martin. It was small, but it was HEAVY—could be gold nuggets! Not quite—eight high-ball glasses with crest of the show on the outside of each glass. It was exactly what everyone of the cast received. Twice in the washer, the crest was gone!

Ellie was crushed, not because of the crest. But she thought, "Perhaps they'll have a Christmas party. Most successful shows do." After all, weren't these men netting (before taxes), *netting*, mind you, almost eighteen thousand dollars a week? They had been netting this amount since the second week after the show opened in New York!

During the Philadelphia tryout, Frank Loesser had given in the Hotel Warwick a sumptuous party for *everyone* connected with the show *and* their wives. Stage hands, musicians, sound men, lighting men, cast top echelon: EVERYONE—and the food layout was something to behold, and champagne flowed like water—European vintage at that! It must have cost, with the hired orchestra and waiters, at least five or six thousand dollars. But there was no Christmas party for us.

Our show HOW TO SUCCEED, will gross twenty to thirty-five million dollars with the additional proceeds from the American road company, the London, Australian and other companies. Our own New York company should keep running for at least three if not four years. And then there are the all-important film rights! So shed no tears for Mr. Feuer and Mr. Martin.

Rather, may you wonder how these two men could "dock" (deduct from her small salary) Bonnie Scott, our lovely young singing star, for the three shows she missed during her two-day *honeymoon* a few months after we came to New York. In their position I would have given her a wedding check of at least two hundred and fifty dollars!

At Christmas, I did what I think was a very normal thing to do. It was no more than what I have usually done at such a time of the year. The *entire* company of performers, the producers, writers, personnel from the office across from the theatre, the box-office men, stage hands, the lighting crew, the sound crew, and the musicians, who with substitutes, number over forty—all of these received gifts, many of them with names of the recipient inscribed thereon to the tune of over twelve hundred dollars! And who did this?—that little old wine maker . . . ME!

Starring in a smash musical is often a rather mixed blessing. The demand for tickets is driving me out of my mind. My daily mail is full of missives from people whom I never knew existed begging for tickets. Many supplicants justify their requests with the statement that one or both of their parents used to buy my records! Some are so desperate to see the opus that they even offer to pay for the seats. My God, *I* have to pay for every one I secure; there are no "free" seats to a hit show. I'm chained to my typewriter explaining why I can't get tickets for the entire Western Hemisphere, but the deluge continues. . . . Help!

CHAPTER XXI

Life Begins at Sixty!

"Life Is Still A Bowl of Cherries"

I HEAR THE TAXI-DRIVER CHARACTER IN the number I used to do saying, "Where to? Where to? Where to?" The twentieth century is sixty-two years old and I am nearly sixty-one and it's "Where to, Rudy?" My God, I remember back in thirty-nine I was eagerly devouring a book called *Life Begins at Forty*. What shall I read now!

I am enjoying hugely my appearance in *Succeed*. After all, how many ex-crooners get a chance to play before the President of the United States and a covey of astronauts! It happens to be the kind of show that does not pall on an actor. It is light, yet penetratingly satirical and somehow always seems fresh to me and the rest of the cast though we play it eight times a week. If this feeling persists and if I and the management can come to mutually acceptable terms in June then I'll stay another year. A third year on Broadway for me is conceivable but rather doubtful. That would be a trifle too much of a good thing.

No, failing a third-year contract I would like to hit the road again in a sort of farewell appearance; you know, play once more my favorite clubs, hotel rooms, and one-night, one-man shows in various auditoria. After a year or so of this I think my bride and I will hang up the gloves, sit around the house, putter in the garden, read, and watch TV every night. And I enjoy California wines. I've got to admit that I am hooked on TV, particularly the old movie reruns.

As to how long this "retirement" will last, your guess is as good as mine. I never want to completely divorce myself from show business— but if the phone doesn't ring, so be it. I have no further burning ambitions as a performer—I don't feel I have to *prove* myself any more. For well over three decades I've had the best and the worst of it in practically all media so there's little challenge left, little mystery, few new fields to conquer.

Still the old fire horse never forgets and the clanging of the alarm bells makes him yearn to be back in harness. Take, for instance, the movie version of *Succeed*. It is almost certainly six or seven years away. (They are just beginning to plan the movie of *My Fair Lady* and it is approaching the start of its seventh year on Broadway!) All the same, if they offer me the motion-picture role of J. B. Biggley, I will bound from my wheel chair and crawl to the studio on my hands and knees if need be. And let's face it, the role is a lovely and challenging one.

Sunday night, June 3, 1962, will always be a major breakthrough in my career. On that night Ed Sullivan had the courage to let me do two out-and-out comedy routines that were apparently well received. They will be repeated (and for top Sullivan money) on his TV program of September 2nd!

Ed now wants me for three or four more comedy spots in the fall, and *if* these go as well as things went on June 3, I'll probably become almost a regular—a sort of gentile Alan King. Then if I do some one-man two-hour concerts, those who normally would stay away (Who wants to hear Vallee sing thru his nose all evening?) may turn out, because the Sullivan exposure could do for me what TV appearances have done for Victor Borge. After all, my show is something like his, except that I sing and play the saxophone!

Just to keep my hand in as a "single," I am planning some solo appearances on Sundays, my day off from *Succeed*. They will be in the East, probably Boston, Hartford, Providence, New York's Carnegie Hall, and a few others. If these performances are profitable and well-received, maybe I will bow out of *Succeed* somewhat sooner than planned.

My old favorite, *Jenny Kissed Me*, has been offered to me during my one-week *Succeed* vacation and maybe I'll do it then in summer stock. The big-tent summer circuit has come through with some terrific offers and I may do them on my Sundays off. The possibilities in the latter medium have come about mainly from the success of *Succeed*.

And so it goes: it certainly does not seem that my future will be a particularly boring one. I am inordinately thankful that this is so.

Failing to find enough to keep me active in the entertainment field will not mean I must languish in unfulfillment. If given the opportunity, I would like to become some sort of public servant—I might even run for office. The hours of work bother me a bit—I don't honestly know whether I could *ever* get into the habit of rising before noon. Also, I am quite idealistic; when I was considering running for Mayor of Los Angeles a politician told me, "The rat race will break your heart!"

The job I would like in public office would be Mayor of L. A. as Jimmy Walker was of New York without, of course, any suspicion of malfeasance. Walker was a "greeter" first and foremost and I believe did a great deal for his city.

I am not really oriented politically one way or another; like so many of us, I vote for the candidate rather than the party label. Same way with religion; I have no great leaning toward any one faith. They all have their good points and their infuriating points. I suppose you might say I am a questioning, free-lance believer.

There are many ways for me to occupy my time other than the more obvious ones. For instance, I am a bug on the provision of seat belts for automobiles. In the many years of my travels by car I have seen some horrible motor accidents, tragedies which could have been mitigated by the use of belts. When time has permitted in the past, I have been active in urging their use, by legislation if necessary. I am eager still to lobby for them wherever possible.

For most of my life I have had a great love of animals, particularly dogs. I hope to have the time and opportunity to work with veterinarians or the Society for the Prevention of Cruelty to Animals in the years to come. I would be happy to work without pay in bringing aid and comfort to those animal inmates of hospitals and shelters.

And what about children? I have never particularly wanted children and it is very difficult to say just why. I can say that I would not have been unhappy had fortune blessed a marriage of mine with issue. But I do not feel a desperate void in my life through lack of young. This is unaccountable but it is the way I happen to feel.

You see, I have a phobia about stupidity. I detest it in myself and in anyone else. I am monumentally impatient about stupidity and, quite naturally, a child does countless stupid things. My God, he's *supposed* to fall into swimming pools, set fire to the house, tear up the family car, or what have you. Maybe I'm too selfish to have the saintly resiliency so necessary in raising an offspring.

Individuals constantly ask me, "Don't you have any children?"

"No," I answer. "I've never particularly cared about them, never particularly wanted them."

There is a shocked pause as if I had just sullied the flag, motherhood, and the New York Yankees.

"But, certainly, Mr. Vallee," they continue doggedly, "you must want to see yourself perpetuated."

I have a simple answer for this. *No!* This really knocks them right on their can because the average man wants a child largely because of his vanity. He wants the child to look like him. You know, cigars, product of his loins, and all that.

"Good God!" I kid them. "Another Vallee! Another adenoidal crooner! God forbid!"

Then they give me the clincher. "What about that mass of mementos you've got in your home, the movies and records and rooms full of clippings and keepsakes? Surely you'd want to have a child to leave that to?"

"Christ, no! After I'm gone I don't care what happens to it. Give it to the Smithsonian Institution or burn it! It makes no difference."

And it does make no difference. I don't kid myself that those rooms full of memorabilia mean very much in the march of history. My mission in life was to entertain, to purvey escapism, if you will, and there is precious little enduring creativity inherent in the career of a wandering minstrel. My recordings, my movies and, I hope, this book will be around for a while; but they will be, inevitably, period pieces, maybe curios at which to chuckle. Tastes change and that is the way of the world.

I am not the least bitter about this. I never look back over my shoulder and shed a nostalgic tear. I like to look ahead. I never mourn the demise of big-time radio; I am too much intrigued over the miracle of television.

I've come a long way from Vermont and Maine on a highway paved, for the most part, with good fortune. Except for a few harrowing detours it has been a ball; I venture to say that a lot of my fans have shared the fun with me and, if I have accomplished nothing more than giving them moments of joy in my performance, then I am accordingly enriched.

There's no point in trying to relive the success of yesteryear. What's past is prologue and, brother, I'm rooting like hell for tomorrow!

THE END